W9-CMN-472

FABLES: THE DELUXE EDITION

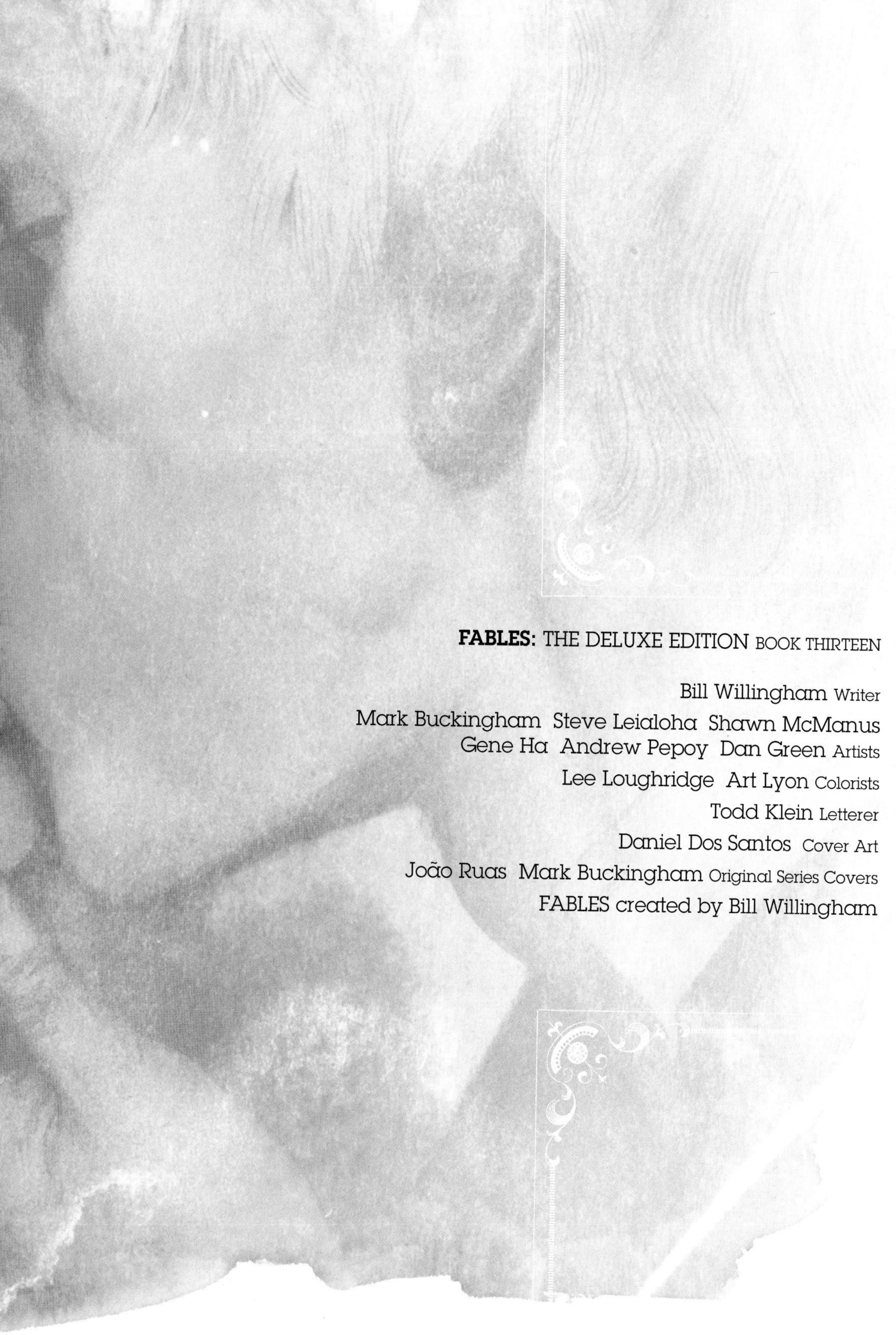

FABLES: THE DELUXE EDITION BOOK THIRTEEN

Bill Willingham Writer

Mark Buckingham Steve Leialoha Shawn McManus
Gene Ha Andrew Pepoy Dan Green Artists

Lee Loughridge Art Lyon Colorists

Todd Klein Letterer

Daniel Dos Santos Cover Art

João Ruas Mark Buckingham Original Series Covers

FABLES created by Bill Willingham

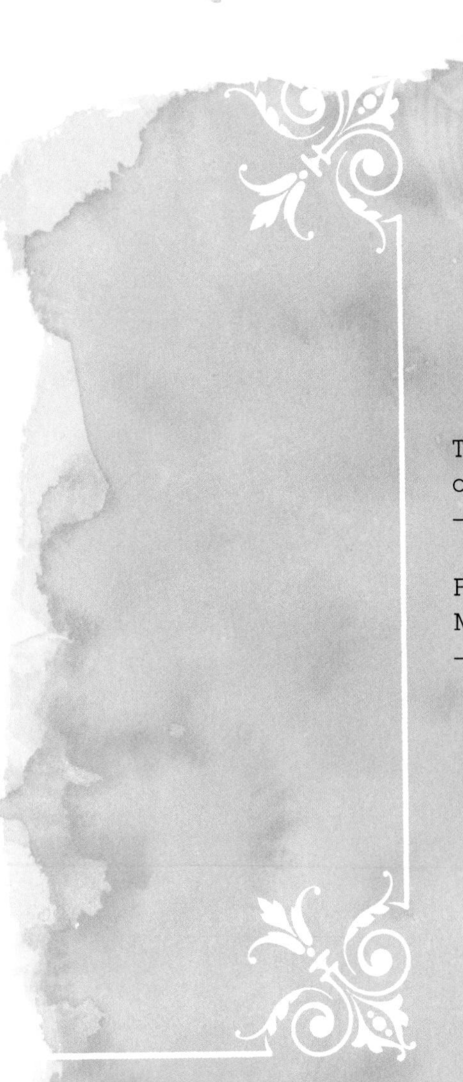

To Mark, who let me do this, even though he could have stopped me.
— Bill Willingham.

For Matilda and Rudy.
My wonderful niece and nephew.
— Mark Buckingham

Shelly Bond Editor – Original Series
Gregory Lockard Associate Editor – Original Series
Jeb Woodard Group Editor – Collected Editions
Scott Nybakken Editor – Collected Edition
Steve Cook Design Director – Books
Louis Prandi Publication Design

Shelly Bond VP & Executive Editor – Vertigo

Diane Nelson President
Dan DiDio and Jim Lee Co-Publishers
Geoff Johns Chief Creative Officer
Amit Desai Senior VP – Marketing & Global Franchise Management
Nairi Gardiner Senior VP – Finance
Sam Ades VP – Digital Marketing
Bobbie Chase VP – Talent Development
Mark Chiarello Senior VP – Art, Design & Collected Editions
John Cunningham VP – Content Strategy
Anne DePies VP – Strategy Planning & Reporting
Don Falletti VP – Manufacturing Operations
Lawrence Ganem VP – Editorial Administration & Talent Relations
Alison Gill Senior VP – Manufacturing & Operations
Hank Kanalz Senior VP – Editorial Strategy & Administration
Jay Kogan VP – Legal Affairs
Derek Maddalena Senior VP – Sales & Business Development
Jack Mahan VP – Business Affairs
Dan Miron VP – Sales Planning & Trade Development
Nick Napolitano VP – Manufacturing Administration
Carol Roeder VP – Marketing
Eddie Scannell VP – Mass Account & Digital Sales
Courtney Simmons Senior VP – Publicity & Communications
Jim (Ski) Sokolowski VP – Comic Book Specialty & Newsstand Sales
Sandy Yi Senior VP – Global Franchise Management

Logo design by Brainchild Studios/NYC

FABLES: THE DELUXE EDITION BOOK THIRTEEN

DC Comics
2900 West Alameda Avenue
Burbank, CA 91505
Printed in Canada. First Printing.
ISBN: 978-1-4012-6449-9

PEFC Certified
Printed on paper from sustainably managed forests and controlled sources
PEFC
PEFC/01-31-106
www.pefc.org

Library of Congress Cataloging-in-Publication Data is available.

Table of Contents

Breadcrumbs and Glass and Bloody Hearts

As a culture, we believe in the fundamental simplicity of folklore. We think of fairy tales as being almost like atomic units: the most basic of all narratives. This is why they're among the first stories we tell our children, and why folklorists try and break them down into archetypal "functions," like physicists identifying subatomic particles. Centuries of use have worn them smooth and stripped away any excess ornamentation. Only pure plot and simple morality remain.

But...It's complicated.

You see, for all their whimsy, fairy tales have always been grim (and also Grimm—although the famous brothers were only the most well-known members of a much larger population of traditional folklore collectors). Yes, there are enchanted slippers and fortune-telling mirrors, determined piggies and brave young orphans, but there's also cannibalism and murder and ogres and witches and terrible, terrible parents. Anyone who tells you otherwise is referencing the sanitized, toothless shadows of the real stories—the ones that we feed to children today because we want to protect them from the darkness.

But the truth is, if we don't confront the imaginary monsters in the safe spaces of stories, eventually we will find ourselves defenseless when the real things with teeth and claws come at us from the world's metaphorical woods—or worse, from the wilderness inside our own minds.

Bill Willingham has always known this. He knows that there's a reason evil queens are intent on eating people's hearts: because our interiors are where the truth of us lies. In the source material he draws on (the Grimms, yes, but also Perrault, Scott, Afanasyev, and the thousand voices speaking through Scheherazade or Anansi), morality is complex and fluid. The ground shifts beneath us. Good wins, except when it doesn't. Evil gets its comeuppance, except when it escapes unscathed to come tapping at the window another night. Determination and integrity are not always enough, because people (and fairies and genies and winds) are fickle and messy and constantly change their minds and motives.

FABLES takes the stories that we thought we knew, the ones threaded into our cultural DNA, and turns them into something strange and new and magical precisely because it gets to the bloody, pounding heart of being human. (Never mind that the cast includes toys and talking animals, dragons and dryads, wolves and tigers.) It's about relationships: family, friendship, love, rivalry, enmity, how characters are tested in the dark places, and how they come out on the other side.

Of course, darkness lacks meaning if there's no light to serve as a contrast. You need whimsy and wonder and humor. You need the signature details that catch in the imagination, like the trail of breadcrumbs, the talking harp, the golden goose and the glass slippers that should have been fur but for a mistranslation from the original French.

That mix of light and dark is something Willingham and his collaborators do extraordinarily well—particularly in this volume, where the status quo has been swept aside and anything can happen. Mr. Dark, the Big Bad of the past forty-odd issues, has been taken out of the picture, along with a few other major players. As a result, it's now time to start squaring things away for the Rose Red vs. Snow White grudge match that FABLES has been foreshadowing from the start, complete with all the swords and oaths and magical transformations that you've come to expect—as well as the decidedly *unexpected* reintroduction of the impressively awful Prince Brandish, last seen in the portents-laden flashbacks of "Rose Red."

This volume also features the strange adventures of "A Revolution in Oz," with Shawn McManus' art placing us on a wholly different visual plane from the iconically delineated realm of Mark Buckingham and Steve Leialoha. This detour to Oz, together with "Cubs in Toyland," the unsettling excursion that follows it, expands the FABLES universe and gives Willingham space to tell his stories at a greater remove. The two tales are also a welcome distraction from the high stakes and heartbreak that plays out in the concluding storyline "Snow White"—though the term "distraction" is misleading, since these seemingly tangential stories are each rich with the elemental features of the most powerful myths and legends: sacrifice, magical tools, kings, blood, death, renewal...all of that *Golden Bough* Fisher King stuff.

These side trips also hint at the ultimate destiny that Willingham has in store for the Wolf family: transformation into a (for lack of a better term) pantheon. Of course, anyone who reads mythology knows that when a family is made up of gods (or wolves, or kings), feuds among its members tend to result in higher-than-normal body counts.

True to its classical roots, there isn't even an obvious villain in "Cubs In Toyland"—just desperate individuals who do terrible, surprising things in order to accomplish what they hold as their sworn duty. Bufkin's adventures in Oz are, thankfully, less devastating, though there are still plenty of moments that make the blood quicken. That ability to shift between horror and comedy—often within the beats of a single page—is one that Willingham (and Buckingham, and McManus, all of whom can switch genres at the drop of a head) polishes to a mirrored sheen.

Here, as in every volume of the FABLES saga, Willingham's *coup de théâtre* is not his transformation of childhood memories into something dark and different. It's not his reimagination of characters like kindly old Geppetto and the Big Bad Wolf into power-mad schemers and beat cops. It's how he reveals the darkness and differences within folklore's archetypes that were always present, at their cores. Stuffed toys, fairy tales, the book you're holding in your hands: all are monstrous and comforting, worrying and beguiling. They aren't smoothed out at all; they're rough and jagged.

How else could they teach you anything?

—Lauren Beukes
June 2016

When You Need a

HERO!

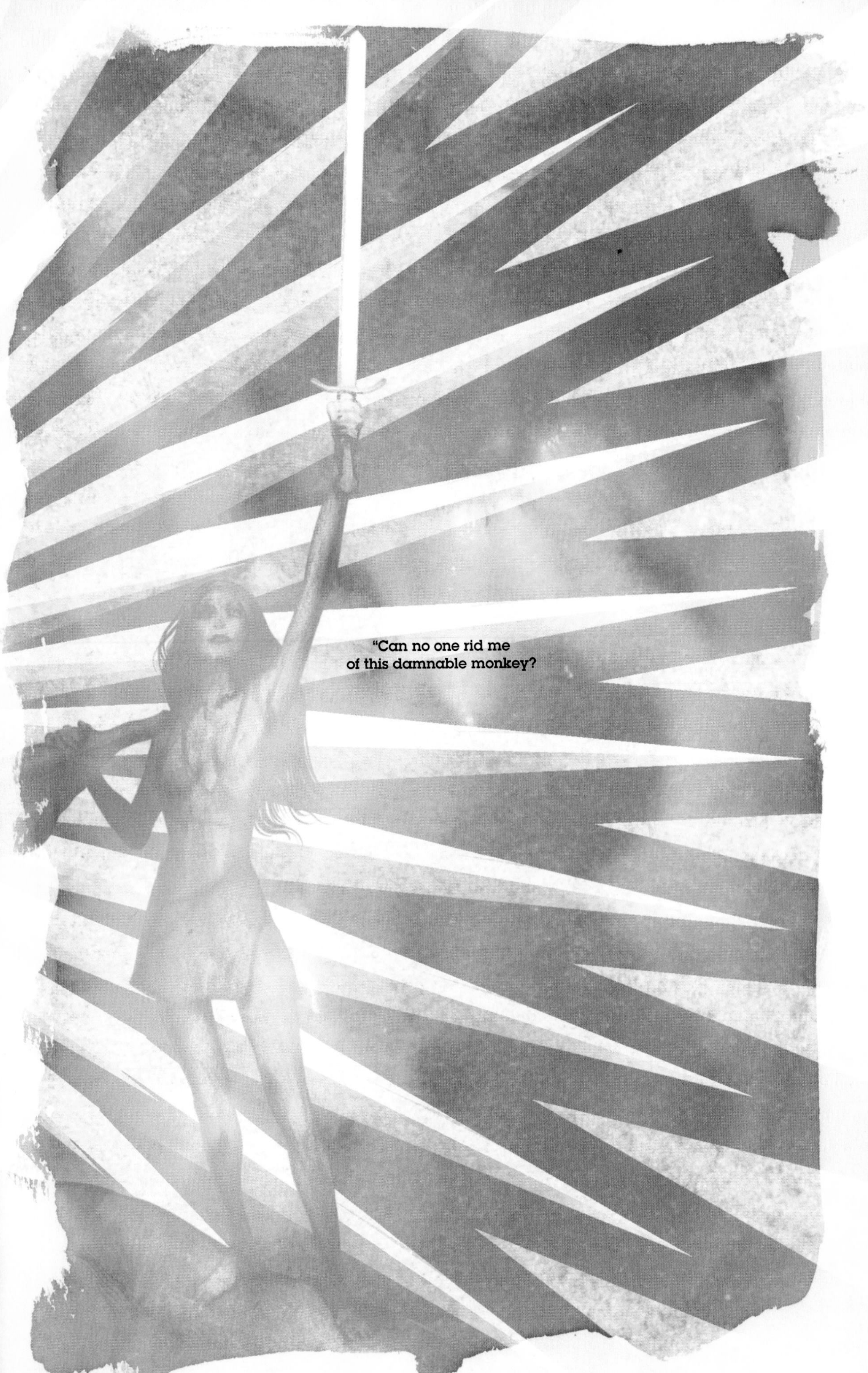
"Can no one rid me
of this damnable monkey?

A REVOLUTION in OZ
Chapter One: THE TREASURE HOUSE
Bill Willingham writer/creator
Shawn McManus artist
Todd Klein letters
Gregory Lockard assistant editor
Shelly Bond editor
LET'S TURN THE CLOCK BACK A FEW DAYS AND SEE WHAT WE CAN SEE...
ATTENTION TO ORDERS!
WHAT NOW?
A DISPATCH DIRECTLY FROM THE FORTY-SECOND UNDER-MINISTER FOR IMPERIAL SECURITY AND SUSPICION. HIGHEST PRIORITY.
AGAIN? BUT WE JUST--
HAVEN'T WE GOT ENOUGH ON OUR PLATE WITHOUT THESE CONSTANT BUREAUCRATIC INTER-FERENCES?
LOOK LIVELY, GENTLEMEN.
TOMS.
THE HIGH MUCKY-MUCKS, IN THEIR INFINITE WISDOM, HAVE ORDAINED YET ANOTHER INVENTORY.

THIS IS GETTING RIDICULOUS.
SECURE THAT MUTINOUS TALK, SOLDIER!
IF THE OVERLORDS NEED REASSURANCE THAT THEIR WEAPONS-GRADE MAGICAL TREASURES ARE SAFE, WE'LL PROVIDE IT WITH THE PROPER MILITARY COMPORTMENT.
LET'S GET THESE DOORS OPEN, TOM.
SWEET SLIPPERS OF DOOM!
IT'S EMPTY, CAPTAIN.
ALL THE MAGIC ITEMS--
I CAN SEE THAT, TOM!
CAN'T I SEE THAT FOR MYSELF?!
OF COURSE I MOST CERTAINLY CAN!
LOOK! A HOLE IN THE FLOOR!
91
SOMEBODY DUG INTO THE BUNKER FROM BELOW!
BLOODY RENEGADE NOMES DID THIS! I'LL WARRANT THAT MUCH!

"WHO MADE OFF WITH OUR WEAPONS?"
WE GOT AWAY WITH EVERY-THING!
EVERYTHING!
THE GOLDEN CAP! WITH THIS WE CAN TURN THE AIR PATROL TO OUR SIDE!
NOT YET. WE'LL HOLD OFF UNTIL THEY CAN BE USED IN A SUDDEN SURPRISE ATTACK.
LOOK! THE POWDER OF LIFE! PRACTICALLY MY OWN FATHER AND MOTHER IN A BOX!
I'M MORE INTERESTED IN THE EXPECTACLES. IF WE CAN SEE WHAT HAPPENED TO BUFKIN--
I'LL TAKE CHARGE OF ALL THE CASKS OF OBLIVION WATER. REVOLUTIONARIES WHO CAN'T REMEMBER SECRETS CAN'T SPILL SECRETS!
THAT'S AN ADVANTAGE WE SHAN'T SQUANDER.
Next: Victory is assured!

A REVOLUTION in OZ
Chapter Two: THE BIG PLAN
Bill Willingham writer/creator
Shawn McManus artist
Todd Klein letters
Gregory Lockard assistant editor
Shelly Bond editor
TAKE A PEEK THROUGH THE MAGIC EXPECTACLES AND ONE CAN SEE THE IMMEDIATE FUTURE.
WHOA!
THE LOVELY AND DARING LILY MARTAGNION SEES GLIMPSES BOTH OBSCURE AND VAGUE, AND NOT OF HERSELF.
...CAUGHT A BIT OF LUCK THERE...
...HANGED TODAY...
...EATEN ALIVE BY TIGER BEETLES...
...ANY FINAL WORDS, SAY THEM NOW!

OH NO!
WAKE UP!
EVERYONE WAKE UP!
GGGRRRRRR-RUMMPHHH?
JACK PUMPKIN-HEAD!
WAKE UP, YOU LAZY GOURD!
HUH?
LILY?
WHAT'S THE MATTER?
THEY'RE GOING TO KILL MY BOYFRIEND, THAT'S WHAT!
THEY'RE GOING TO HANG BUFKIN!

A WEE BIT LATER...
WE HAVE TO MOUNT AN IMMEDIATE PLAN TO RESCUE HIM, OF COURSE.
FIRST WE'LL MAKE USE OF THE POWDER OF LIFE TO--
HOLD ON! NOT SO FAST!
I'VE BEEN AT WAR WITH THE EMPEROR SINCE BACK WHEN HE WAS STILL JUST ANOTHER KING.
AND I'VE LEARNED A THING OR TWO ABOUT REVOLUTIONARY WAR IN THAT TIME.
SPECIFICALLY, OUR STRUGGLE IS BIGGER THAN THE FATE OF ANY ONE MEMBER. WE'RE NOT READY TO STRIKE YET.
YOUR GROUNDED AIR MONKEY WILL JUST HAVE TO FEND FOR HIMSELF, KNOWING THAT HIS NOBLE SACRIFICE WILL SERVE THE GREATER GOOD.
WE'LL HONOR HIM OF COURSE--A GREAT MARTYR TO THE CAUSE.
HOW DARE YOU?!
HE'S OUR LEADER! WE HAVE TO--
AND, AS OF NOW, I'M IN COMMAND OF IT.
NO!!
HOW DARE YOU, LITTLE BUG!
THIS IS A WAR, NOT A ROMANCE!
Next: Those who dare...

A REVOLUTION in OZ
Chapter Three: AT THE END OF HIS ROPE
Bill Willingham writer/creator
Shawn McManus artist
Todd Klein letters
Gregory Lockard assistant editor
Shelly Bond editor
THAT FATEFUL DAY CAME WHEN BUFKIN, PRINCE OF THE REVOLUTIONARIES, WAS HANGED FOR TREASON.
HANGMAN, CARRY OUT THE SENTENCE OF THIS COURT.
SEE YOU ALL IN HELL!
NOTHING COULD SAVE HIM.
UNLESS...
...THE ROPE REFUSED TO COOPERATE.

YOWCH!
BONK!
HOW...?
DON'T TRY TO FIGURE IT OUT! JUST RUN FOR IT, SWEETIE!
ARE YOU TRYING TO GET CAUGHT AGAIN? MOVE YOUR ASS, YOU SAD SACK OF MONKEY-FLAVORED FECES!
HOW IS IT THERE ISN'T A DEAD MONKEY AT THE END OF THIS ROPE?
I COULDN'T SAY. I TIED THAT NOOSE MYSELF.
I'M ALIVE!
JUST LIKE THE LITTLE GIRL PROMISED!

HAVE A POKE IN THE EYE, HANGMAN!
AND YOU, TOO, YOU STUFFY OLD BASTARD!
YOU HAVE A POKE IN THE EYE, TOO!
BINK!
OW!
THIS HANGMAN'S ROPE IS FREE FROM HUMAN BONDAGE!
HUZZAH!
I'M FREE!
ODD THAT I'M STILL FEELING SORT OF MURDERY, THOUGH. I GUESS I'M A TRUE HANG-MAN'S ROPE BY NATURE.
HOW'D YOU DO THAT, LILY?
POWDER OF LIFE APPLIED TO THE ROPE IN THE WEE HOURS!
AM I ONE HOT AND SASSY GIRLFRIEND, OR WHAT?
Next: What about that nome general who wanted to take over the revolution?

A REVOLUTION in OZ
Chapter Four: GENERAL ORDERS
Bill Willingham writer/creator
Shawn McManus artist
Todd Klein letters
Gregory Lockard assistant editor
Shelly Bond editor
ONCE UPON A TIME THERE WAS A REVOLUTION WHOSE LEADERS WERE AT ODDS ON HOW BEST TO PROCEED.
SO I SAYS TO MY WIFE WITH THE WOODEN LEG; "PEG," I SAYS, "WHY DON'T YOU GET ON THE STICK?"
I DON'T GET IT.
NEITHER DO I, BUT IT SEEMED REALLY FUNNY WHEN SAWHORSE TOLD IT TO THE OTHERS.
I'D NEVER MARRY A WOMAN WITHOUT TWO GOOD STONE LEGS.
HERE'S YOUR LUNCH, GENERAL BLUG.
PRIVATE BONDLE! CORPORAL ZAN! YOU STINKERS!

UNTIE ME AT ONCE!
CAN'T DO THAT, SIR. YOU'LL JUST GET ALL TREASONY AGAINST THE REVOLUTION AGAIN.
AT LEAST QUIT FEEDING ME!
CAN'T DO THAT EITHER, SIR. ORDERS ARE TO KEEP YOU BLOATED, SLEEPY AND LISTLESS.
SO YOU CAN'T ESCAPE THROUGH THE ROCK, AND SELL US OUT TO THE EMPIRE.
OPEN WIDE, SIR. THERE'S A GOOD GENERAL.
GUGG! NGUH!
THAT'S IT, SIR. EAT EVERY BITE OR NO DESSERT.
WE'LL BE BACK IN TEN MINUTES WITH SECOND LUNCH, FOLLOWED CLOSELY BY EARLY DINNER.

WELCOME BACK, BOSS!
WELL, LOOK WHO'S HERE!
HOW WAS THE ESCAPE?
DARING.
BUFKIN WAS MARVELOUS!
YOU SHOULD HAVE SEEN HIM, DODGING EMERALD CITY GUARDS, KEEPING OUT OF SIGHT FROM THE AIR PATROL!
I HAVE THE BEST BOYFRIEND EVER!
I THOUGHT WE TALKED ABOUT THAT.
NOT ENOUGH. DON'T YOU KNOW ANYTHING ABOUT WOMEN? THAT CONVERSATION ONLY ENDS WHEN YOU SAY, "YES, LILY, MY LOVE. ANYTHING YOU SAY, LILY MY SWEET."
ANYTHING EXCITING HAPPEN HERE WHILE I WAS GONE?
NOT TOO MUCH.
ALTHOUGH WE'VE MANAGED TO REACH THE STEREOTYPICAL YET INEVITABLE "FALLING OUT" STAGE OF THE REVOLUTION.
ARE SHOW TRIALS NEXT? OH, I DO HOPE SO!
Next: Battle Plans!

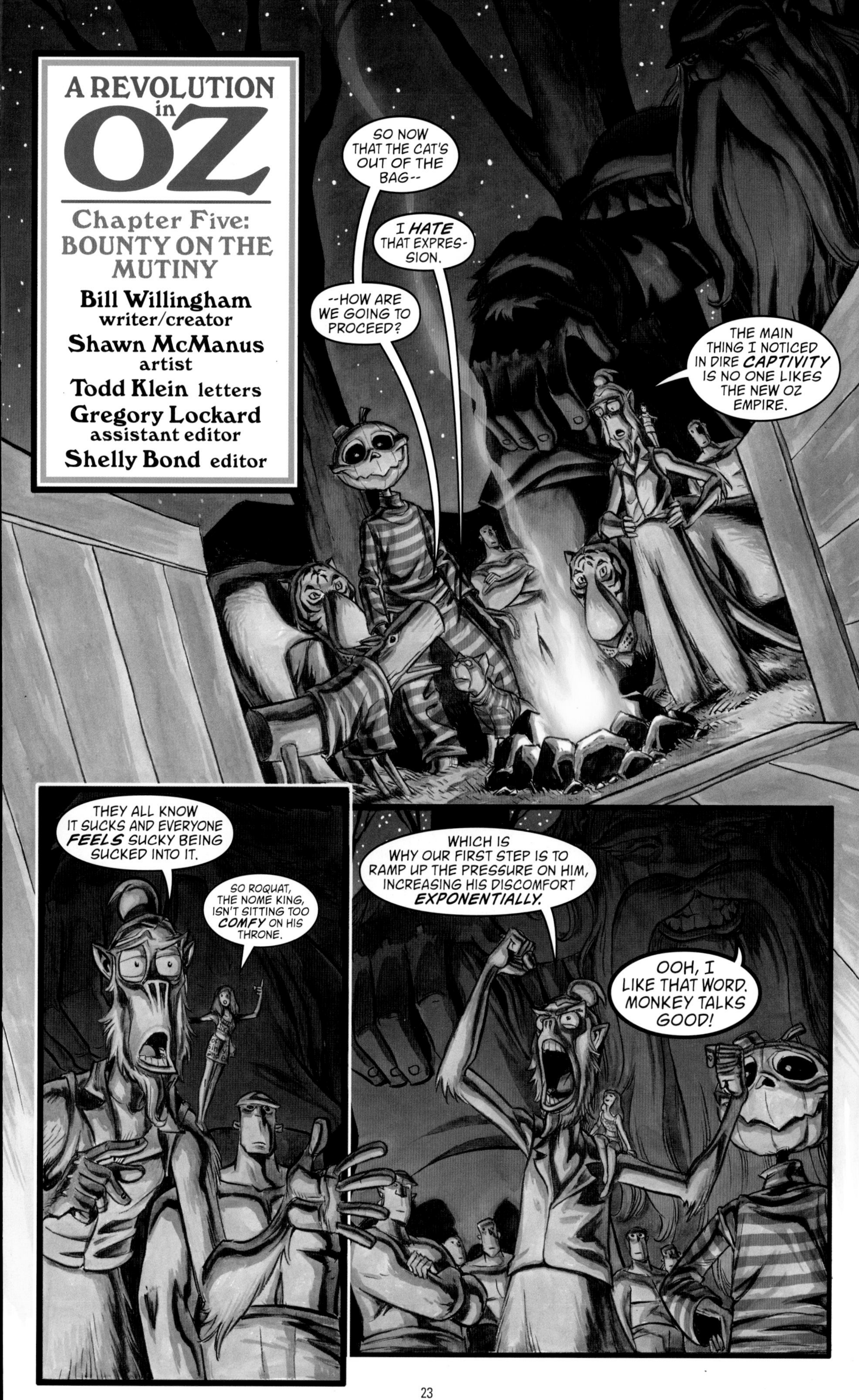
A REVOLUTION in OZ
Chapter Five: BOUNTY ON THE MUTINY
Bill Willingham writer/creator
Shawn McManus artist
Todd Klein letters
Gregory Lockard assistant editor
Shelly Bond editor
SO NOW THAT THE CAT'S OUT OF THE BAG--
I HATE THAT EXPRES-SION.
--HOW ARE WE GOING TO PROCEED?
THE MAIN THING I NOTICED IN DIRE CAPTIVITY IS NO ONE LIKES THE NEW OZ EMPIRE.
THEY ALL KNOW IT SUCKS AND EVERYONE FEELS SUCKY BEING SUCKED INTO IT.
SO ROQUAT, THE NOME KING, ISN'T SITTING TOO COMFY ON HIS THRONE.
WHICH IS WHY OUR FIRST STEP IS TO RAMP UP THE PRESSURE ON HIM, INCREASING HIS DISCOMFORT EXPONENTIALLY.
OOH, I LIKE THAT WORD. MONKEY TALKS GOOD!

I PROPOSE WE OFFER A FAT BOUNTY ON ROQUAT'S STONY HEAD.
THAT'S A LOVELY IDEA!
EXCEPT WE'VE GOT NO TREASURE TO USE FOR THE BOUNTY.
NOTHING?
NOT UNLESS YOU WANT TO START GIVING AWAY ALL THE BIG MAGIC STUFF WE RISKED SO MUCH TO CAPTURE.
NO, WE CAN'T DO THAT. WE NEED EVERY SCRAP OF THAT FOR THE FIGHTING.
OH DEAR. I DO BELIEVE OUR CONUN-DRUMS HAVE INCREASED EXPONEN-TIALLY.
SO, IF WE DON'T HAVE THE CASH TO FLOAT A BIG PAYOUT, WHAT IF WE WENT THE OTHER WAY?
WADDAYA MEAN, LILY?
WHAT IF WE LOUDLY AND PUBLICLY OFFERED A REALLY SMALL PRICE ON HIS HEAD? WOULDN'T THAT HUMILIATE AS WELL AS ENRAGE HIM?
GENIUS!

TWO LOLLIPOPS?
TWO LOLLIPOPS FOR MY HEAD?
THIS INSULT TO MY MOST AUGUST AND EXTRAORDINARY PERSONAGE CANNOT BE ENDURED!
GUARDS! SOLDIERS OF THE REALM! DIVERSE MONSTERS AND MECHANISMS!
REWARD!
CAN NO ONE RID ME OF THIS DAMNABLE MONKEY?!
TWO LOLLIPOPS FOR THE CAPTURE OR DEATH OF THE STINKY POOP UPSTART EMPEROR, ROQUAT!
Bufkin THE liberator.
NEXT: The pressure increases (exponentially)!

A REVOLUTION in OZ
Chapter Six: THE LOLLIPOP KILLED
Bill Willingham writer/creator
Shawn McManus artist
Todd Klein letters
Gregory Lockard assistant editor
Shelly Bond editor
THE EMERALD CITY, CAPITAL OF THE NEW OZIAN EMPIRE.
ARE YOU SURE ABOUT THIS, YOUR IMPERIALNESS? THE PEOPLE HAVE BEEN ACTING PRETTY RESTLESS LATELY.
IT'S SECOND SHOE DAY.* I ALWAYS PARADE BEFORE MY LOYAL SUBJECTS ON THE SECOND SECOND SHOE DAY OF EVERY MONTH.
TRADITIONS UNITE EMPIRES. EVEN THE MOST SUPERFICIAL ONES MUST BE UPHELD.
HERE I AM, YOU NOTHINGS AND MEANINGLESS, WRETCHED CRAWLERS AND SCRAPERS!
THERE HE IS NOW.
OPPRESSIVE MOOP.
SHHHHH! BE CAREFUL, PALLIODINO. HIS SPIES ARE EVERY-WHERE.
*Celebrating when the "other shoe" dropped, of course, when Roquat first declared himself no longer the governor of one district of Gep-petto's foundering empire, but the new Emperor in full of his own, more localized empire.

BASK IN THE GLORY OF YOUR LIBERATOR!
DID YOU SEE THAT PAPER POSTING A REWARD FOR HIS STONY MELON ON A PLATTER?
THE ONE OFFERING TWO LOLLIPOPS? SURE I DID. IT'S EVERY-WHERE, NO MATTER HOW OFTEN THEY TEAR THEM DOWN.
WELL, WATCH THIS.
HEY, MISTER EMPEROR!
HERE!
SUCK ON THIS!

PLOP!
HUH?
NOW YOU'RE WORTH THREE LOLLI-POPS!
HAR HAR!
WHO DID THIS?!
WHO SHOUTED?!
NO ONE?
NOT ONE OF YOU HAS THE STONES TO SPEAK UP?
VERY WELL!
GUARDS!
KILL ALL OF THEM UNTIL SOMEONE CONFESSES!
NEXT: The bloodiest day in Oz!

A REVOLUTION in OZ
Chapter Seven: A SINGLE LOOSE ROCK
Bill Willingham writer/creator
Shawn McManus artist
Todd Klein letters
Gregory Lockard assistant editor
Shelly Bond editor
ON THE SECOND SECOND SHOE DAY, IN THE MONTH OF BASALT, THERE WAS A GREAT SLAUGHTER IN THE EMERALD CITY.
KEEP GOING!
KILL THEM ALL!
THEY SAY A GREAT AVALANCHE CAN START FROM A SINGLE LOOSE ROCK.
CHOP INTO THEM WITH CHOPPY FERVOR!
DON'T STOP UNTIL EVERY MISERABLE HEAD IS SEPARATED FROM ITS DESPICABLE, IGNOBLE, LICE-RIDDEN PEASANT BODY!
YES, SIRE!
11

SOME SAY THE BLOODY REVOLUTION AGAINST ROQUAT THE FIRST WAS BORN OF A SINGLE THROWN LOLLIPOP.
NO ONE WHO'S SEEN MY HUMILIATION MAY LIVE TO TELL ABOUT IT!
CAPTAIN, HAVE THE AIR PATROL SEARCH AMONG THE CORPSES FOR SURVIVORS AND THOSE FAKING DEATH!
AND HAVE THEM CIRCLE THE AREA FOR ANYONE WHO SCAMPERED AWAY.
YES, S-- HUH?
WHERE IS THE AIR PATROL?
HOLY KRAKAMUNGO! THERE'S NO AIR COVER AT ALL OVERHEAD!
OKAY, I'M SENSING SUCCESS ACROSS THE BOARD.
ALL FLYING MONKEYS ARE GROUNDED AND IN HIDING.
AND YOU'RE CONTROLLING EVERY ONE OF US THROUGH THE GOLDEN CAP?
NO, JUST THE OFFICERS SO FAR, USING THEM TO COMMAND THE RANK AND FILE IN THE OLD-FASHIONED WAY OF BARKING ORDERS.
I BELIEVE I COULD EASILY DIAL THE CAP UP TO ELEVEN AND DIRECTLY CONTROL EACH AND EVERY MONKEY...
...BUT I DON'T WANT TO GO MAD AND DRUNK WITH POWER.

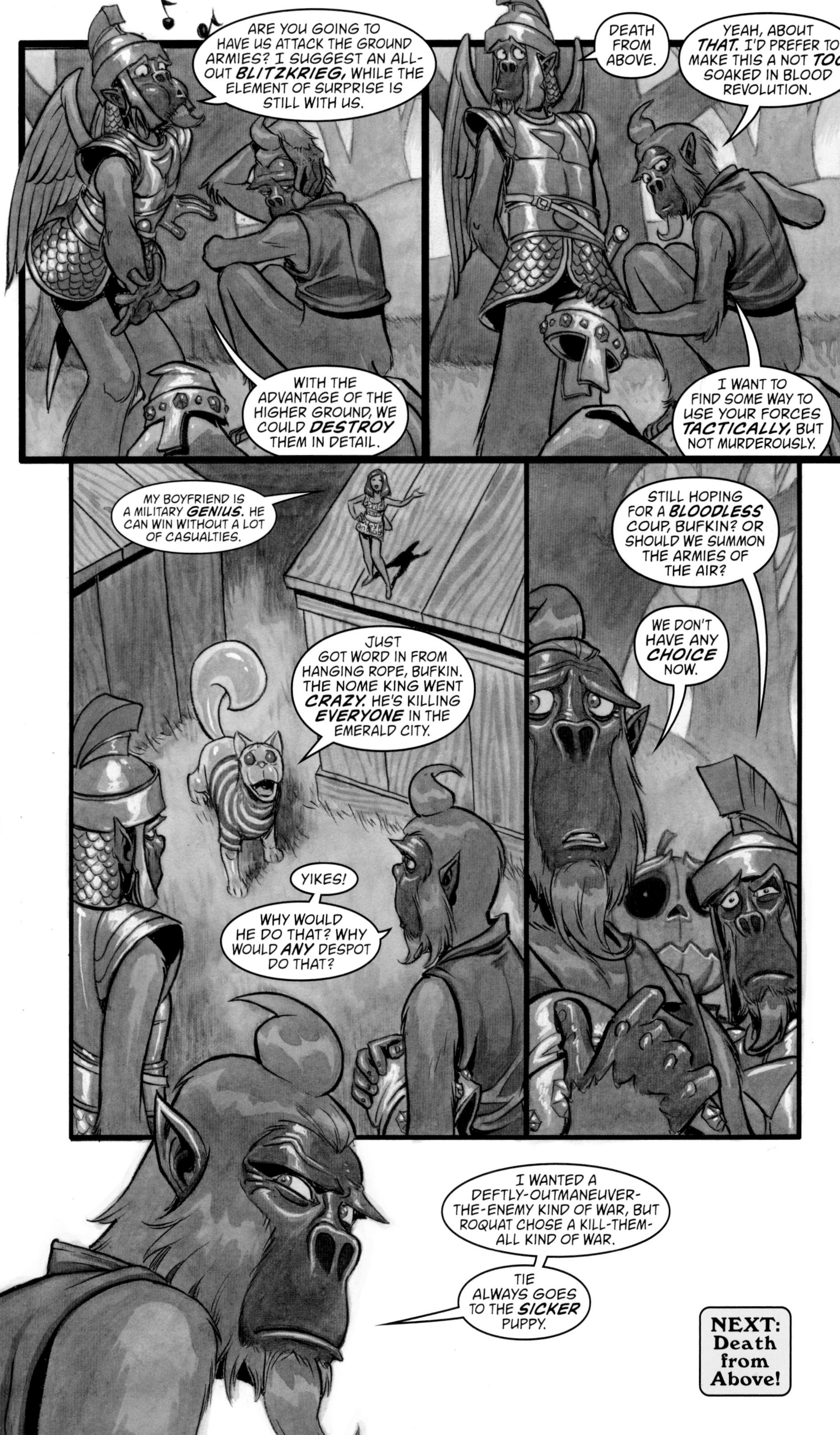
ARE YOU GOING TO HAVE US ATTACK THE GROUND ARMIES? I SUGGEST AN ALL-OUT BLITZKRIEG, WHILE THE ELEMENT OF SURPRISE IS STILL WITH US.
WITH THE ADVANTAGE OF THE HIGHER GROUND, WE COULD DESTROY THEM IN DETAIL.
DEATH FROM ABOVE.
YEAH, ABOUT THAT. I'D PREFER TO MAKE THIS A NOT TOO SOAKED IN BLOOD REVOLUTION.
I WANT TO FIND SOME WAY TO USE YOUR FORCES TACTICALLY, BUT NOT MURDEROUSLY.
MY BOYFRIEND IS A MILITARY GENIUS. HE CAN WIN WITHOUT A LOT OF CASUALTIES.
JUST GOT WORD IN FROM HANGING ROPE, BUFKIN. THE NOME KING WENT CRAZY. HE'S KILLING EVERYONE IN THE EMERALD CITY.
YIKES!
WHY WOULD HE DO THAT? WHY WOULD ANY DESPOT DO THAT?
STILL HOPING FOR A BLOODLESS COUP, BUFKIN? OR SHOULD WE SUMMON THE ARMIES OF THE AIR?
WE DON'T HAVE ANY CHOICE NOW.
I WANTED A DEFTLY-OUTMANEUVER-THE-ENEMY KIND OF WAR, BUT ROQUAT CHOSE A KILL-THEM-ALL KIND OF WAR.
TIE ALWAYS GOES TO THE SICKER PUPPY.
NEXT: Death from Above!

A REVOLUTION in OZ
Chapter Eight: FLIGHT WITHOUT WINGS
Bill Willingham writer/creator
Shawn McManus artist
Todd Klein letters
Gregory Lockard assistant editor
Shelly Bond editor
THREE MONTHS LATER...
WE SHOULDN'T MARCH IN THE OPEN, SIR.
WE'RE VISIBLE TO ANY OF THE ENEMY'S AIR PATROLS THAT MAY HAPPEN BY.
WE'VE NO CHOICE. OUR EMPEROR COMMANDS IT.
WANTS US TO SHOW THE COLORS.
PROVE THAT HE STILL RUNS THINGS.
2

DOES HE?
I'M NOT SURE, MAJOR BUBBIC. STILL, BEST NOT BE OVERHEARD TALKING LIKE THAT.
LOOK!
MONKEYS!
TROOP WILL FORM RANKS!
TRY TO--
2
TRY TO DO WHAT YOU CAN.

I DIDN'T WANT THIS.
THERE ARE WAYS TO DO A REVOLUTION THAT DON'T *REQUIRE* A HIGH BODY COUNT.
HOW DO *YOU* KNOW?
MY BOYFRIEND IS VERY WELL-READ.
REALLY? LOOKS SORT OF *BLUISH* TO ME.
ANOTHER VICTORY FOR *BUFKIN* THE LIBERATOR!
ALL HAIL BUFKIN--THE ONLY MONKEY WHO CAN *FLY WITHOUT WINGS!*
WHAT DOES *THAT* MEAN?
I--WELL, UH, I WAS TRYING FOR SOMETHING *POETIC.*
STIRRING, WITHOUT--Y'KNOW--BEING SO LITERAL.
NEXT: All the Marbles!

Chapter Nine: ALL THE MARBLES

Bill Willingham writer/creator
Shawn McManus artist
Todd Klein letters
Gregory Lockard assistant editor
Shelly Bond editor

WHERE ARE WE GOING, TOM?
I DON'T HAVE THE FAINTEST IDEA, TOM.
FAR AWAY FROM HERE IS THE BEST I CAN PURPOSE.
SOMEWHERE SAFE, RIGHT?

THAT'S THE PLAN.
WELL, IT'S MY HOPE AT LEAST. OLD TOM NUMBER FOUR ALWAYS SAID, "HOPE ISN'T A PLAN."
WE SHOULD HAVE WAITED FOR TOM THIRTY-SEVEN. HE WANTED TO GO WITH US.

WE DID WAIT! TOO LONG!

WE'LL HAVE TO PRESUME THIRTY-SEVEN WAS TAKEN, JUST LIKE NINE, EIGHTEEN, FORTY-FOUR AND SIXTY-ONE.
OUR ENTIRE POKER CLUB.
ALONG WITH HUNDREDS OF OTHER RUMBLE TUMBLE TOMS OVER THE PAST FEW DAYS.
SOMETHING TERRIBLE IS SINGLING US OUT IN PARTICULAR. SOMETHING FROM--
LOOK OUT, TOM!
YYYAAAII-IIIGGHHH!!
ANOTHER ONE!
YIPPEE!
MMMMMM!
OW! OW!
MURDER MOST FOUL!
PHEW!

AND A LOW NUMBER, TOO!
THOSE ARE THE BEST ONES!
MORE COLLECT-IBLE!
YOOP'S BUILDING THE BEST BAG OF MARBLES EVER!
NOW WHERE DID THAT OTHER MARBLE-RIDING MAN GO?
CRASH!
TOM?
WHAT DID THAT MONSTER DO TO YOU?!
ROLL, TOM. ROLL FOR YOUR LIFE. BUT I THINK 'TIS FOR NAUGHT. THE DAY OF TOMS IS PAST.
93
NEXT: The End of the Emperor?

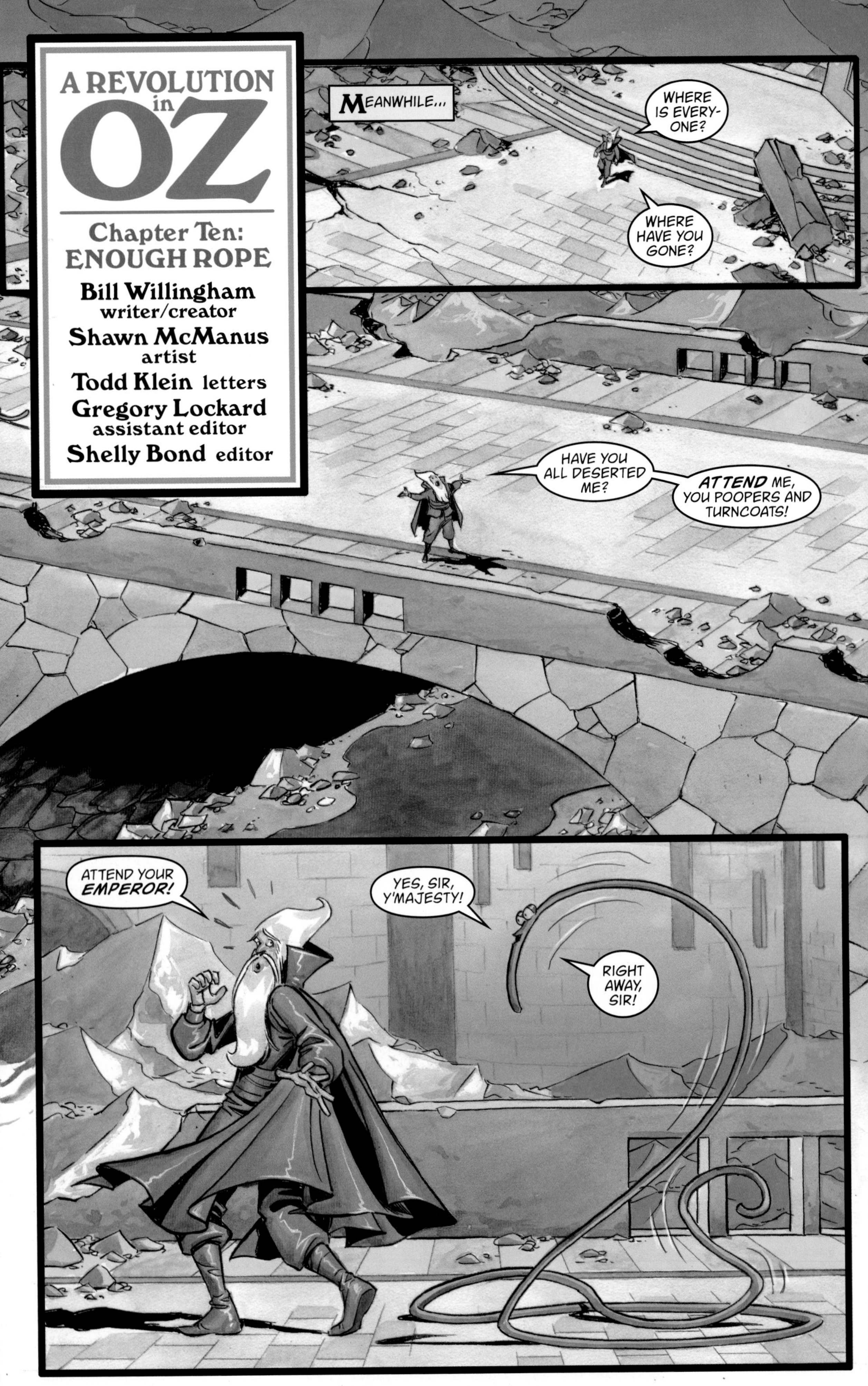
A REVOLUTION in OZ
Chapter Ten: ENOUGH ROPE
Bill Willingham writer/creator
Shawn McManus artist
Todd Klein letters
Gregory Lockard assistant editor
Shelly Bond editor
MEANWHILE...
WHERE IS EVERY-ONE?
WHERE HAVE YOU GONE?
HAVE YOU ALL DESERTED ME?
ATTEND ME, YOU POOPERS AND TURNCOATS!
ATTEND YOUR EMPEROR!
YES, SIR, Y'MAJESTY!
RIGHT AWAY, SIR!

WHO ARE YOU?
YOUR IMPERIAL HANGING ROPE, EMPEROR!
HERE TO PERFORM MY FINAL SERVICE TO THE EMPIRE.
WHAT'S THAT?
HANGING THE CORRUPT, BLOODY-HANDED DESPOT, OF COURSE!
HANGING YOU FROM THE VERY BRIDGE OF YOUR MOST GENO-CIDAL ACT!
HOW DARE YOU, I--!
YAAHHHH!

UUUUUR-RRRGG...
YOU'RE NOT DEAD?
AFTER THAT FALL AND SNAP?
MY NECK'S MADE OF STONE, YOU NINCOMPOOP! OF COURSE I'M NOT DEAD!
FINE!
SO I'LL HAVE TO TRY A LITTLE HARDER! BUT HANGING'S MY PROFESSION, AND HANG YOU I WILL!
EVEN IF I HAVE TO SNAP YOU LIKE A WHIP!
OR...
POP!
UH...SOMETIMES THE SUBJECT'S HEAD POPPING OFF HAPPENS TO BE AN OCCASIONAL RESULT OF A PROPERLY CONDUCTED HANGING.
TRUST ME. IT'S OFTEN TO BE EXPECTED.
NEXT: A full-sized issue bringing it all to the grand finale!

A REVOLUTION in OZ
Chapter Eleven: Emperor Bufkin
Bill Willingham writer/creator
Shawn McManus artist
Todd Klein letters
Gregory Lockard assistant editor
Shelly Bond editor
THAT NIGHT, AND ALL THROUGH THE NEXT DAY, WE CELEBRATED!
WE WON! WE WON!
DING DONG, THE NOME KING IS DEAD!
MY BOYFRIEND PARTIED HARDER THAN ANYONE.
WHICH NOME KING?
OUR MEAN NOME KING!
NOME KING COULDN'T HAVE BEEN ALL THAT BAD, CONSIDERING HE KEPT A HUGE STOCKPILE OF BOOZE AND DIDN'T LOCK NONE OF IT AWAY!
WELL, THAT DOESN'T NARROW IT DOWN MUCH. TRUTH BE TOLD, ALL THE NOMES TEND TOWARDS MEANINESS. WHOEVER THEY ELECT IS LIKELY TO BE JUST AS--
HEY!

DO WE EVEN GET TO HAVE A NEW NOME KING? WILL BUFKIN LET US?
WHY NOT? AND WHY WOULD BUFKIN HAVE A SAY IN IT, ONE WAY OR THE OTHER?
WELL, BECAUSE HE'S GOING TO BE THE NEW EMPEROR OF THE COMBINED OZIAN EMPIRE.
ISN'T HE?
WHO SAYS?
LET ME TELL YOU ONE THING RIGHT NOW, BUDDY BOY!
IF YOU THINK MY FELLA BUFKIN IS GOING TO STEP INTO THE OLD DESPOT'S SHOES AND DECLARE HIMSELF UNOPPOSED EMPEROR OF THE ENTIRE GREATER OZIAN FANDANGO...
THAT'S A GREAT IDEA!
I AGREE!
ALL HAIL BUFKIN THE FIRST!

HEY!
HOLD ON THERE! REIN IT IN!
WAIT JUST A NOSE-PICKING MINUTE!
I HAVE NO NOTION OF BECOMING EMPEROR OF OZ! ZERO! NADA! NEIN!
I'M NOT GOING TO BE ANYONE'S EMPEROR!
SURE, I'D BE GOOD AT IT. HOW COULD I NOT BE?
I MEAN-- JUST LOOK AT ME.
OH, I'M LOOKING, MONKEY MAN.
I'M LOOKING ALLA DAMN TIME.
I'M BUILT OF AWESOMINITY! BORN TO LEAD!
BUT NOT HERE AND NOT NOW.
EXCELLENT! SO I CAN BE EMPEROR, SINCE YOU DON'T WANT IT?
NEXT: Monkey gives a speech.

A REVOLUTION in OZ
Chapter Twelve: The Talking Monkey
Bill Willingham writer/creator
Shawn McManus artist
Todd Klein letters
Gregory Lockard assistant editor
Shelly Bond editor
LONG AFTER WE SOBERED UP, MY BOYFRIEND STILL HAD A BEE IN HIS BONNET ABOUT THAT "CROWNING HIM THE NEW EMPEROR OF OZ" BUSINESS.
I CALLED YOU HERE, BACK TO THE OLD CAMP, BECAUSE YOU WERE THE FIRST MEMBERS OF THE GRAND AND GLORIOUS STRUGGLE.
SURE, I GOT A LITTLE CARRIED AWAY. WHAT GIRL DOESN'T WANT HER GUY TO DO WELL? BUT BUFKIN NEVER LETS ANYTHING DROP UNTIL HE'S THOROUGHLY CHEWED IT TO DEATH.
IT'S HIS WAY, GOD BLESS THE BIG CUTIE.
IT WAS REALLY YOUR REVOLUTION ALL ALONG. I WAS JUST A HIRED GUN--A BEOWULF TO YOUR HROTHGAR.
I DON'T THINK I HAVE ONE OF THOSE. MAYBE PUMPKINS DON'T COME DOWN WITH HROTHGARS.

JUST YOUR AVERAGE MIGHTY DEMIGOD SUPER HERO WHO **HAPPENED BY** WHEN YOU NEEDED ME MOST.
DO TELL.
SHUSH, YOU.
HE'S JUST ABOUT TO GET TO THE **HUMBLE** PART.
I'VE SEEN HIM DO THIS BEFORE.
UHM...SO THEN ANYWAY, EVEN THOUGH I CAME FROM OZ, I DON'T **BELONG** HERE ANYMORE--WHETHER AS EXALTED LORD EMPEROR OR JUST ANOTHER AVERAGE CITIZEN.
GRANTED: MORE **EX-TRAORDINARY** THAN MOST, BUT YOU GET MY MEANING.
THE REVOLUTION IS OVER AND SO IS MY BUSINESS HERE.
THE HARD WORK OF GOVERNING REMAINS, AND THAT'S WHERE **YOU** COME IN, MY FINE TRIO OF DOUGHTY LIEUTENANTS.
DOUGHY? DID YOU CALL US DOUGHY?
THAT MAKES NO SENSE. BETWEEN THE **THREE** OF US, WE'RE MOSTLY STICKS AND GLASS.

IF YOU WANT TO KEEP THE EMPIRE INTACT, THEN ONE OF YOU WILL HAVE TO BECOME THE NEW EMPEROR.
I RECOMMEND WHICHEVER TWO OF YOU AREN'T CHOSEN, KEEP READY AGAINST THE DAY YOU'LL HAVE TO RAISE A NEW ARMY TO OVERTHROW THE POWER-MAD BUM.
OR BETTER YET, BREAK THE BLOODY DAMN THING APART, BACK INTO ITS ORIGINAL COMPONENT KINGDOMS. OR EVEN FORM NEW ONES.
MAKE THEM SMALL ENOUGH AND I SUSPECT YOU'LL FIND THEY'RE NICER PLACES THAN OTHER-WISE.
YOU AND JUST ABOUT EVERYONE WHO HELPED US COULD BE A KING THEN. WHO KNOWS? GIVE IT A SHOT.
BUT WHAT ABOUT--?
BUT WHAT ABOUT ME?
I MAY SETTLE DOWN AND RULE SOMEPLACE SOMEDAY, BUT NOT YET.
THE ADVENTUROUS ROAD STILL CALLS TO ME FOR NOW.
WHEREVER THERE ARE PEOPLE IN DIRE BONDAGE, I'LL BE THERE.
WHEREVER THERE'S INJUSTICE TO MAKE JUSTIFIABLE AGAIN, I'LL BE THERE!
I WASN'T GOING TO ASK THAT.
NEXT: The departure.

A REVOLUTION in OZ
Chapter Thirteen: The Departure
Bill Willingham writer/creator
Shawn McManus artist
Todd Klein letters
Gregory Lockard assistant editor
Shelly Bond editor
AFTER HIS BIG SPEECH, MY BOYFRIEND ANNOUNCED HE AND I WOULD BE LEAVING IMMEDIATELY, WHICH IS WHAT WE DID.
BUT WE DIDN'T GET FAR.
SO WHEN ARE WE ACTUALLY LEAVING?
SOON, LILY. SOON.
A HERO NEEDS HIS ***RESTORATION*** BETWEEN THRILLING ADVENTURES.
BOTTLE A GENIE AND KILL BABA YAGA: TAKE A BREAK.

OVERTHROW AN EVIL EMPIRE: TAKE ANOTHER BREAK.
AND WHAT BETTER PLACE IN ALL THE WORLDS TO RESTORE ONESELF THAN UNDER THE CARING BOUGHS OF THE LUNCHBOX TREE?
IF I EVER RETIRE, AFTER ALL THE QUESTS ARE QUESTED, ALL THE WARS WON, AND AFTER I'VE GROWN TIRED OF WHATEVER KINGDOM I COME TO RULE, WITH PERFECT BENEVOLENCE--
--I THINK I'LL BUILD ME A COTTAGE NEXT TO THIS TREE AND NEVER WANT FOR ANYTHING AGAIN.
BUILD US A COTTAGE, YOU MEAN. US, MONKEY BOY, OR WE'RE ABOUT TO HAVE WORDS AGAIN!
RELAX, LILY. OF COURSE IT WILL BE FOR THE BOTH OF US. BUT AS LIFELONG FRIENDS, NOT LOVERS.
WE TWO AREN'T BUILT FOR ROMANCE. NOT WITH EACH OTHER.
PARTNERS IN ADVENTURE, BUT NOT THE OTHER THING. ROBIN AND LITTLE JOHN, BUT NOT ROBIN AND MARION.
SHERLOCK AND WATSON, BUT NOT SHERLOCK AND THAT RED-HEADED WOMAN WHOSE NAME ALWAYS ESCAPES ME.

RED SONJA.
I THINK THAT WAS HER NAME.
OR WAS IT JEAN GREY?
THERE YOU ARE!
DO YOU KNOW HOW LONG IT TOOK ME TO TRACK YOU TWO DOWN?
YOW!
RELAX, LOVER, IT'S JUST HANGY THE ROPE. HE'S HARMLESS.
MOSTLY HARMLESS, TO MY FRIENDS AT LEAST.
I WAS BUILT FOR MURDER, THOUGH.
AND WHY EXACTLY ARE YOU HERE?
TO GO WITH YOU, OF COURSE. THE LONG ROAD'S A RAINBOW, BOSS.
AND THAT'S HOW WE WERE FINALLY INSPIRED TO SET OUT FOR ADVENTURES UNKNOWN.
SEE? I CAN CARRY MOST OF THE SUPPLIES WE NEED.
ARE YOU KIDDING? THAT'S BARELY ENOUGH LUNCHBOXES TO GET MY FELLA THROUGH A SINGLE LUNCH.
SHUSH, YOU.
ONWARD!

Let me tell you what I know about the nearly legendary couple, Bufkin and Lily, and the adventures I shared with them. The *real* version.
Not that fabricated nonsense which appeared in the series of dollar novels written by the disreputable Marcus Thomas Buckingwill,* who never actually met any of us, though he claimed to on four occasions.
I got no flowery prose in me. All I can give you is the undecorated facts.
YOU SAVED OUR VILLAGE!
IT'S WHAT WE *DO.*
*Not to be confused with his delightful and celebrated son, Tommy Buckingwill, who invented the Etheric Autodoubler.
AFTER
Being an account of the life and adventures of Bufkin, Lily and Hangy the Rope, in the days and years following certain incidents of note that took place in Oz and its immediate environs.
BILL WILLINGHAM WRITER-CREATOR
SHAWN McMANUS ARTIST
TODD KLEIN LETTERS
GREGORY LOCKARD ASST. EDITOR
SHELLY BOND EDITOR

I have no idea how old Bufkin was before I came to life in Oz with my coils around his throat.
SHHHHHH.
He'd never say.
CAREFUL NOW.
YOU BE CAREFUL, BUDDY BOY. I WON'T BE STUCK RAISING A BUNCH OF FATHER-LESS KIDS.
But he lived another seven hundred and forty-two years (by your reckoning) following the revolution in Oz.
WE DON'T HAVE ANY KIDS.
NOT YET. I LIVE IN HOPE.
OKAY, LET'S GO!
In that time our doughty trio of heroes accomplished quite a bit.
CHARGE!
We freed the seven Wilding Trees of the Black Forest from their ages-long servitude to the Sorcerer Wyrm, Kel Yarowm.
WE'RE FIXIN' TO MAKE YOU LOSE WOOD, PAL!

We caught and caged Zorgo Quoot, the Gentleman Wendigo.
NO MORE DINING ON LIBRARY PATRONS FOR ***YOU***, ZORGO!
STAND BY YOUR WAVE-MAKERS!
Helped turn the tide against Wanderharth, the living Drift.

Of course we weren't always heralded as heroes. Meddlers and interlopers were among the terms we heard most often.

WE HAVE TO ***FEND*** FOR OURSELVES NOW?

BUT THE TYRANT PROVIDED FOR ALL OUR NEEDS!

BUT WE JUST FREED YOU.

YOU CAN CHART THE COURSE OF YOUR OWN LIVES NOW.

DON'T YOU GET IT? ***ALL*** OUR NEEDS! FOR GENERATIONS!

HOW THE HELL CAN WE BE EXPECTED TO DO FOR OURSELVES NOW? WE HAVE NO SKILLS!
THEN YOU'D BEST LEARN QUICKLY, FOLKS. FREEDOM IS MESSY, BUT WORTH IT.

Most of the time they were only hero and companion, though Lily seemed to take perverse joy in calling him "her boyfriend" at all times.
DON'T LET THE RABBLE GET YOU DOWN, SWEETIE.
DOING THE RIGHT THING IS THE RIGHT THING TO DO, EVEN WHEN NO ONE APPRECIATES IT.

But there were three occasions when the odd circumstances of their lives made possible the romance she'd always sought.
AH HA! I KNEW IT!
YOU WERE JUST HELPING ME TO GET TO MY...AH... SPECIAL FRIEND!
KRAKK!
The first time was when Lily was captured by the evil Doctor Karlo Von Kongmacher, who Bufkin hired to grow his arm and wings back.
HERE'S TO YOU, KARLO!
KLIK
BOFF
AHHAA-HAHAHAHA-AGGGH!
TEND TO LILY! I'VE GOT THE FIEND ALL TIED UP!
Bufkin made short work of the mad scientist, but not before he transformed Lily into a giant ape.

When you start with a woman only three inches tall, being turned into a giant monkey made her just right for hero and heroine to hook up.
WHY, LILY!
OUR STARS HAVE FINALLY ALIGNED.
YOU'RE GORGEOUS!
That romance lasted a good thirty years and produced a dozen offspring before the effects wore off, returning Lily to her previous species and stature.
THAT'S THE LAST OF THEM. ALL GROWN UP AND FLED THE NEST.
YEAH, BUT WE DID GOOD BY EVERY ONE OF THEM, LILY DARLING. THEY EACH GOT INTO GOOD SCHOOLS.
The second woo-possible interlude happened when Lily came across the wishing fork of Ladeedah and yielded to temptation.
I WISH MY MAN BUFKIN WAS SIZE AND SPECIES APPROPRIATE FOR SOME GOOD OLD-FASHIONED HOW-DO-YOU-DO.

That lasted for a dozen years, but we lived in a dangerous place then.
WE NEED HANGY! WHERE THE HELL IS THAT DAMNED ROPE?
VISITING HIS STUPID FRIENDS!
No children lived long enough to come of it.
NO, SILLY, I'M NOT GETTING FAT. I'M PREGNANT AGAIN.
REALLY?
WAHOOOOO!
YEAH, BEING A MALE BARLEYCORN BRIDE IS OKAY, BUT I WISH I WERE TALLER.
YOU ARE GETTING TALLER. I THINK THE WISH IS WEARING OFF.
WHY DO THE GOOD TRANS-FORMATIONS ALWAYS WEAR OFF?

The third and final time they got together, in any sort of physical way, was near the end, when they both got a big dose of Umpamas Gas.
GOOD CLUTCH THIS TIME, LILY DARLING.
TELL ME ABOUT IT. I FEEL LIKE I DROPPED AN URBAN SUB-DIVISION.
Turned them into giant Korob Birds, as that particular gas is wont to do.
HE'S ABOUT TO JOG LEFT!
CUT HIM OFF, SMIGLEY!
Hundreds of their children survived from those years. I guess that inspired me.
YEAH, KEEP SNIPPING OFF SMALL LENGTHS OF MY TAIL.
TRUST ME. THIS CAN WORK--I KNOW IT. THEY'LL GROW AUTONOMOUSLY TO BE MY KIDS!

I see already that I left so much out--like the time we conquered the floating cities of Dabb. I warned you I was no natural storyteller.
REMEMBER, DON'T KILL THE SLAVES. WE'RE ALL ABOUT LIBERATING THEM.
THEY'RE THE ONES IN THE PURPLE TUNICS AND THE NECK COLLARS.
SO? WHAT DO WE CARE ABOUT SPARING THEM?
LOOK AT IT IN A STRICTLY SELF-SERVING WAY, THEN. SACRIFICING THEM IS WHAT POWERS THE NECROMANCY THAT KEEPS THE ISLANDS AFLOAT, AMONG OTHER THINGS.
KILL THE SLAVES AND YOU'RE JUST POWERING THE SAME COMBAT SPELLS THE BAD GUYS ARE ABOUT TO USE AGAINST US.

Bufkin and Lily never quite found their way back to Fabletown, but some of their kids did in time.
YOU'RE THE SON OF--?
BUFKIN. YOU DON'T REMEMBER BUFKIN?
AND HE'S REALLY OKAY?
I ASSURE YOU, HE'S DOING GREAT, AND HE WOULD HAVE SENT YOU HIS BEST REGARDS IF HE'D KNOWN I'D END UP HERE.
And they never found where the lost Business Office had gotten itself off to, but I did once, during the Flipping Days incident.
LOOK OUT! IT'S SPINNING WEBS AS FAST AS YOU CAN ROPE IT!
NONSENSE, FRANKY! I'M THE FASTEST ROPE IN THE WEST!
I had many grand adventures with Franky, The Mirror, and the rest of the gang before the next Flip Day took me away again to a new world.
From time to time I went back to my beloved old profession, both to make money for our travels...
...and to keep the skill set fresh.
HELLO?
CAN SOMEONE UNTIE AND INTER THIS MOOK SOON? I GUARANTEE HE'S STONE COLD DEAD, AND I HAVE A TWO-THIRTY LUNCH DATE.

Finally, after their wars were all won, and his adventures long played out, Bufkin and Lily returned to Oz and that beloved lunchbox tree.

ARE YOU JUST GOING TO LIE THE DAY AWAY OUT HERE?

CAN'T SEE WHY NOT.

True to his word, he built a cottage there, where he lived out his final days in peace and plenty.

AND THE *CHORES* ARE GOING TO DO THEMSELVES, ARE THEY?

THAT'S WHAT *OFFSPRING* ARE FOR. MY WORK'S ALL DONE IN THIS LIFE, DARLING O' MY HEART.

YOU MAKE A GOOD POINT, DEAREST.

After Bufkin passed away, Lily barely lived another twenty days--just long enough to write a few letters to the children, grandchildren and great-grandchildren.

We buried her beside him, the way she asked.

BUFKIN THE BRAVE * HERO TO THE OPPRESSED * THREE TIMES BELOVED HUSBAND TO LILY

LILY MARTANION * SHE FREED MANY FROM BONDAGE * THREE TIMES BELOVED WIFE TO BUFKIN

The End

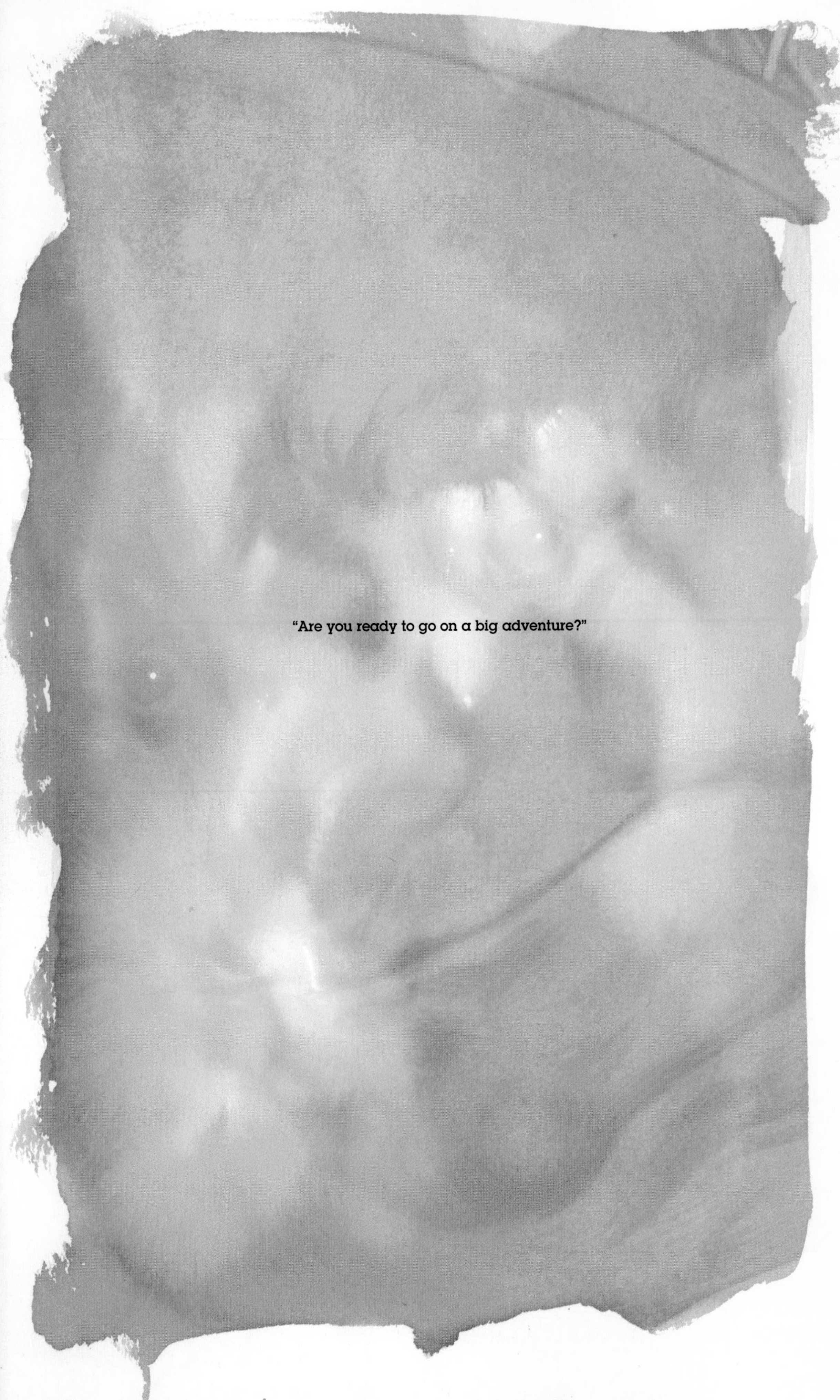

"Are you ready to go on a big adventure?"

WOLF MANOR IN THE CLOSING DAYS OF JANUARY.
GHOST!
STOP THAT! NO ROUGHHOUSING IN THE WAR ROOM.

MOMMY NEEDS TO WORK.
GO SEE WHAT YOUR BROTHERS AND SISTERS ARE...

...DOING.
THANKS, SWEETIE.

THE DAY AMBLES ALONG, AS DAYS ARE APT TO DO.
YOU KIDS HAD BETTER BE FINISHED CLEANING YOUR ROOMS.
NOK NOK

UH OH.
OH.
I SEE.

MONSTERS TO THE FINISH.
HEY!

GIVE ME BACK MR. GROWLY!
SPLASH!

TOY BOAT
Chapter 1 of CUBS in TOYLAND
In which we begin our tale with the promise of a fantastical, magical journey.
ALL RIGHT!
THAT'S DONE IT!
EVERYONE IS BANISHED TO HIS OWN ROOM! AND NO DINNER UNTIL EACH ROOM CAN PASS A DOUBLE DADDY-LEVEL MILITARY INSPECTION!
BUT DADDY'S NOT HERE.
IT WASN'T MY FAULT! THEY TOOK MR. GROWLY!
DON'T MAKE HER MADDER THAN SHE IS, CONNOR!
REMEMBER WHAT HAPPENED THE LAST TIME! RESTRICTIONS FOR A MILLION, BILLION YEARS!
BILL WILLINGHAM writer/creator
MARK BUCKINGHAM pencils
STEVE LEIALOHA inks
LEE LOUGHRIDGE colors
TODD KLEIN letters
GREGORY LOCKARD asst. ed.
SHELLY BOND editor

DIDN'T YOU HEAR ME, THERESE?
I DID, BUT I WANTED TO ASK YOU SOMETHING.

OKAY, BUT THIS ISN'T GOING TO GET YOU OUT OF--HEY, WHAT'S THE MATTER, LEMON PIE? YOU LOOK SCARED.
IT'S BECAUSE OF THE TOY BOAT I GOT FOR CHRISSMISS. IT'S NOT A PRESENT FOR A GIRL.

NO, I SUPPOSE NOT SO MUCH, BUT THAT'S OKAY. WITH SO MANY WILDINGS FILLING THE HOUSE, SOMEONE PROBABLY JUST GOT MIXED UP ON WHICH TOY WENT TO WHICH CUB.
YOU GOT LOTS OF OTHER GIFTS.
BUT NONE I CAN PLAY WITH.

THE BOAT DOESN'T LIKE ME TO PLAY WITH OTHER TOYS.
OH, THAT'S NOT TRUE. IT'S JUST A SILLY PLASTIC THING. TOYS CAN'T GET JEALOUS.

MEANWHILE, IN THE WORLD OF THE NORTH WIND...
IS THE TRAINING TOO SCARY AGAIN? YOU REMEMBER I TOLD YOU TO TELL ME IF THEY TRIED PUSHING YOU TOO HARD.

NO, THAT'S NOT IT, DADDY.
IT'S JUST--
I DON'T THINK IT'S TOO SCARY ANYMORE. MOSTLY IT'S FUN.

BUT YOU MISS HOME. ME TOO, WINTER.
YES, I MISS MOMMY, AND THERESE, AND GHOST, AND AMBROSE, AND BLOSSOM, AND CONNOR, AND EVEN DARE.
I LIKE MOMMY'S SCHOOL-TIME BETTER, AND PLAYING WITH NOT SO MANY RESPON-- RESPONSIBLEES.

WE'LL SEE THEM ALL AGAIN SOON. EVEN NORTH WIND SCHOOL DOESN'T LAST FOREVER. WE'LL MAKE THESE PIRATES GIVE US A BREAK IN A FEW DAYS.
AND SOMETHING ELSE...

I'VE BEEN HAVING THE SAME SCARY DREAM EVERY NIGHT.
ONLY I KNOW THEY AREN'T DREAMS.

"IT'S ME WHEN I'M ALL GROWN UP.
"I'M THE NORTH WIND, JUST LIKE THEY WANT ME TO BE.
"BUT I'M ALSO **NOT** LIKE THEY WANT ME TO BE, BECAUSE I'M MEAN AND ALWAYS HAVE MY OWN WAY.
"I MAKE EVERYONE DO ONLY WHAT ***I*** WANT.
"AND I'M NEVER AFRAID EVER AGAIN, BECAUSE I MAKE EVERYONE AFRAID OF ***ME.***"

DON'T WORRY, TINY SCARECROW. IT'S JUST A DREAM.
NO IT ISN'T. IT'S WHAT **HAPPENS.** SOMEHOW I KNOW IT'S WHAT HAPPENS WHEN I GROW UP.
YOU'RE TALKING ABOUT DESTINY.

BUT HERE'S A SECRET: DESTINY ISN'T REALLY ABSOLUTELY WHAT WILL HAPPEN. IT'S MORE LIKE WHAT'S **AVAILABLE,** BUT ONLY IF YOU ACCEPT IT.
HUH?

IT'S LIKE A--SORT OF A **MENU.** IT'S A GREAT BIG DINNER, WITH LOTS OF DIFFERENT FOOD. AND YOU'RE FREE TO TAKE WHAT YOU WANT AND LEAVE EVERYTHING YOU DON'T.

BUT, DADDY, YOU AND MOMMY ALWAYS MAKE US EAT **EVERY-THING** ON OUR PLATE.
OH NO.

THAT NIGHT...
THERESE.
THERESE.

TIME TO WAKE UP, LITTLE GIRLY GIRL.
TIME FOR US TO GO.

WHA--?
HUH?
IT'S DARK NOW AND EVERY-ONE'S ASLEEP, SO WE CAN SNEAK AWAY.

YOU CAN TALK?
OF COURSE I CAN. NOW GET DRESSED.
SAVE THE QUESTIONS FOR LATER.

BUT I CAN'T GO OUT AT NIGHT. I'M NOT ALLOWED.
YOU CAN'T BE AFRAID OF BREAKING THE RULES. DARE WOULDN'T BE AFRAID.
DO YOU WANT ME TO BE HIS MAGIC TOY INSTEAD?

NO!
THEN DARE WOULD HAVE MORE TOYS THAN ME!
DON'T GO!
RELAX.

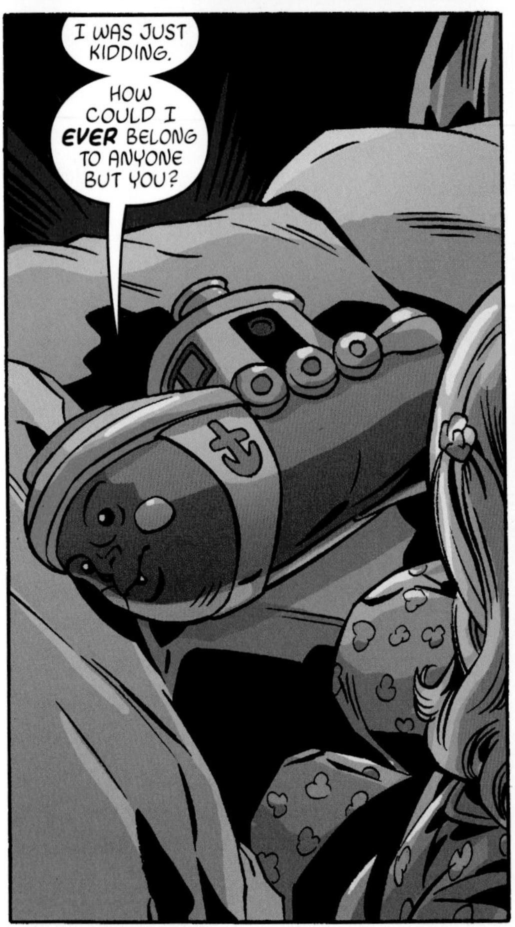
I WAS JUST KIDDING.
HOW COULD I EVER BELONG TO ANYONE BUT YOU?

IT'S A MEAN THING TO SAY, EVEN IN PRETEND.
I'M SORRY, THERESE.
I'M JUST EAGER TO BE OUTSIDE, PLAYING. WHAT GOOD IS A TOY YOU DON'T PLAY WITH?
BUT IF WE HAVE TO WAIT UNTIL MORNING, I GUESS THAT'S OKAY.

EARLY THE NEXT MORNING...
WITH A SINGLE PHRASE, MISTER DARK BUILT A SERIES OF MISDIRECTION SPELLS THAT WILL KEEP CASTLE DARK HIDDEN FROM THE MUNDYS FOR ALL TIME.

REMARKABLE.
YES, MADDY. UH... I SUPPOSE IT IS.
IS IT SAFE TO GO IN?

OH, YEAH. HE DIDN'T PLACE A SINGLE WARDING AGAINST FABLES.
IT'S AS IF HE WANTED US TO SHOW UP-- EVENTUALLY.
COURTYARDS WITHIN COURTYARDS! LIKE NESTING DOLLS! SO MUCH ROOM!

IF THIS IS TO BE THE NEW FABLETOWN, WE SHOULD STOP CALLING IT CASTLE DARK.
BAD OVERTONES AND SUCH.

AND WE'LL WANT TO GET RID OF SOME OF THE MORE GRUESOME... UH... DECORATIONS.

HEY, Y'ONNER! THIS WAY!
C'MERE!
I HEARD SOMETHING!

HELLO?
DID YOU HEAR THAT?

CAN YOU HELP ME? CAN YOU--
HOLD ON THERE! WE'RE HERE!
WE'LL HELP YOU!

RRRRRRRRRRRRIP!
LOCKED OR NOT, NO STEEL DOOR CAN KEEP ME OUT!
THANK GOD.

IT'S BEEN SO LONG. SO MANY HORRORS.
BUT I NEVER GAVE UP. NEVER STOPPED PRAYING YOU'D COME.
UH...
WHO ARE YOU?

AT ABOUT THAT SAME TIME...
WE'RE WAY AHEAD! WE'RE *BEATING* YOU SO BAD!
ARE NOT!

'BYE, MOMMY!
I'M GOING OUT NOW!

HEY, THERESE, IT'S A *RACE!* COME HELP US BUILD OUR SNOWMAN AND BEAT THOSE DINKS!
I CAN'T.
BECAUSE NO ONE WILL EVER *CATCH* US.
I HAVE TO GO FIND A PLACE TO FLOAT MY BOAT.

WOW, IS SHE ACTING LIKE A COMPLETE GOONY OR *WHAT?*
ZOMBIE GIRL.

IT'S STILL SNOWY EVERYWHERE. THERE'S NO LAKES OR PUDDLES YET.
KEEP GOING UNTIL WE FIND SOMETHING. ANY TRICKLE OF WATER WILL DO.

HEY, LOOK.
DON'T STOP NOW. I CAN ALMOST HEAR WATER NEARBY.

WHAT DO YOU THINK THIS IS?
ALL RUSTED AND--
OH!

IT'S THE TICKY TOCKY TIGER THING MR. MOOGLI BROUGHT HOME FROM THE FARAWAY JUNGLE!

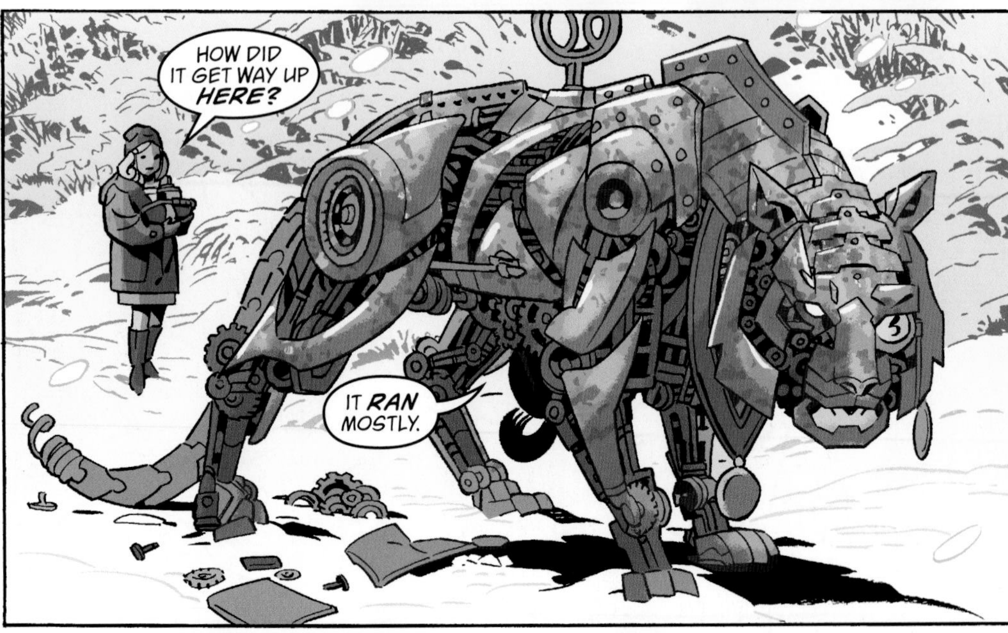
HOW DID IT GET WAY UP HERE?
IT RAN MOSTLY.

TRYING TO GET AWAY FROM MISTER DARK.

MADE IT A LONG WAY BEFORE BREAKING DOWN AGAIN.

BECAUSE I WASN'T HERE TO KEEP HIM--OOH!
I NEED THAT!

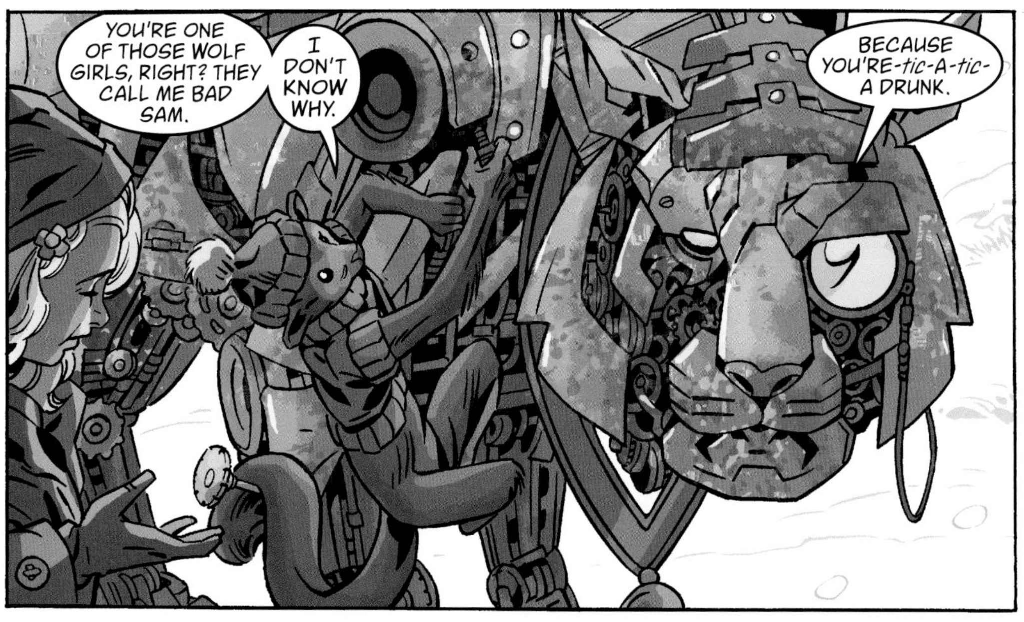
YOU'RE ONE OF THOSE WOLF GIRLS, RIGHT? THEY CALL ME BAD SAM.
I DON'T KNOW WHY.
BECAUSE YOU'RE-tic-A-tic-A DRUNK.

WELL, SURE... I SUPPOSE THAT COULD BE ONE REASON.
HEH. YOU'RE FUNNY.

THANK YOU...I THINK.
NOTHING TO DRINK NOW THOUGH, SO I MIGHT AS WELL GET HIS LORDSHIP BACK IN ACTION.

RUSTED SOLID FOR NEARLY A YEAR, HE WAS.
I HAVE TO GO.

OKAY, THEN. TAKE CARE.
I HAVE TO FIND THE WATER.

IN THE LAND OF THE NORTH WIND...

THIS IS A DISASTER!

WE'RE GOING TO BE SADDLED WITH A *TIMID* NORTH WIND!

OH NO!

WHAT WILL WE DO?

THIS IS MARVELOUS!

THEY'RE GOING TO GIVE US A *TIMID* NORTH WIND.

OUR DAY OF ***ASCENDANCY*** HAS COME AT LONG LAST!

LOOK!
THERE'S A STREAM, FINALLY.
BUT WE'RE AN AWFUL LONG WAY FROM HOME.

IT DOESN'T MATTER.
HOME IS FOR SISSIES AND LITTLE BABIES.
ARE **YOU** A CRYING LITTLE BABY?

NO!
I'M NEARLY NINE!
THEN PUT ME IN THE WATER. QUICK!

OKAY, BUT IT'S NOT A VERY BIG STREAM.
THAT WON'T MATTER, IT'S--
AHHHHHHHHH.
THAT'S BETTER.

STEP BACK, NOW.
OH!

SEE?
WHAT DID I TELL YOU?

I'M A MAGIC BOAT.
NOW, ARE YOU READY TO GO ON A BIG ADVENTURE?
I DON'T KNOW, I--

HOW DID THE WATER GET SO BIG?
MAGIC!

NOW, CLIMB ABOARD!
HURRY!
WELL...I GUESS.
BUT ONLY FOR A LITTLE WHILE, OKAY?

NEXT: THE HAPPY WONDERLAND

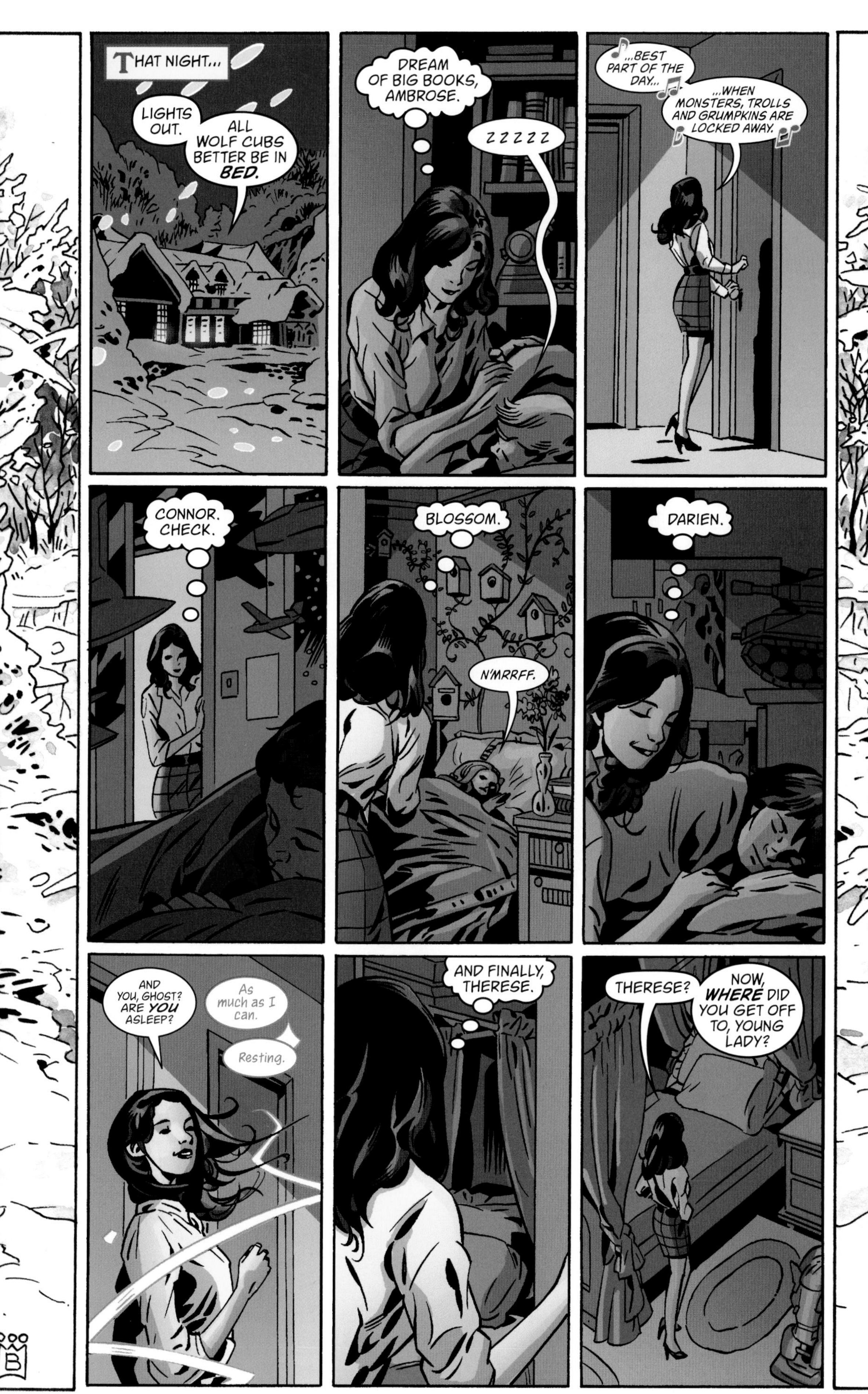
THAT NIGHT...
LIGHTS OUT.
ALL WOLF CUBS BETTER BE IN BED.
DREAM OF BIG BOOKS, AMBROSE.
ZZZZZ
...BEST PART OF THE DAY...
...WHEN MONSTERS, TROLLS AND GRUMPKINS ARE LOCKED AWAY.
CONNOR. CHECK.
BLOSSOM.
N'MRRFF.
DARIEN.
AND YOU, GHOST? ARE YOU ASLEEP?
As much as I can.
Resting.
AND FINALLY, THERESE.
THERESE?
NOW, WHERE DID YOU GET OFF TO, YOUNG LADY?

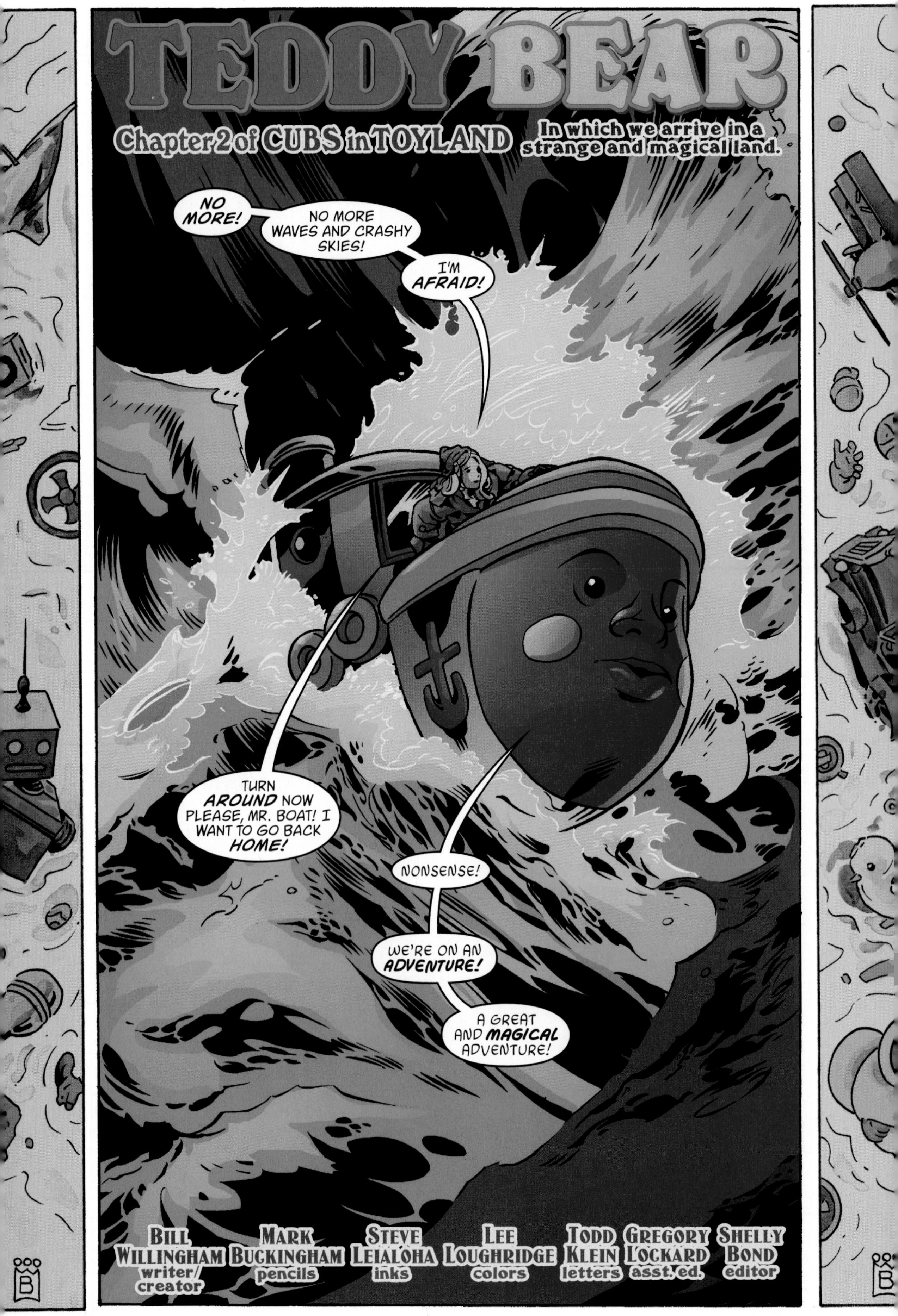

TEDDY BEAR

Chapter 2 of CUBS in TOYLAND

In which we arrive in a strange and magical land.

NO MORE!

NO MORE WAVES AND CRASHY SKIES!

I'M AFRAID!

TURN AROUND NOW PLEASE, MR. BOAT! I WANT TO GO BACK HOME!

NONSENSE!

WE'RE ON AN ADVENTURE!

A GREAT AND MAGICAL ADVENTURE!

BILL WILLINGHAM writer/creator
MARK BUCKINGHAM pencils
STEVE LEIALOHA inks
LEE LOUGHRIDGE colors
TODD KLEIN letters
GREGORY LOCKARD asst. ed.
SHELLY BOND editor

AND STILL IN THAT SAME NIGHT...
I DON'T KNOW HOW LONG I'VE BEEN HERE, CHAINED IN THE DARK.
MAYBE YOU CAN TELL ME.

HOW LONG AGO DID YOU LEAVE ME BEHIND AT THE FARM?
DID ANYONE EVEN THINK TO LOOK FOR ME?

WE DIDN'T ABANDON YOU INTENTIONALLY, MRS. SPRATT.
BUT THOSE WERE TERRIBLE, CONFUSING DAYS.
AND NO ONE GAVE A SINGLE THOUGHT TO MAKE SURE THE PLODDING OLD FAT WOMAN MADE IT TO THE DEPARTURE POINT IN TIME.
HMMMM.

IT WASN'T LIKE THAT.

I UNDERSTAND, MR. MAYOR. I HAD NO FRIENDS TO MAKE SURE I WAS THERE, AND RAISE THE ALARM.

MY OWN FAULT, I SUPPOSE.
CARE TO TELL US WHAT HAPPENED?

I SHOULD HAVE HID.
OR TRIED TO RUN AWAY.

"INSTEAD I STUPIDLY WAITED AT THE RENDEZVOUS POINT, THINKING SOME-ONE WOULD EVENTUALLY NOTICE AND COME BACK FOR ME.
"I WAS RIGHT OUT IN THE OPEN WHEN HE ARRIVED.

"HELPLESS."
THEY'LL REGRET LEAVING YOU.
I NEED BUT ONE OF YOU TO LEAD ME TO THE REST.

"WHEN I WOKE AGAIN, I WAS HERE."
I SUSPECT THE SUPPER DISH IS THE KEY TO YOUR COOPERATION.

"AND SO HE STARVED ME.

"NOTHING BUT CRUMBS AND SCRAPS, UNTIL I AGREED TO GIVE YOU UP."

YOURS MUST HAVE BEEN A TERRIBLE ORDEAL.
AND LARGELY OUR FAULT.
EVERY TIME I LOST HOPE -SOB- WHEN I COULDN'T -SOB- I TRIED SO OFTEN TO DIE! BUT HE WOULDN'T LET ME. HE'D DO JUST ENOUGH TO KEEP ME ALIVE.

ALL THAT'S BEHIND YOU NOW.
MISS DUGLAS?

WHAT THE HELL--?

LEIGH!
WHO ARE THESE PEOPLE?
HOLD IT, BUDDY!

HANDS WHERE I CAN SEE THEM!
WHO--?
NO, WAIT!
DON'T HURT HIM!

I'VE NEVER SEEN WHAT HE LOOKS LIKE BEFORE, BUT HIS VOICE!
I KNOW HIM!

YOU'RE WERIAN HOLT, AREN'T YOU?
THAT'S ME. AND YOU HAVE TO BE LEIGH.

"I WAS A PRISONER, TOO. MISTER DARK CAPTURED AND ENSLAVED ME TO BE HIS SERVANT."
FEED THE WOMAN, BOY.
BE QUICK ABOUT IT, AND THEN GO JUST AS SWIFTLY ABOUT YOUR OTHER DUTIES.

"AS OFTEN AS I COULD, I STOLE FOOD FROM MY OWN MEAGER PLATE TO SNEAK TO HER.
"WHEN HE CAUGHT ME, HIS PUNISHMENTS WERE INVENTIVE, TO SAY THE LEAST."

BUT I COULDN'T SIMPLY STAND BY AND WATCH HER WITHER AWAY.
YOU--YOU WERE THE ONLY FLICKER OF HOPE IN THE ENDLESS DARKNESS.

WITHOUT YOUR KINDNESS, I'M CERTAIN I WOULD HAVE GONE MAD.
IN TIME HE WOULD HAVE SHATTERED ME LIKE GLASS.

FAR AWAY, IN THE KINGDOM OF HAVEN...
FLY HAS ONLY HIMSELF TO BLAME THAT WE WEREN'T READY TO GO WITH THE LAST GROUP.
BETWEEN HIM AND WEYLAND, THEY LOADED US WITH SO MUCH STUFF FOR THE BABY I HAVEN'T GOT HALF OF IT PACKED YET.

THE HAND-CARVED CRIB. THE ROCKER. THE TOYS.
YEAH, ABOUT THAT.
WHAT IF YOU DIDN'T FINISH PACKING?

MEANING WHAT?
WHAT IF WE STAYED HERE INSTEAD?

WHAT WOULD YOU SAY IF, INSTEAD OF GOING BACK TO THE GRIND AND DANGER OF FABLETOWN, WE DECIDED TO LIVE HERE?
SERIOUSLY?
IT'S SAFE AND PEACEFUL IN HAVEN. PERFECT PLACE TO RAISE A DAUGHTER.
goobs!

ELSEWHERE...
WAKE UP, THERESE.

WAKE UP, PRETTY PRETTY PRINCESS.

WE'RE HERE.
NHUH?

WE'VE PASSED THROUGH THE STORM AND NOW FIND OURSELVES ON THE WONDERFUL SHORE!
WHERE? YOU PROMISED TO TAKE ME HOME!

AND SO I DID.
THIS ISN'T HOME!

IT IS NOW.
YOUR NEW HOME.
YOUR NEW KINGDOM!
WHAT?!

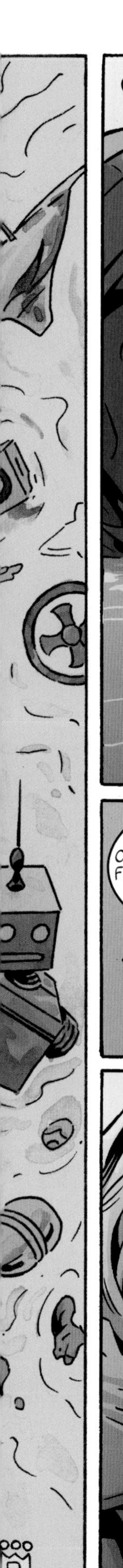

A KINGDOM?
MY KINGDOM?

YUPPERS.
A MAGICAL LAND FOR YOU TO RULE.
BUT--?

AFTER ALL, AREN'T YOU AS GOOD AS YOUR SISTER WINTER? WHY SHOULD SHE BE THE ONLY ONE TO HAVE A KINGDOM ALL HER OWN?
YOU'RE GETTING SMALL AGAIN.
MY JOB IS DONE.

I MOVED THE STARS FOR YOU, AND CRAFTED VAST OCEANS TO CROSS. I BROKE YOU FREE FROM YOUR DULL, ORDINARY WORLD, AND DELIVERED A QUEEN TO THIS ONE.
TIME TO REST.

A QUEEN?
ME?

BUT THIS PLACE--
--IT'S SO DIRTY.
MUDDY AND DARK.
IT'S BEEN MISSING ITS QUEEN FOR A LONG TIME NOW.

WHAT MAGICAL KINGDOM CAN BE LOVELY LACKING ITS QUEEN?
BUT THERESE IS THE PRETTIEST DAUGHTER OF THE FAIREST WOMAN. THE LAND WILL WAKE TO YOUR BEAUTY--IN TIME.
I DON'T KNOW...
MOVE ALONG, YOUR HIGHNESS. MOVE UP THE BEACH.
LOOK.
HERE COMES SOMEONE.
OH!
THEY'RE LIKE YOU.
LOOK SHARP NOW, LADS.
TOYS.
LET'S HAVE EVERYONE ON HIS BEST BEHAVIOR.

GREETINGS AND MOST SPLENDID SALUTATIONS, YOUR MAJESTY.
ALLOW ME TO INTRODUCE MYSELF. I AM YOUR MOST HUMBLE SERVANT, THEODORE CLEMENT VON BENIOT AND DOWN, OF SAINT BASTIEN AND SAINT IVES.
WARDEN OF THE SHIFTY SHORE, AND KNIGHT INERRANT OF THE YONDER PLUSH.
MOST CALL ME MR. IVES FOR SHORT.
UHM...
HELLO.
CAN IT BE?
AT LONG LAST?

I'M THERESE.
WE KNOW.
WHERE AM I? WHERE ARE **WE?**
ARE YOU MY MAMA?
HUSH, CHILD. NOT YET.
WHERE **ARE** YOU? DIDN'T MR. STEAMPUDDLE SAY?
YOU'VE COME TO THE **MAGICAL LAND,** SOMETIMES CALLED FAR MATTAGONIA.

SOMETIMES CALLED MADLAND.
BUT NOT MUCH LONGER, MAY IT BE.
MAY IT BE.
MAY IT BE.
YOU'RE IN TOYLAND, YOUNG LADY.
TOYLAND?
REALLY?
TRULY SO.
ARE YOU MY MAMA?
NOT NOW, SILLY NAN.
HUSH, NAN.
ALL THINGS IN THEIR TIME.
THIS IS VERY EXCITING-- A LOVELY ADVENTURE-- BUT I CAN'T STAY.
WE CAN TALK MORE AFTER YOU'VE RESTED FROM YOUR LONG JOURNEY.

COME WITH US TO YOUR **PALACE** ON TOP OF PLAYLAND HILL.
EVERYTHING WILL BE EXPLAINED THERE.
I DON'T KNOW, MR. IVES.

I SHOULDN'T STAY AWAY FROM HOME FOR SO LONG WITHOUT **TELLING** ANYONE.
OH?

WHO WOULD YOU TELL?
MY **MOMMY,** OF COURSE. SHE WORRIES AND GETS REALLY **MAD** WHEN WE STAY OUT TOO LATE, OR GO SOMEWHERE WITHOUT TELLING HER FIRST.

I SEE.
BUT THAT DOESN'T MATTER HERE.

THIS IS THE LAND WHERE **NO ONE** WORRIES FOR YOU.
NO ONE **CARES** WHERE YOU'VE DISAPPEARED TO, OR EVEN **REMEM-BERS** YOU'VE GONE AWAY.
THIS IS THE LAND OF THE **DISCARDIA.**

BUT SOMEWHERE FAR AWAY, SOMEONE DOES WORRY.
THERESE!
THERESE!
WHERE ARE YOU, SWEETIE?
IT'S VERY LATE! YOU HAVE TO COME HOME NOW!
THERESE!
HONEY?
I DON'T THINK SHE CAN HEAR YOU, MOMMY.
DARIEN?
WHAT ARE YOU DOING OUT OF BED?

I SAW HER EARLIER, WHEN WE WERE MAKING SNOWMEN.

"SHE WENT OFF BY HERSELF TO PLAY WITH HER STUPID TOY BOAT. I FOLLOWED HER, BECAUSE SHE WAS ACTING ***WEIRD.***

"THERESE ***NEVER*** WANTS TO BE BY HERSELF. SHE CAN'T STAND HAVING NO ONE AROUND TO TELL HER HOW ***PRETTY*** SHE IS."
I HAVE TO GO NOW, MR. SAM.
TAKE CARE THEN, YOUNG MISSY.

"I FOLLOWED HER TO A STREAM, ALMOST ALL THE WAY OUT OF WOLF VALLEY."
QUICK! PUT ME IN THE ***WATER!***

THAT'S WHERE THE ***SCARY*** THING HAPPENED.

NEXT: THE DISCARDED

CLOCKWORK TIGER
Chapter 3 of CUBS in TOYLAND
In which lunch is finally served.
SO THERESE CAME THIS WAY?
PROLLY CAME TO PLAY ON MR. TICKY TOCKY TIGER AGAIN!
WHO WOULDN'T?
MY TURN!
BILL WILLINGHAM writer/creator
MARK BUCKINGHAM pencils
STEVE LEIALOHA inks 1-9,12-14
ANDREW PEPOY inks 10-11,17
DAN GREEN inks 15-16
LEE LOUGHRIDGE colors
TODD KLEIN letters
GREGORY LOCKARD asst. ed.
SHELLY BOND editor
IT'S ALWAYS YOUR TURN, DARIEN!
OH DEAR.
AGAIN?
TINKER'S SAKE, THEY CAN FLY! HOW CAN CLIMBING BE SO MUCH FUN?
HEY, YOU MONKEYS!
I TOLD YOU BEFORE, STAY OFF LORD MOUNT-BATTEN!
OH NO!
ANY TOY IN WOLF VALLEY BELONGS TO US! THAT'S LIKE A BIG FAT RULE!

HE'S NOT A TOY, YOU BRATS! HE'S THE RIGHTFUL GOVERNOR OF ALL THE INDU!
BAD SAM! BAD SAM!
THEY'RE GONE, BOY.
HURRY NOW.
CLIMB ABOARD.
WE NEED TO BE OFF, BEFORE SAM OR YOUR LITTER-MATES RETURN.
OKAY, BUT I CAN'T PLAY VERY LONG. I NEED TO LOOK FOR MY SISTER.
YOU THINK I BROUGHT YOU HERE THIS MORNING TO PLAY?
BROUGHT ME?
GIRD YOUR HEART FOR ACTION, BOY, IT'S TIME FOR THE GREAT ADVENTURE.
OUR QUEST HAS COMMENCED.

YOU CAN COME OUT NOW.
YOU CAN TALK?
SOMETIMES.
WHEN MY REPAIRS ARE KEPT UP, OR THE MAGIC IS STRONG UPON ME.
WOW!
HANG ON!

YOOP!
WHEN THE SHRILL, PIERCING CLARION OF DUTY SOUNDS, THOSE OF A HEROIC SOUL HAVE NO CHOICE BUT TO ANSWER THE CALL.
WHERE ARE WE GOING?
SHITFIRE! WHERE ARE WE NOW?
THIS ISN'T OUR VALLEY!
DON'T FALL OFF.

THESE ARE PERILOUS LANDS WE'RE PASSING THROUGH.
AND I'VE NO ABILITY TO STOP IN ONE OF THEM TO FETCH YOU BACK INTO THE SADDLE.
ONE STEP IN EACH WORLD IS ALL I'M ALLOWED.
FOR THESE LANDS ARE THE STEPPING STONES BETWEEN THE TWO DISTANT POLES OF MY DIVIDED NATURE.
UNDERSTAND?

NO!
SAM MEANS WELL, BUT HE'S WRONG. I AM A TOY.
A PRODUCT OF TWO DISCIPLINES, SORCERY AND THE WATCH-MAKER'S ARTS.
CREATED TO BE A SULTAN'S GIFT TO THE CHILDREN OF THE VICEROY (MAY THE BICKERING GODS OF EAST AND WEST REST HIS SOUL).
TWO THINGS, BOY. GET IT?
ALWAYS TWO, WHICH ENCAPSULATES THE ETERNAL STRUGGLE FOR BALANCE. THE NUMBER OF UN-CERTAINTY.
INDECISION.
CONFLICT.
I WAS BROUGHT BACKWARDS INTO LIFE.
WHAT DOES THAT MEAN?
I'M CURSED TO LIVE OPPOSITELY IN TWO REALMS. IN THE REAL WORLD I'M A CLEVER TOY. IN THE TOY WORLD I'M A REAL TIGER. AND ALWAYS ONE FOOT IN EACH.
DOESN'T THAT GIVE YOU TWO FEET LEFT OVER?
BRIGHT BOY. NO, I WAS SPEAKING METAPHORI-CALLY.
OH. MY BROTHER AMBROSE KNOWS HOW TO TALK METALFORK. DOES IT ALL THE TIME TO MAKE ME LOOK DUMB. I ONLY KNOW A LITTLE SPANISH.
AND SO HERE WE ARE. THE TERRIBLE SHORE.

"MADLAND."
THIS IS A GREAT AND GLORIOUS DAY, YOUR MAJESTY.
HOW I'VE LONGED FOR IT, WAITING THROUGH THE YEARS.
WE NEVER GAVE UP HOPE.
BUT THERE WERE TIMES WE DESPAIRED THAT HOPE HAD GIVEN UP ON US.
HERE THEY COME!
CAN YOU SEE HER? WHAT DOES SHE LOOK LIKE?
MAY IT BE SHE LOOKS LIKE MOMMY.
MAY IT BE.

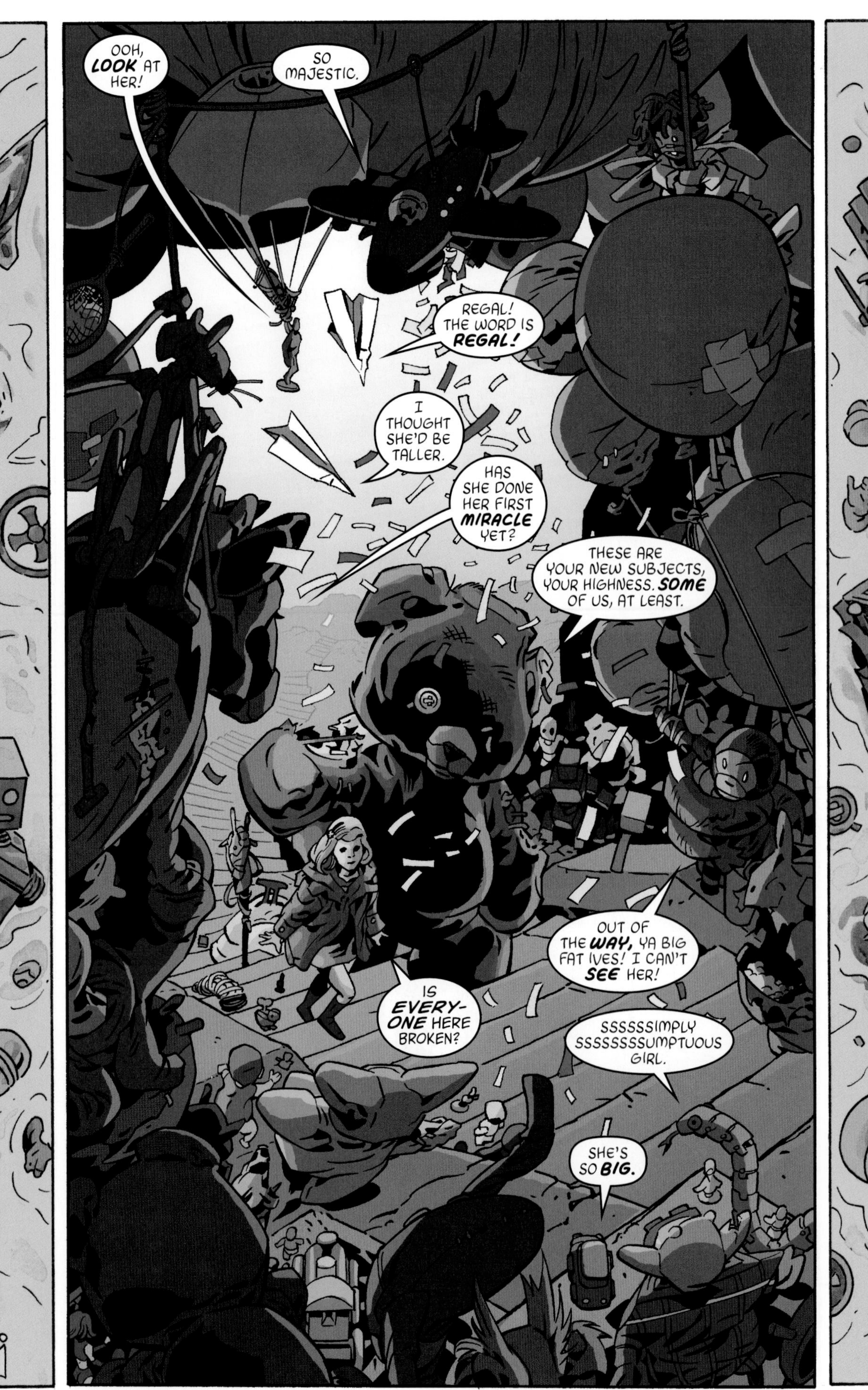
OOH, LOOK AT HER!
SO MAJESTIC.
REGAL! THE WORD IS REGAL!
I THOUGHT SHE'D BE TALLER.
HAS SHE DONE HER FIRST MIRACLE YET?
THESE ARE YOUR NEW SUBJECTS, YOUR HIGHNESS. SOME OF US, AT LEAST.
OUT OF THE WAY, YA BIG FAT IVES! I CAN'T SEE HER!
IS EVERY-ONE HERE BROKEN?
SSSSSSIMPLY SSSSSSSSUMPTUOUS GIRL.
SHE'S SO BIG.

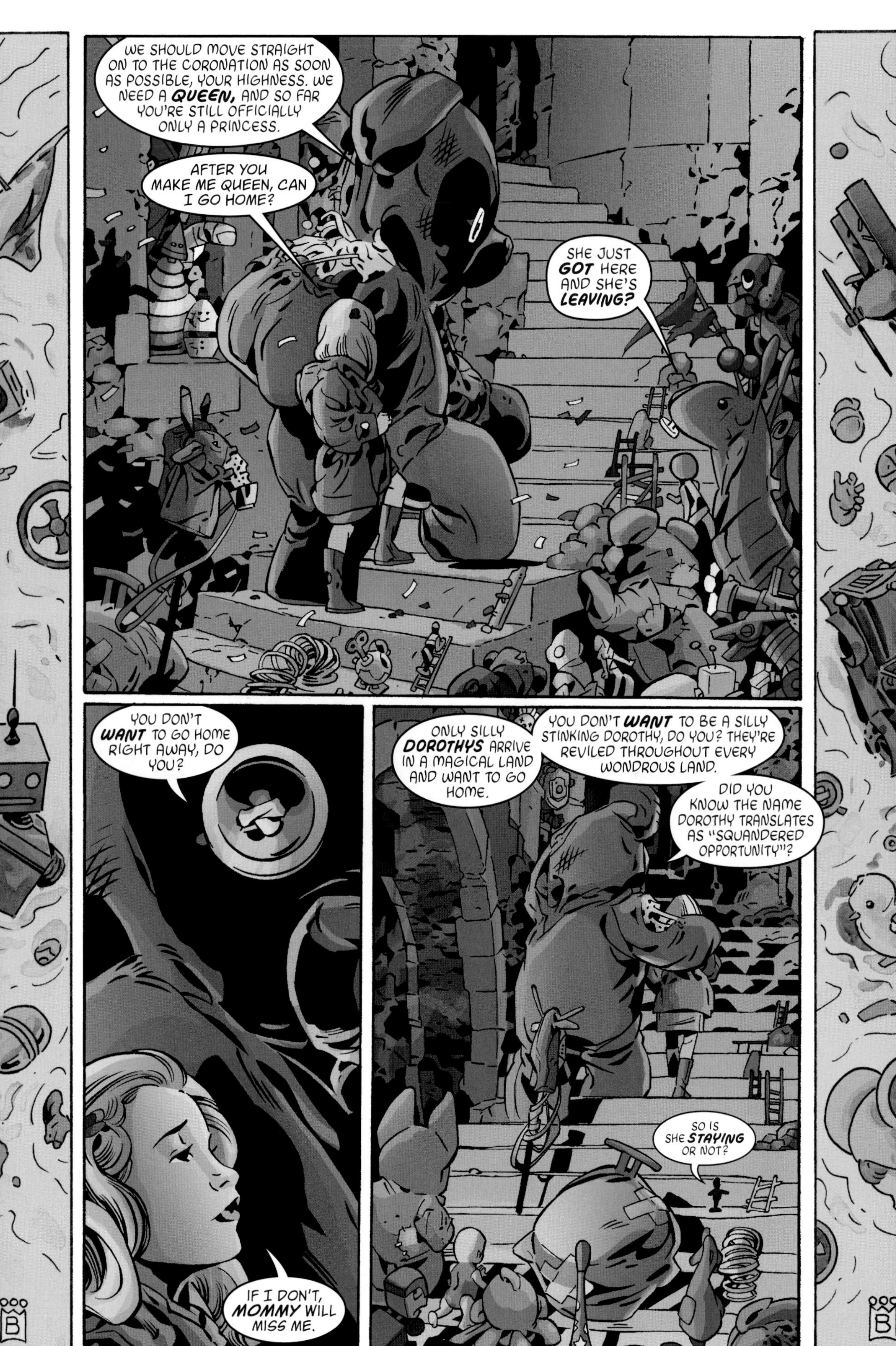
WE SHOULD MOVE STRAIGHT ON TO THE CORONATION AS SOON AS POSSIBLE, YOUR HIGHNESS. WE NEED A QUEEN, AND SO FAR YOU'RE STILL OFFICIALLY ONLY A PRINCESS.
AFTER YOU MAKE ME QUEEN, CAN I GO HOME?
SHE JUST GOT HERE AND SHE'S LEAVING?
YOU DON'T WANT TO GO HOME RIGHT AWAY, DO YOU?
IF I DON'T, MOMMY WILL MISS ME.
ONLY SILLY DOROTHYS ARRIVE IN A MAGICAL LAND AND WANT TO GO HOME.
YOU DON'T WANT TO BE A SILLY STINKING DOROTHY, DO YOU? THEY'RE REVILED THROUGHOUT EVERY WONDROUS LAND.
DID YOU KNOW THE NAME DOROTHY TRANSLATES AS "SQUANDERED OPPORTUNITY"?
SO IS SHE STAYING OR NOT?

AT THAT SAME TIME, FAR AWAY...
THERESE!
THERESE!
SPREAD OUT, BUT KEEP IN SIGHT OF EACH OTHER.
I'VE GOT NO SCENT. THE SNOW'S TOO NEW TO TELL IF SHE CAME THIS WAY.

BIGBY WOULD BE ABLE TO PICK UP HER SCENT IN SECONDS.
HE NEEDS TO BE HERE.

I CAN SEE YOU'RE WORRIED, SIS, BUT ONE THING I'VE LEARNED RECENTLY.
THERE'S ALWAYS HOPE.
AND ODDLY ENOUGH, I CAN PROMISE THIS TIME, HOPE WON'T RUN OUT ON YOU.

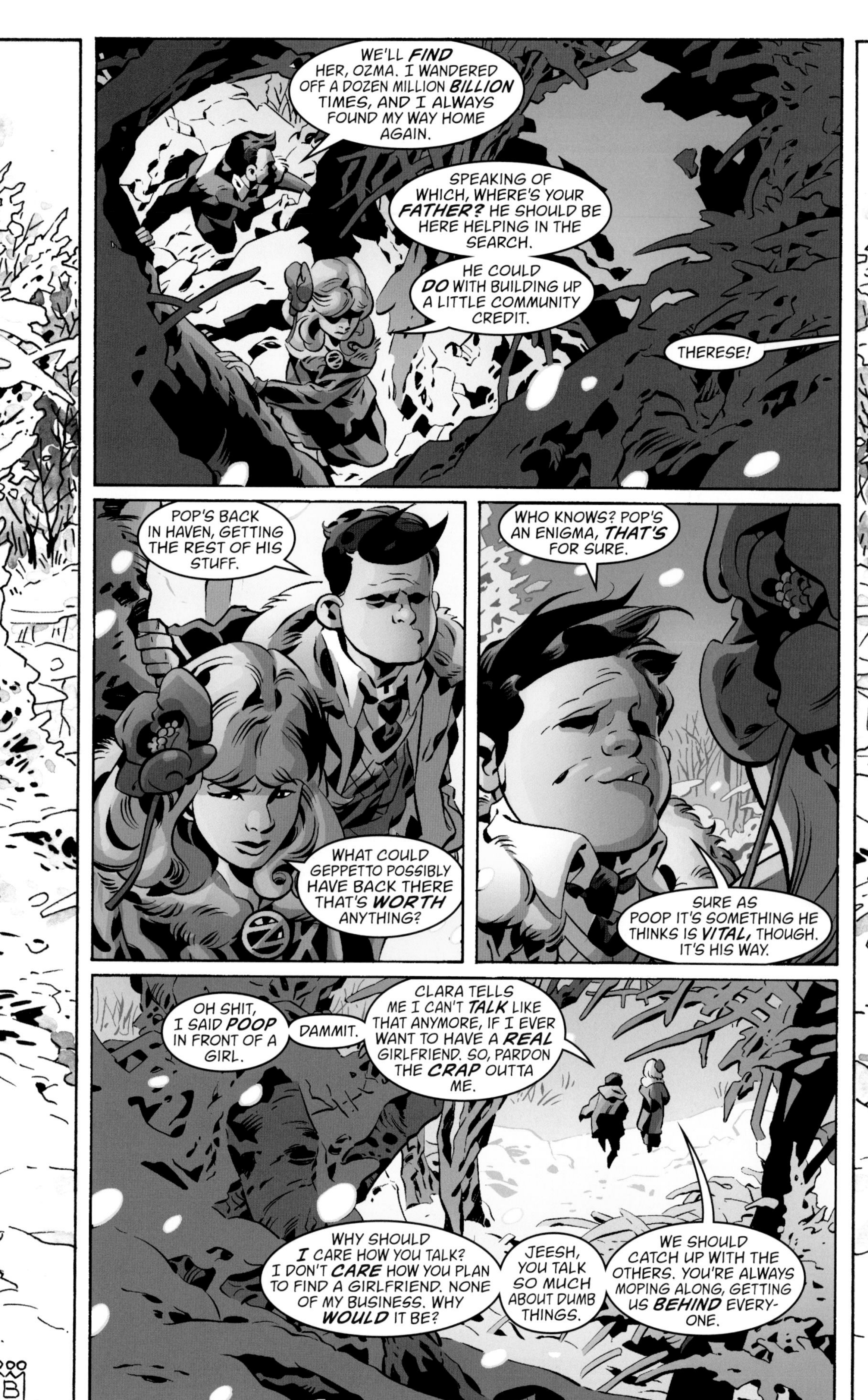
WE'LL FIND HER, OZMA. I WANDERED OFF A DOZEN MILLION BILLION TIMES, AND I ALWAYS FOUND MY WAY HOME AGAIN.
SPEAKING OF WHICH, WHERE'S YOUR FATHER? HE SHOULD BE HERE HELPING IN THE SEARCH.
HE COULD DO WITH BUILDING UP A LITTLE COMMUNITY CREDIT.
THERESE!
POP'S BACK IN HAVEN, GETTING THE REST OF HIS STUFF.
WHAT COULD GEPPETTO POSSIBLY HAVE BACK THERE THAT'S WORTH ANYTHING?
WHO KNOWS? POP'S AN ENIGMA, THAT'S FOR SURE.
SURE AS POOP IT'S SOMETHING HE THINKS IS VITAL, THOUGH. IT'S HIS WAY.
OH SHIT, I SAID POOP IN FRONT OF A GIRL.
DAMMIT.
CLARA TELLS ME I CAN'T TALK LIKE THAT ANYMORE, IF I EVER WANT TO HAVE A REAL GIRLFRIEND. SO, PARDON THE CRAP OUTTA ME.
WHY SHOULD I CARE HOW YOU TALK? I DON'T CARE HOW YOU PLAN TO FIND A GIRLFRIEND. NONE OF MY BUSINESS. WHY WOULD IT BE?
JEESH, YOU TALK SO MUCH ABOUT DUMB THINGS.
WE SHOULD CATCH UP WITH THE OTHERS. YOU'RE ALWAYS MOPING ALONG, GETTING US BEHIND EVERY-ONE.

THIS IS MY PALACE? REALLY?
BUT IT'S ALL CRUMBLY AND WITH BROKEN PARTS. REAL FAIRY TALE PRINCESSES DON'T HAVE BROKEN-DOWN PALACES.
IT'S SOMETHING OF A FIXER-UPPER, I'LL WARRANT THAT MUCH. BUT IT WILL BEGIN TO CHANGE ONCE YOU'RE CROWNED AND ENTHRONED.
WAVE AT YOUR SUBJECTS, MAJESTY. THEY'VE WAITED FOR THIS DAY FOR A LONG TIME. GIVE THEM SOMETHING FOR THEIR DEDICATION.
HELLO. THANK YOU ALL.
AND HERE WE ARE. YOUR THRONE AWAITS.
OH.
THIS-- THIS IS REAL, ISN'T IT?
LET ME TAKE YOUR COAT, YOUR HIGHNESS.
I'M REALLY ABOUT TO BECOME A REAL QUEEN OF A WHOLE COUNTRY?
RIGHT NOW?
WINTER WON'T EVEN BE CROWNED FOR YEARS AND YEARS.

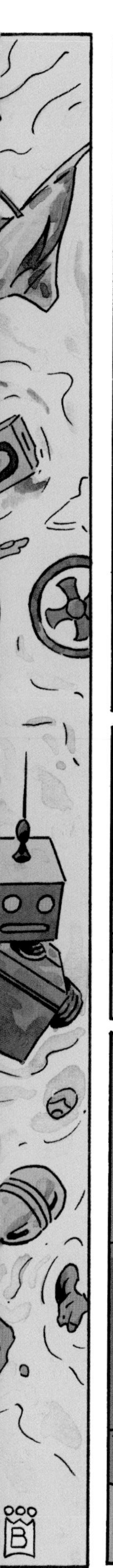

SIT AND WE'LL BEGIN.
SHE WON'T EVEN BE A REAL QUEEN. SHE HAS TO BECOME A KING. YUCK!
OH, THIS THRONE IS A BIT SPIKEY!

OH, OF COURSE. ALLOW ME TO REMEDY THAT.

MR. WELLSTUFFED, WILL YOU STEP UP TO SERVE YOUR QUEEN?
OF COURSE, TEDDY SAINT IVES, OF DARKSLIDE AND PUFFBOTTOM DELL.

I'LL JUST--
HOLD ON AND--

UPSY-DAISY!
ALL CUSHIONED NOW, Y'R GREAT-NESS.

PLEASE SIT.
ARE YOU SURE?
UHM... THANK YOU, MR. WELLSTUFFED.
GLAD TO BE OF HELP, MA'AM.

PRESENTLY...
BY THE SACRED MAINSPRING AND HIS COHORTS, WOUND AND WINDING; BY THE FOUR COURTS OF THE CARVED, SEWN, GLUED AND VACUUM-MOLDED; BY THE AUTHORITY OF HEFT AND WEAVE; BY THE BATTERIES BOTH INCLUDED AND NOT; AND WITH SOME ASSEMBLY REQUIRED...
...BY THE CONCORD OF THE BOXED, BAGGED AND BLISTER-PACKED...
...I HEREBY CROWN YOU THERESE THE FIRST, UNCONTESTED QUEEN OF TOYLAND, FAR MATAGONIA, AND THE WONDROUS SHORE!
FURTHERMORE, I DECLARE YOU MONARCH EXTRAORDINARY OF THE DISCARDIA, WHERESOEVER THEY MIGHT BE FOUND.

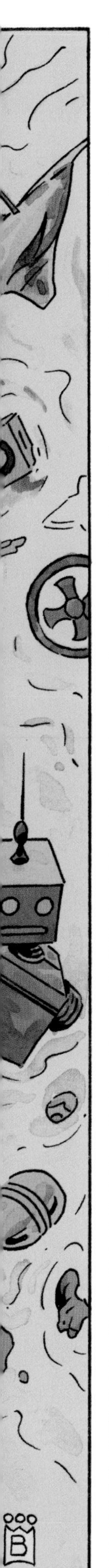

CONGRATULATIONS, YOUR HIGHNESS.
WHAT IS YOUR FIRST COMMAND?
MMMMM.

OH, I KNOW!
I'M **HUNGRY!**
I HAVEN'T HAD ANYTHING TO EAT SINCE BREAKFAST **DAYS** AGO.

ATTENTION THE COURT.
BRING **FOOD!**

HERE Y'GO, Y'R **SPECIALNESS.**
FINEST THE KITCHEN HAS T' OFFER. SURE, Y'BET.

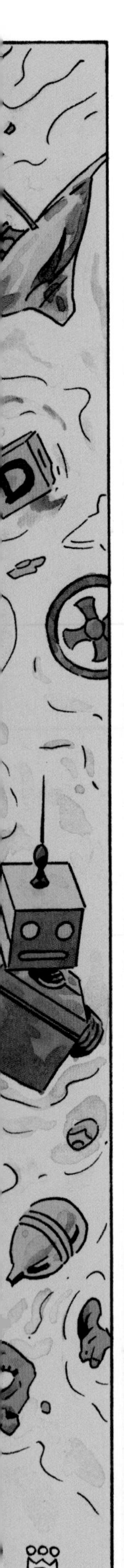

I TRUST THIS WILL BE TO YOUR LIKING.
THANK YOU SO MUCH, MR. IVES.
NNNNRG

THIS IS ALL SO LOVELY!

HUH?
squeek!

SOMETHING THE MATTER, MA'AM?
I CAN'T EAT THIS! IT'S PLASTIC!

OF COURSE IT IS. THIS IS TOYLAND AND EVERYTHING IN IT IS A TOY.
NOTHING GROWS HERE. NOTHING EXISTS HERE BUT THAT WHICH IS WASHED UP.
IS THIS NOT THE LAND OF THE DISCARDIA?
BUT--

--I'M REALLY HUNGRY.

NEXT: THE FORLORN HOPE

Once upon a time, Therese, the daughter of Snow White and Bigby Wolf, ruled a magical kingdom of lost toys.
I'm STILL hungry.
And I'm bored. Being a queen isn't fun after all.
You could always start your great mission, your majesty, blessing the land and restoring it to beauty and power.
Restoring US too. Don't forget that.
May it be.
What's it like being HUNGRY, ma'am? I've often tried to imagine it, to better play my part.
Is it like when your yarn gets tangled, or your stuffing gets wet and moldy?
ACTION FIGURES
Chapter 4 of CUBS in TOYLAND
In which we take the heights and save the girl.
BILL WILLINGHAM writer/creator
MARK BUCKINGHAM pencils
STEVE LEIALOHA inks 1-6,9-13,17
ANDREW PEPOY inks 7-8,14-16
LEE LOUGHRIDGE colors
TODD KLEIN letters
GREGORY LOCKARD asst. ed.
SHELLY BOND editor

IT'S TRUE, MY QUEEN. IT'S TIME TO **BEGIN** THE RESTORATION. THE DISCARDIA HAVE BEEN BROKEN, TORN, AND MISSING PARTS FOR TOO LONG.
IT'S YOUR GREAT UNDERTAKING. THE **REASON** WE BROUGHT YOU ACROSS WAVES AND WORLDS BEYOND NUMBERING, TO BE OUR SOVEREIGN.
WELL, WHAT ABOUT WHAT *I* WANT? I'M HUNGRY.
THAT'S WHAT WE NEED TO SOLVE.
HERE, MAJESTY. DRINK.
IT'S WATER.
DRINK.
DRINK.
YOU'LL LIKE IT.
"THE RAINY RAIN DRIPS, DRIPS, DRIPS DOWN OUR STONY WALLS.
"STONY WALLS FILTER IT SO GOOD, GOOD, GOOD."
THIS IS FIT FOR A QUEEN, OR NOTHING IS.
YOU MUST LEARN TO USE YOUR IMAGINATION, YOUNG QUEEN.
PRETEND TO EAT AND YOU'VE EATEN.
JUST AS EVERY TOY IS GIVEN LIFE BY THOSE WHO PRETEND TO HAVE IT.
THAT'S CRAZYPANTS TALK, MR. IVES.
THERE.
NOW TASTE IT. IS IT GOOD?

HERE.
TAKE THIS AWAY.
I DON'T WANT STUPID WATER. I NEED TO EAT.
I CAN'T PRETEND TO EAT. I NEED SOMETHING FOR REAL.
I NEED REAL HAMBURGERS AND MACARONI AND CHEESES!

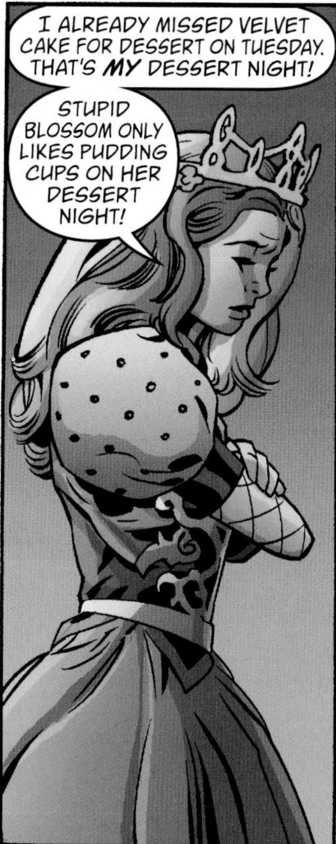
I ALREADY MISSED VELVET CAKE FOR DESSERT ON TUESDAY. THAT'S MY DESSERT NIGHT!
STUPID BLOSSOM ONLY LIKES PUDDING CUPS ON HER DESSERT NIGHT!

SOMETIMES GREAT SACRIFICES MUST BE MADE FOR THE GOOD OF THE REALM, HIGHNESS.
NO!
I DON'T WANT TO SACRIFICE. I WANT TO EAT!
NOW!

I'LL TRY TO FIND YOU SOMETHING.

THIS ISN'T GOING WELL. SHOULD WE TELL HER ABOUT THE OTHER THING?
NOT YET, MR. WELL-STUFFED. SHE'S NOT READY.

MEANWHILE...
LET'S GET THIS DONE WITH EXPEDITION, SHALL WE?

IT'S MOVING DAY INTO FABLETOWN: THE SEQUEL.
I WANT TO GET BACK UP TO THE FARM TO HELP LOOK FOR LITTLE THERESE. AND NOW WITH DARIEN MISSING, TOO--
I WOULDN'T WORRY. NOW THAT BIGBY'S BACK, HE'LL FIND THEM.

THIS WAY.
PLENTY OF ROOM. YOU CAN UNLOAD HERE AND THEN PARK OUTSIDE.
YOU AND MR. HOLT ARE DOING A WONDERFUL JOB, MRS. SPRATT.
CALL ME LEIGH.

I MUST ADMIT, I FEEL LIKE WE'RE INTRUDING INTO YOUR HOUSE, MRS...ah... LEIGH.
OH NO, YOUR HONOR. YOU CAN'T FEEL THAT WAY. AT LEAST YOU MUSTN'T.

CASTLE DARK WASN'T MY HOUSE. IT WAS MY PRISON. YOU CAN'T HELP BUT IMPROVE IT BY MOVING IN.

AND DOWN ON TOYLAND'S SALTY SHORE...
SO WHAT DO WE DO NOW, MISTER MONKBATTER?
MOUNTBATTEN. CALL ME MONTY, THOUGH.
DO WE JUST RUN UP THERE TO THE CASTLE AND TELL MY SISTER TO COME HOME WITH US?
I HOPE IT CAN BE DONE THAT EASILY.
AND WE CAN RIDE ALL THE WAY BACK WITH YOU, JUST LIKE HOW WE GOT HERE?
YES-- IF THE CHILD IS FREE TO GO.
BUT THERE'S SOMETHING ELSE AT PLAY HERE, ALMOST LIKE I CAN SMELL A PROMISE OF BLOOD AND BATTLE ON THE MORNING MIST.
WELL, WHO HAVE WE HERE? A YOUNG LORD OF ADVENTURE, ASTRIDE A FIERCE TIGER, NO LESS.
HUH?
WAIT!
I KNOW YOU!
I SHOULD THINK SO, DARIEN.

WE'VE ALREADY HAD SO MANY ADVENTURES TOGETHER, I'D BE DEVASTATED IF YOU DIDN'T RECOGNIZE YOUR OLD COMRADE IN ARMS.
RANGER MIKE DANGER REPORTING FOR DUTY, COMMANDER!
IT LOOKS LIKE THIS MAY BE OUR TOUGHEST MISSION YET, DON'T YOU THINK SO, SIR?
NOT TO WORRY, THOUGH. I BROUGHT OUR TRUSTED COMPANION ALONG.
MMD
THAT'S ME!
NO WAY! HE'S TALKING ABOUT ME!
BUT--
--YOU'RE SO BIG!

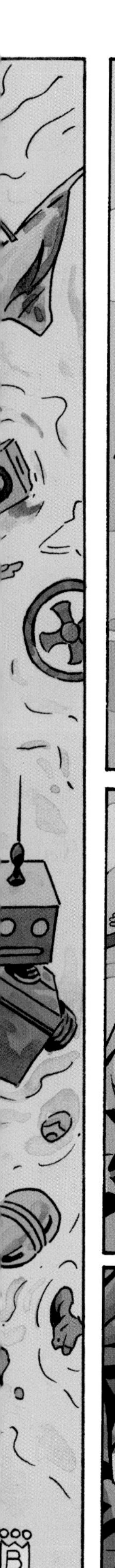

IF I'VE INCREASED IN STATURE OVER THE YEARS, IT'S BECAUSE OF THE TRUST AND RESPONSIBILITY YOU'VE PLACED IN ME, SIR!
WOW!
YOU'RE LIKE THE COOLEST TOY EVER!
AND WHO ARE THESE TWO?

AS I SAID: MY FAITHFUL COMPANION AND MAN FRIDAY, KARATE NINJA NOBU.
BOTH VERSIONS.
DWW

I'M THE REAL NOBU! ORIGINAL SERIES!

NO! I'M THE REAL ONE!

THE NEWER VERSION WITH KUNG FU ACTION FIST!

UHM... SPRING'S A BIT WORN.
CAN SOMEONE HELP ME PUSH THIS BACK IN?

THEY'RE SO SMALL COMPARED TO YOU.
EVER THE FATE OF SIDEKICKS.

SO, ARE YOU HERE TO HELP ME, RANGER MIKE?

I SURE AM, COMMANDER.
WOULDN'T LET YOU GO INTO DANGER ALONE.
MMD

NO AVOIDING IT, I SUPPOSE.

DANGER?

NO SENSE PUTTING IT OFF.
WHEN A MISSION IS NIGH, IT ONLY HELPS THE ENEMY TO DELAY.
DIRECTLY INTO THE FRAY IS THE BEST WAY.
ONCE MORE UNTO THE BREACH AND ALL THAT.

AT ABOUT THAT SAME TIME...
WHAT'S BIGBY DOING NOW?
WHAT HE DOES BEST. SNIFFING OUT THE TRUTH.
HELLO?
HE CAN'T TALK ANYMORE, SAM?
NOT A WORD SINCE THE KIDS PLAYED HERE.
NONE OF THE REPAIRS I'VE MADE SINCE THEN HAVE HELPED. THE LORD GOVERNOR IS AS INERT AS I'VE EVER SEEN HIM.
ALL THIS RUST COULD ACCOUNT FOR THAT.
DARIEN WAS HERE, AND THERESE PASSED HERE BEFORE HIM.
BUT MY SON'S TRAIL STOPS COLD. CUT OFF LIKE A KNIFE.
DEAD IN WAYS BEYOND WHAT ANY CREATURE COULD DO TO HIDE FROM ME.
DARE'S NO LONGER ON THIS WORLD.

AN HOUR OR SO LATER...
THERESE CAME THIS WAY.

STOPPED HERE.

ALONG WITH SOMETHING ELSE, MADE OF PETROLEUM PLASTIC AND...
...SOMETHING.

ANOTHER DAMNABLE THING THAT I CAN'T IDENTIFY.

AND ANOTHER CHILD LIFTED ENTIRELY OUT OF THE MUNDY WORLD.

IN TOYLAND...
YOU HAVE TO BE MORE **REASONABLE,** QUEEN THERESE.
NO I DON'T!
THE **QUEEN** IS IN CHARGE OF EVERYONE! ISN'T THAT SO?
AM I THE QUEEN OR NOT?
OF **COURSE** YOU ARE, YOUR GRACE.
OUR DUTY IS TO SERVE YOUR EVERY WHIM.
THEN, WHEN I **ORDERED** YOU TO GET ME FOOD, AND YOU SAID YOU WOULD, AND THEN YOU DIDN'T **FIND** ANYTHING AT ALL, YOU DISOBEYED ME.
THAT'S WHAT YOU DID, **DIDN'T** YOU, MR. IVES?
GIVEN A CERTAIN INTERPRETATION, YES, BUT--
NO BUTS!
MOMMY SAYS THE ONLY BUTS THAT MATTER ARE THE ONES THAT WILL GET **PADDLED** IF YOU DON'T DO AS YOU'RE TOLD!
SO I GAVE YOU A THOUSAND HUNDRED CHANCES AND YOU **BETRAYED** ME EVERY TIME. NO MORE CHANCES, **EVER!** I'M FLYING HOME RIGHT NOW!
YOU CAN'T!
YOU'RE NOT THE BOSS OF ME!

NO, I MEANT YOU LITERALLY CAN'T!
YALP!
YUG!
MRPHH!
UHOOOOH!
I FELL DOWN! I ACTUALLY FELL DOWN! I NEVER DID THAT! IT HURT!
I CAN'T FLY NO MORE!
YOU CAN FLY IN YOUR IMAGINATION, YOUR GRACE. YOU CAN STILL DO THAT.
HERE IN THE LAND OF HAPPINESS, EVERYTHING IS PRETEND.

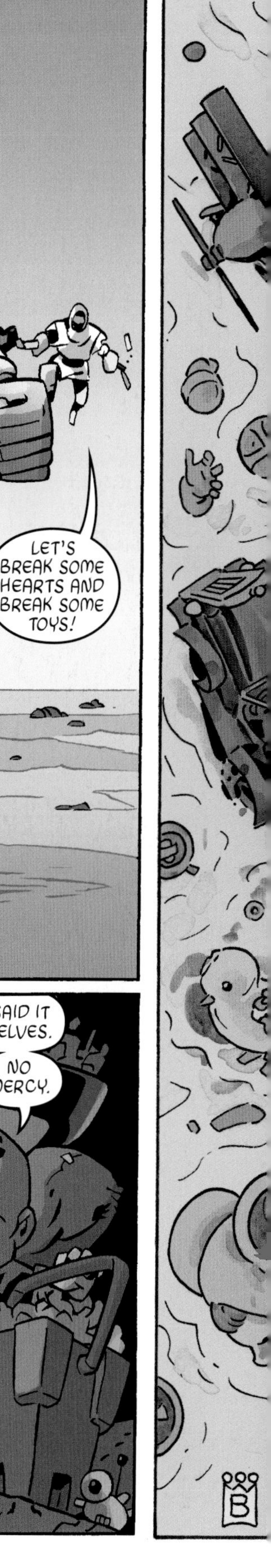
HERE WE GO!
GUNG HO!
MMD
MURDERIZE THE BUMS!
TALLY HO!
LET'S BREAK SOME HEARTS AND BREAK SOME TOYS!
REMEMBER THE PLAN!
RUN IT STRAIGHT UP THE MIDDLE AND **POUND** THEM WITH AN ASTONISHING LACK OF MERCY!
DON'T FORGET, THEY'RE JUST TOYS! THEY DON'T ACTUALLY **FEEL** PAIN!
HERE THEY COME. ORDERS, COMMANDER KID?
THEY SAID IT THEMSELVES.
NO MERCY.

TAKE THE HEIGHTS! SAVE THE GIRL!

PUSH!
HERE WE GO!
INCOMING!

SHRAPNEL ATTACK!
MMD
DIABOLICAL!
UNIMAGINABLE!
LOOK OUT, BOY!
IT'S JUST LITTLE PLASTIC BITS!

I'M OKAY!
I GOT A SHIELD!
PLASTIC STUFF AGAINST A REAL SHIELD HAS LIKE NO HIT POINTS AT ALL!

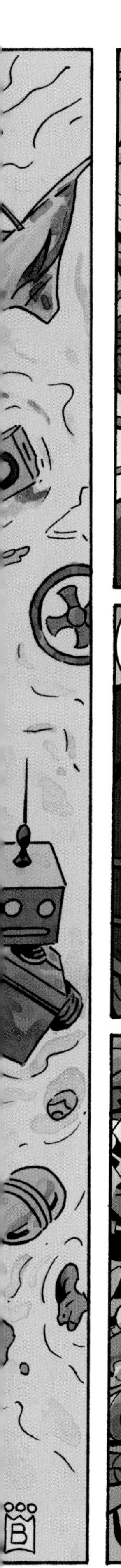

AIR FORCE ATTACK!
DEPLOY THE BADMINTON NET!

UH-OH!
THIS COULD BE A SETBACK!
WRAP THE BIG ONE UP GOOD AND TIGHT!
EVERY ONE OF THE ENEMY WE DELAY IS A NET GAIN FOR US!

I'M FINE, COMMANDER! I'LL GET OUT OF THIS IN A BIT, BUT WE CAN'T LOSE THE MOMENTUM OF OUR ATTACK.
KEEP GOING!
GRRRROOWWL!
OKAY, RANGER MIKE!
WILL DO!

I CAN FIGHT THESE THINGS PRETTY GOOD!
GRRROO-OOOOWWWW-WRRRR!

FOR QUEEN AND COUNTRY!
HERE COME A WHOLE BUNCH MORE!

CARRY ON, BOY! DON'T FALTER!

I'LL DISPATCH THESE PLUSHY DASTARDS AND BE RIGHT ALONG!
OKAY, MR. MONTY!
YOU CAN COUNT ON ME!
I'M DARE! THE SON OF BIGBY WOLF!
AND Y'KNOW WHAT MY DADDY TOLD ME?
WHO DARES WINS!
PREPARE TO LAUNCH.
LAUNCH THE KILL TRAIN!
WHA-HOOOO! RIDE ON THE KILL TRAIN!
WHOA!

NEXT: THE HUNGRY GAMES

BROKEN KITE
Chapter 5 of CUBS in TOYLAND
DARIEN!
OOAH!
HEY!
I'M NOT FLYING!
NOPE! THIS IS GOING TO KNOCK THE STUFFING RIGHT OUT OF YOU!
RIDE ON THE KILL TRAIN!
BET YOU WISH YOU HAD PROPER STUFFING NOW, HUH, BOY?
BILL WILLINGHAM writer/creator
MARK BUCKINGHAM pencils
STEVE LEIALOHA inks 1-4,7-15
ANDREW PEPOY inks 5-6,16-17
LEE LOUGHRIDGE colors
TODD KLEIN letters
GREGORY LOCKARD asst. ed.
SHELLY BOND editor

YOWTCH!
I CAN'T FLY AT ALL!
NOT MUCH GOOD AT **PRETENDING,** ARE YOU?
I NEED--
HEY!
CUSHION!
HANDS **OFF,** MEAT BOY!
YOOF!
NO FAIR!
OW!

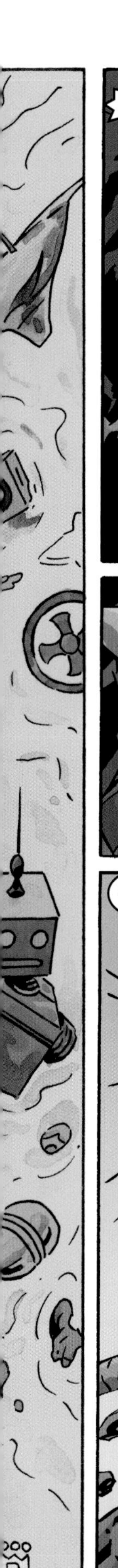

AAAAGGH!

YOU PACK OF PUFF-BELLIED CUTTHROATS!
YOU'VE **KILLED** THE BOY!

AN INFESTIOUS PESTILENCE ON THE **LOT** OF YOU!

YOU'VE GOT QUITE THE FANCY **MOUTH** ON YOU, TONY!
RRRR-RROOOWW-WERRR!

YOU DARE?
YOU COME TO THE WONDERFUL SHORE, TO RAKE AND HARRY AMONG THE DISCARDIA, AND IMAGINE YOU CAN DO SO WITH IMPUNITY?
BASE ANIMAL!
NOT TODAY!
NO, SIR! NOT ON MY WATCH!
I ASK FOR QUARTER, SIR!
LET ME SEE TO THE BOY, THEN WE CAN CONTINUE OUR DUEL AS HONORABLE SOLDIERS.

NO QUARTER!
RIP 'IM INNA FACE, MR. IVES!
NEVER!
NO QUARTER WILL BE ALLOWED TO ENEMIES OF QUEEN THERESE'S REALM!
FINE!
HAVE IT YOUR WAY, THEN.
FANG AND CLAW SHALL BE THE SINGLE ORDER OF THE DAY!
REND THE LOT OF YOU!
WHOOF!
AGREED.
FANG AND CLAW!

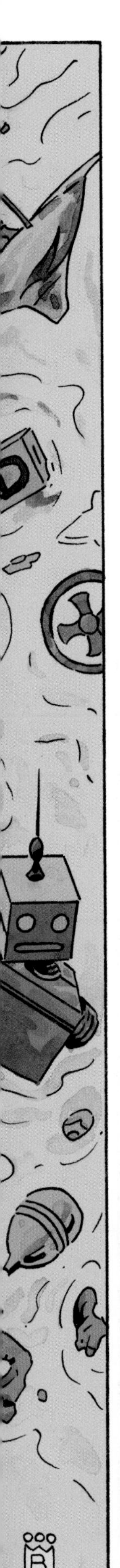

YYRRUGGK!
ALONG WITH THE STRENGTH OF LIMBS IMBUED WITH THE VIRTUE OF MY NOBLE STATION!

BY MY PUISSANT GRACE!
CRAAACCKK!

AND FIDELITY TO QUEEN AND COUNTRY.

WOW!
MR. IVES IS A GIANT BAD-ASS!

IT'S DONE.
BIND THIS CREATURE OF TRUE MEAT AND BONE. BIND HIM WELL.
I HAVE AN IDEA.
Y'OKAY, BOSS.

THE MUNDY WORLD.
FEI LIAN! EURUS! WIND OF THE EAST!
YORUBA! LADY NOTUS! STORM MOTHER! SOUTH WIND!
YAPONCHA! ZEPHYRUS! WEST WIND!
I KNOW YOU'RE NEAR.
I KNOW YOU CAN HEAR ME.
LET'S TALK.
WE'RE HERE, WOLF.
WHAT WOULD YOU HAVE OF US NOW?
THIS CREATURE SHOULD HAVE NOTHING OF US. WE'RE GODS! SO HOW THEN ARE WE TO BE AT HIS BECK AND CALL?

WHAT SAY, FOR ONCE, WE CALL A MORATORIUM ON THE PISSING CONTEST?
I NEED YOUR HELP.

BEGGING?
HUMBLED?
VULNERABLE?
SURE, IF BEGGING IS WHAT IT TAKES, FEEL FREE TO CALL IT THAT.

IF THREATENING WILL WORK, I'LL FIND A WAY TO MAKE MY THREATS STICK.
I'M A DAD, WITH TWO MISSING CUBS. I'LL DO WHAT IT TAKES TO FIND THEM.

YOU'RE ALSO FATHER OF THE NORTH WIND.
IN RESPECT OF THAT, WE'LL CONSIDER YOUR PLEAS.

IN A NUTSHELL, THEN.
FIND THEM.

DARIEN AND THERESE AREN'T ON THIS WORLD ANYMORE. I HAVE NO IDEA HOW.
WINTER SAYS SHE CAN'T SENSE THEM IN ANY OF THE WORLDS IN HER--WHAT DO YOU CALL THEM? JURISDICTION? TERRITORY?
SO, I WANT YOU TO SEARCH THE WORLDS YOU CONTROL. EVERY WORLD YOU CAN GET TO, IN FACT.
FIND MY KIDS AND I'LL FIND A WAY TO REWARD YOU.
SOME-HOW.
AND IF WE REFUSE TO RUN YOUR INCONSEQUENTIAL ERRANDS?
THEN I'LL FIND A WAY TO PUNISH YOU.

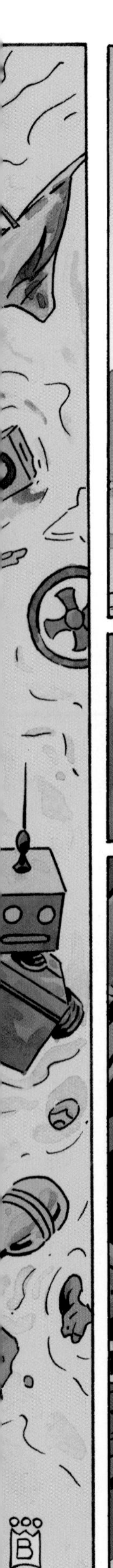

MEANWHILE...
GET OUT!
ALL OF YOU!
YOU TOO, MR. IVES!

LEAVE ME ALONE, UNTIL YOU CAN FEED ME!
I DON'T WANT TO BE HERE ANY-MORE!
I WANT TO GO HOME AND I PROMISE FROM NOW ON I'LL EAT EVERY-THING ON MY PLATE EVERY NIGHT! EVEN MEATLOAF AND PEAS!

I DON'T WANT TO DIE HERE! I DON'T.

LISTEN, YOU LITTLE BRAT!
I'VE HAD JUST ABOUT ENOUGH OF YOUR TANTRUMS AND BLUBBERING!

THIS IS DEADLAND! EVERY CHILD HERE DIES! WHY DO YOU THINK WE WERE SENT HERE IN THE FIRST PLACE?
NO, MR. IVES! NOT YET! SHE ISN'T READY!

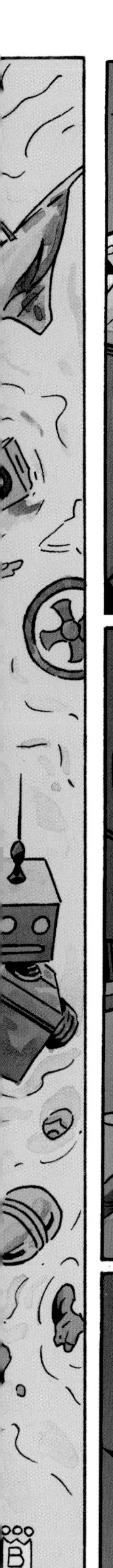

YOU WONDER WHY WE'RE NOT PRETTY, **HAPPY** TOYS? ISN'T IT OBVIOUS?

IT'S BECAUSE WE'RE KILLERS.

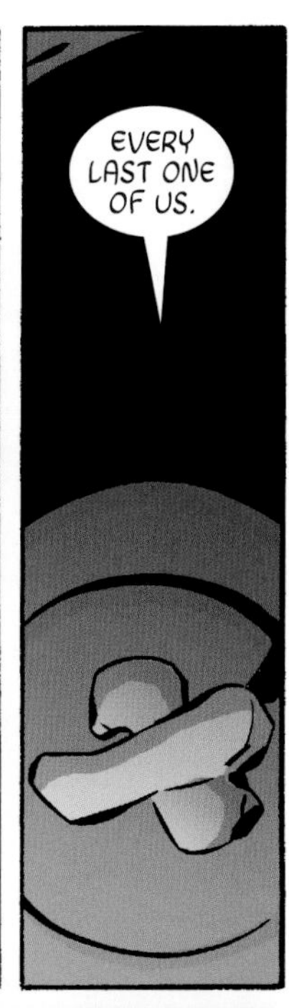
EVERY LAST ONE OF US.

"I WAS PLACED TOO NEAR A FRAYED ELECTRICAL WIRE AND CAUGHT FIRE, RIGHT IN MY PLUSH."

RIGHT **HERE.**

"OF COURSE I WAS CHEMICALLY TREATED AND PASSED ALL THE SAFETY TESTING, SO MY STUFFING BURNT OUT WITHIN THE REQUIRED TWO SECONDS.

"BUT NOT BEFORE THE FIRE SPREAD TO THE BLANKET, THEN TO THE ENTIRE BEDROOM.
"IT'S REMARKABLE I SURVIVED, BUT THROUGH THE WHIMS OF CHANCE AND AIR CURRENTS, MY CORNER OF THE ROOM REMAINED MOSTLY UNTOUCHED, WHILE ALL AROUND ME BURNED.

"BILLY AND BOBBY LINDER DIED SCREAMING IN THEIR TWIN CRIBS, WHILE I WATCHED."

THAT'S WHY I'M HERE.

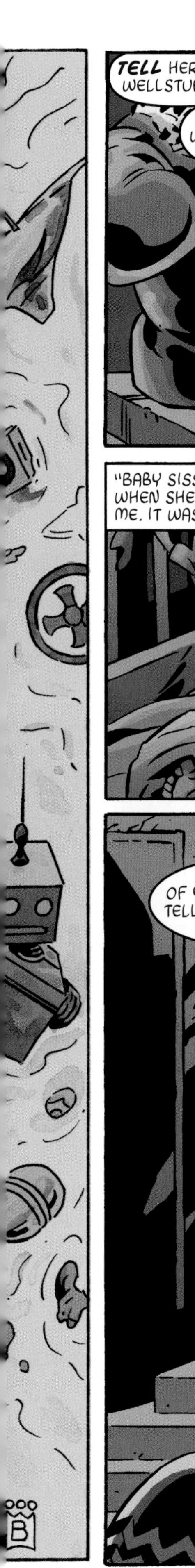

TELL HER, MR. WELLSTUFFED.
TELL HER WHAT YOU DID.
UH...I DON'T--
TELL HER!

"BABY SISSY SUFFOCATED WHEN SHE ROLLED UNDER ME. IT WAS AN ACCIDENT."

IT'S ALWAYS AN ACCIDENT. BUT WE'RE STILL BLAMED. WE'RE STILL BANISHED HERE.

THE REST OF YOU, SPEAK UP. TELL HER YOUR TALES OF WOE.
NO MORE HOLDING BACK.

MY CHILD GOT TANGLED AND STRANGLED ON MY REINS.
BETHANY CHOKED ON ME.
ME, TOO. CHOKING DEATH.
CHOKING.
LUKE RODE ME INTO THE POOL AND DROWNED.
YOUNG JACOB FELL OFF THE ROOF. CLIMBED UP THERE TO MAKE ME FLY.
MY KID WAS RUN OVER WHILE PLAYING WITH ME IN THE DRIVEWAY.
BLUNT FORCE TRAUMA.
MR MEGA TRUCK

MONICA SKATED TOO NEAR THE PINE PARK STAIRS.
WE FELL TOGETHER, BUMPITY, BUMPITY, BUMPITY, ALL THE WAY DOWN.
I WAS PAINTED WITH LEAD-BASED PAINT.
ETHAN CUT HIMSELF ON MY SHARP CORNER. IT BECAME INFECTED.
THIS--
I CAN'T--
I HAVE TO GO!
WAS IT ENTIRELY NECESSARY TO DO THAT, MR. IVES?
SHE NEEDED A SHARP DOSE OF REALITY.
A SLAP TO WAKE HER UP.

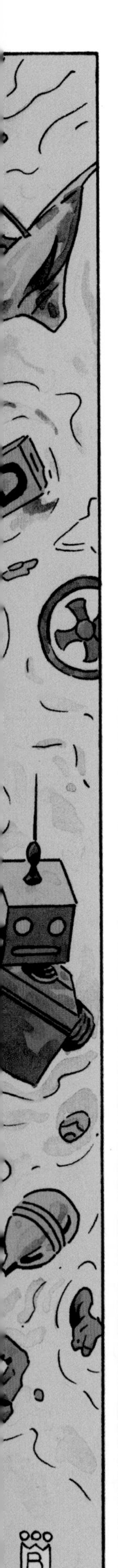

HER WILL IS BROKEN NOW. SHE CAN BE REMADE TO DO WHAT WE NEED OF HER.

WE MUST PROCEED CAREFULLY THOUGH, MR. IVES. SHE CAN BE BROKEN, BUT NOT SHATTERED.
IF SHE WERE TO FIND OUT WHAT WE DID TO HER BROTHER... WE SHOULD SEND A WORK CREW TO DISCREETLY DISPOSE OF HIS BODY.
HHHRRRGH

THERESE.
I'M NOT DEAD.

REMEMBER WHAT DAD SAID.

YOU'RE STILL ALIVE--

--YOU STILL FIGHT.

NEXT: THE PRICE

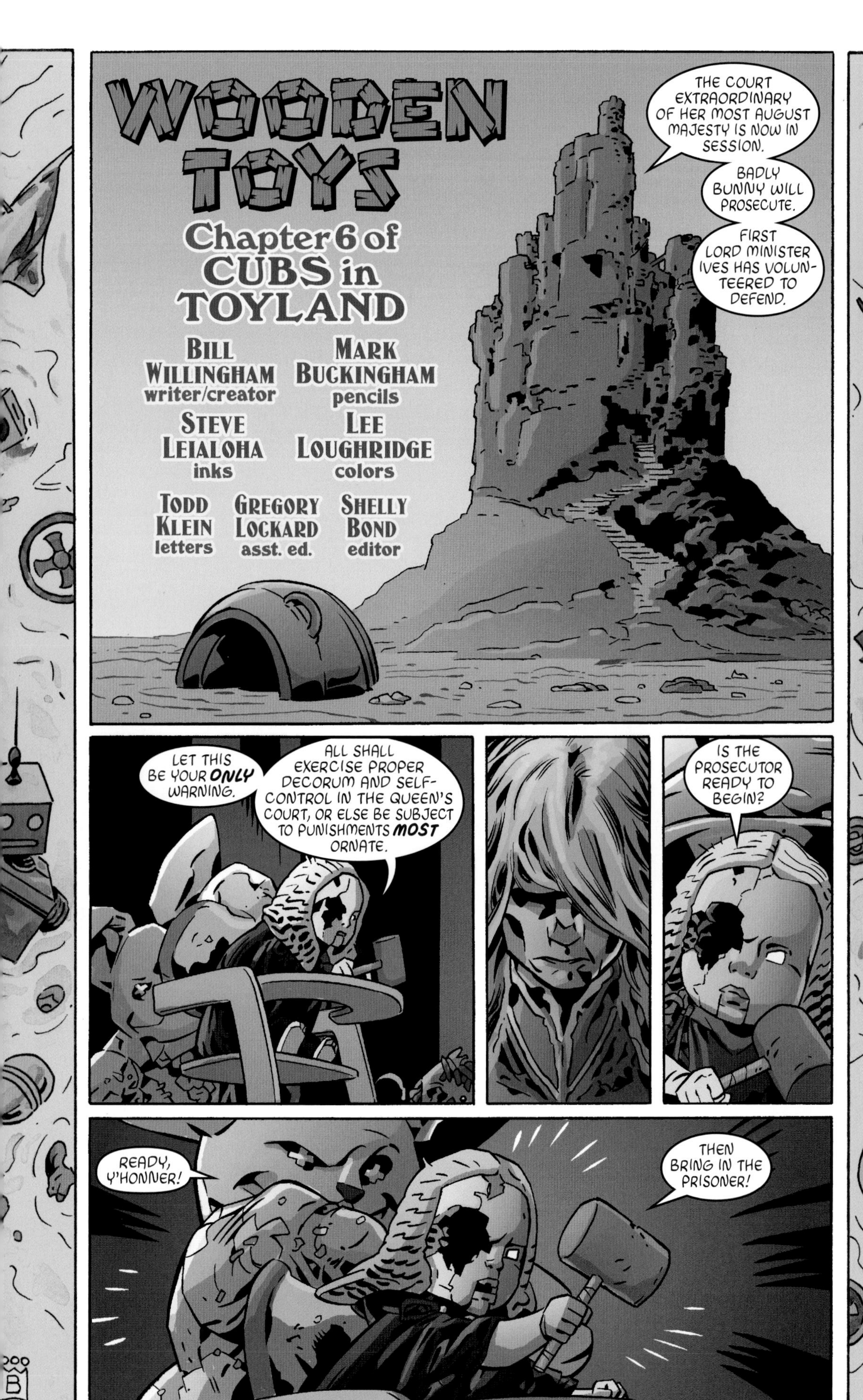
WOODEN TOYS
Chapter 6 of CUBS in TOYLAND
BILL WILLINGHAM writer/creator
MARK BUCKINGHAM pencils
STEVE LEIALOHA inks
LEE LOUGHRIDGE colors
TODD KLEIN letters
GREGORY LOCKARD asst. ed.
SHELLY BOND editor
THE COURT EXTRAORDINARY OF HER MOST AUGUST MAJESTY IS NOW IN SESSION.
BADLY BUNNY WILL PROSECUTE.
FIRST LORD MINISTER IVES HAS VOLUNTEERED TO DEFEND.
LET THIS BE YOUR ONLY WARNING.
ALL SHALL EXERCISE PROPER DECORUM AND SELF-CONTROL IN THE QUEEN'S COURT, OR ELSE BE SUBJECT TO PUNISHMENTS MOST ORNATE.
IS THE PROSECUTOR READY TO BEGIN?
READY, Y'HONNER!
THEN BRING IN THE PRISONER!

BEHOLD THIS WRETCH. THIS TIGER.
NOT EXACTLY LOOKING VERY TONY NOW, IS HE?
HE ATTACKED OUR REALM AND MADE WAR ON THE QUEEN'S ROYAL FORCES, WHICH IS TANTAMOUNT TO WARRING AGAINST THE QUEEN HERSELF.
WE ALL SAW IT. THERE'S NO DENYING. THEREFORE, HE'S GUILTY.
THE PROSECUTION RESTS.

MR. IVES. THE DEFENSE WILL ARGUE ITS CASE.

MY CLIENT'S DEFENSE IS THIS:
THOUGH GUILTY OF ALL YOU SAY, HE'S CLEARLY DONE IN. HE LOST.

HE'S BEEN BEATEN MILITARILY AND PUNISHED PHYSICALLY.
I ASK THAT WE RELEASE HIM, PROVIDED HE PROMISES TO LEAVE OUR SHORES AND NEVER RETURN.

WILL THE ACCUSED SPEAK?

I THROW MYSELF ON THE MERCY OF THE COURT.

AND WHERE IS THIS MERCY TO BE FOUND?
WAS IT INSERTED INTO US WITH OUR BATTERIES? ADDED INTO OUR BLISTER PACK AS A SPECIAL BONUS ATTACHMENT?
I'M CLOTH, STITCHING AND STUFFING. WHAT PART OF THAT CONTAINS SUCH A SUBSTANCE AS YOU SEEK?

I SEEK IT IN THE HEART OF THE QUEEN.
SHE'S MORE THAN CLOTH AND STUFFING. DO YOU REMEMBER ME, MAJESTY?

THERESE?

ANYTHING ELSE, SIR? MATTERS OF MITIGATION OR EXTENUATION?
WERE YOU ADDLED OR MIS-LED?
NO, I ACTED WITH PURPOSE. SHE NEEDS TO BE SAVED FROM THIS TERRIBLE PLACE.

IT APPEARS WE'VE NOTHING MORE, JUDGE KIDD.
THE DEFENSE RESTS.

THEN CLEARLY WE'RE DONE HERE.
YOUR JUDGMENT, MA'AM?

DEATH.
OUR SENTENCE IS DEATH.
MR. IVES, KILL THIS THING AND SERVE IT TO US TO SATE OUR HUNGER.
I OBEY, YOUR GRACE!
HEY!
PLEASE.
MERCY.
HHH-HARRR-OUU!

OH.
OH MY.
LET ME GET IN ON THIS!
THE CARCASS STILL NEEDS TO BE CHOPPED UP!
THE COURT ORDERS EVERYONE TO HELP!
RRRRRR!
MAKE STEAKS AND TIGER CHOPS!
NUGGETS AND MEATBALLS!
MEALS FOR OUR QUEEN!

IS IT DONE?
YES, MAJESTY.
THEN GIVE ME SOME. GIVE ME SOME NOW!
I'M STARVING.
IMMEDIATELY, MA'AM.
JOEY, SERVE THIS TO YOUR SOVEREIGN.
Y'BETCHA, I'LL DO JUS' THAT T'ING!
HERE Y'GO, Y'R QUEENI-NESS.
VER' GOOD, THIS'LL BE IN Y'R BELLY, Y'BET.
THANK YOU.
UH...

HHHURRRNNK.
NGGRRRR.
THIS IS RAW.
I DON'T LIKE RAW MEAT.
COOK THE NEXT PART.

I'M SORRY, YOUR GRACE, BUT THERE ARE NO TREES IN TOYLAND. NOTHING GROWS **NATURALLY** HERE. WE'VE NO WOOD WITH WHICH TO START A FIRE.

YES YOU DO, LIAR, **LIAR!**

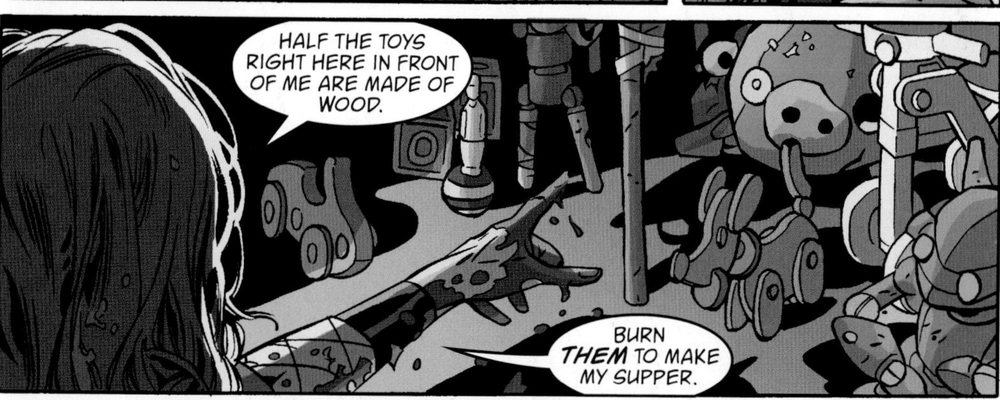
HALF THE TOYS RIGHT HERE IN FRONT OF ME ARE MADE OF WOOD.
BURN **THEM** TO MAKE MY SUPPER.

MR. WELLSTUFFED, I...UH...
OBEY YOUR **QUEEN.**

BUILD A FIRE.
OF COURSE, MR. IVES. RIGHT AWAY.
WE'LL USE ONLY THOSE BROKEN BEYOND ANY HOPE OF REPAIR, AND THE BROKEN PARTS THAT HAVE FALLEN OFF OTHER TOYS.
THEN ASK FOR VOLUNTEERS WILLING TO GIVE UP PARTS THEY DON'T REALLY NEED.
ANYTHING MERELY DECORATIVE, TO BEGIN WITH.
WE'LL COLLECT USEFUL APPENDAGES ONLY IF WE HAVE TO. THOSE WITH TWO ARMS CAN STILL GET BY WITH ONLY ONE.
BETTER TO GUARANTEE A THOUSAND OF US GO THROUGH LIFE PERMANENTLY LAMED THAN OUTRIGHT KILL EVEN A FEW.
WHY GO TO ALL THAT TROUBLE
WHY NOT JUST LET THIS ONE DIE LIKE THOSE WHO'VE COME BEFORE?
BETTER YET, TOSS HER OVER THE CLIFF, LIKE WE DID WITH HER BROTHER.
EVENTUALLY WE'LL GET ONE THAT LIVES JUST LONG ENOUGH TO FIX US BEFORE SHE STARVES.
STOP IT!

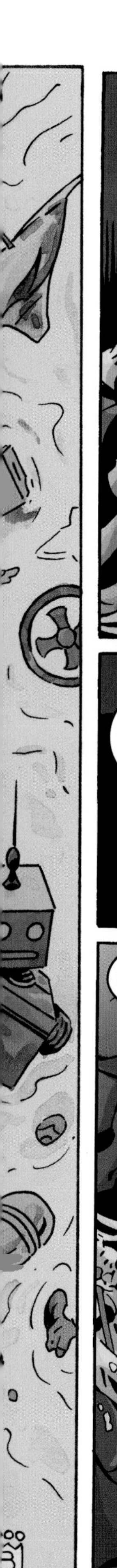

ENOUGH TREASONOUS TALK! SHE'S OUR SOVEREIGN QUEEN!
SO WHAT? SEND MR. STEAMPUDDLE TO GET US A NEW ONE WHO DON'T ORDER US TO KILL OUR OWN, JUST BECAUSE SHE'S FEELING PECKISH.

DO YOU IMAGINE IT'S THAT SIMPLE?
WE LIVE THROUGH THE BELIEF OF CHILDREN.

AND OUR CURRENT QUEEN IS OUR ONLY CONDUIT TO THAT BELIEF, FLOWING TO US FROM OUT BEYOND THE WONDERFUL SHORE.
BREAK THAT LINK WILLINGLY AND WE MAY NOT SURVIVE LONG ENOUGH TO RECRUIT A NEW QUEEN, AFTER THIS ONE IS GONE.

REGICIDE IS SUICIDE, CITIZENS.

INSCRIBE THAT IN YOUR HEARTS.

THE GREAT PRETEND IS A FRAGILE CONSTRUCT.

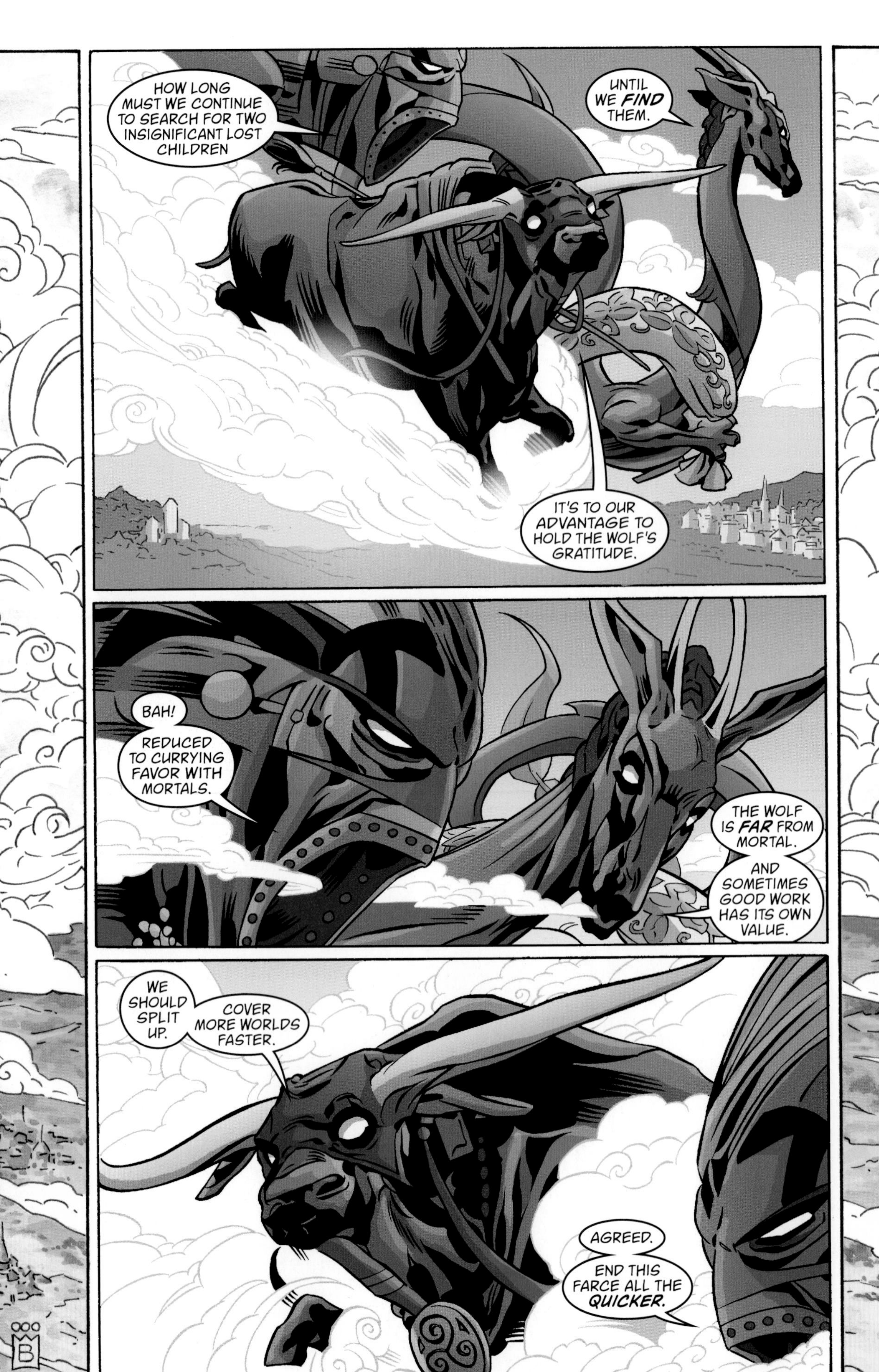
HOW LONG MUST WE CONTINUE TO SEARCH FOR TWO INSIGNIFICANT LOST CHILDREN
UNTIL WE FIND THEM.
IT'S TO OUR ADVANTAGE TO HOLD THE WOLF'S GRATITUDE.
BAH!
REDUCED TO CURRYING FAVOR WITH MORTALS.
THE WOLF IS FAR FROM MORTAL.
AND SOMETIMES GOOD WORK HAS ITS OWN VALUE.
WE SHOULD SPLIT UP.
COVER MORE WORLDS FASTER.
AGREED.
END THIS FARCE ALL THE QUICKER.

SOMEONE STARTED A FIRE.
WHAT?
I DON'T UNDERSTAND.
THE PRICE?
THE PRICE OF FISHING? FISHING FOR A KING?
FISHER PRICE KING?
MAKE SENSE!
OH.
THE PRICE OF BECOMING A KING.
I HEARD YOUR STUPID PROPHECY, WHEN BLOSSOM TOLD ME. BUT IT ONLY SAID ONE OF US BECOMES KING, AND WINTER ALREADY DID THAT.
NOW THERESE IS THE QUEEN OF TOYLAND AND I'M GOING TO BE A KING, TOO?
SHIT FIRE ON POP TARTS. DOES EVERY ONE OF US GET TO BE A KING?

CRAZY TALK.
IF EVERYONE GETS TO DO IT, THEN BEING A KING SURE DOESN'T **MEAN** MUCH.

YES, I KNOW YOU AREN'T REALLY **HERE,** AMBROSE.

I'M NO DUMMY.
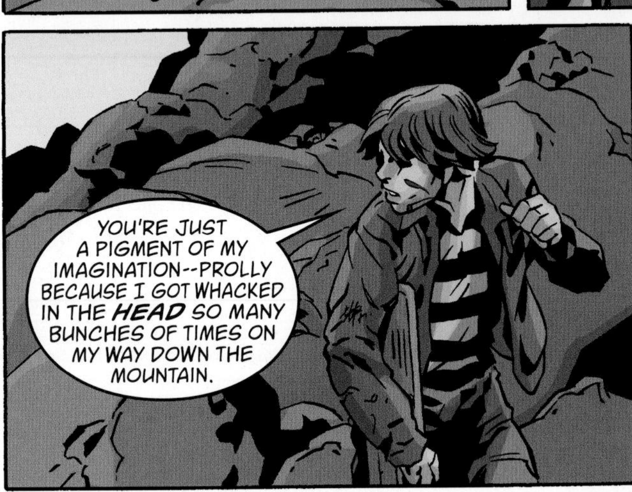
YOU'RE JUST A PIGMENT OF MY IMAGINATION--PROLLY BECAUSE I GOT WHACKED IN THE **HEAD** SO MANY BUNCHES OF TIMES ON MY WAY DOWN THE MOUNTAIN.

BUT THIS...

...THIS PROVES I DO SO **TOO** HAVE AN IMAGINATION AFTER ALL.

SOMETHING YOU WERE **DEAD WRONG** ABOUT, MR. SMARTY BRITCHES.
HA!

NO SIGN OF EITHER OF THEM FOR DAYS.
AND NOW TO LEARN THEY'RE NOT EVEN ON THIS--ON *OUR* WORLD.

WE WON'T STOP LOOKING FOR THEM.
PROMISE ME THAT. BRING MY BABIES *HOME,* BIGBY.

ONE WORLD OR A MILLION--IT'S ALL THE SAME. I'LL *FIND* THEM.
THEY HAVE TO BE TERRIFIED.

WHEREVER THEY ARE.

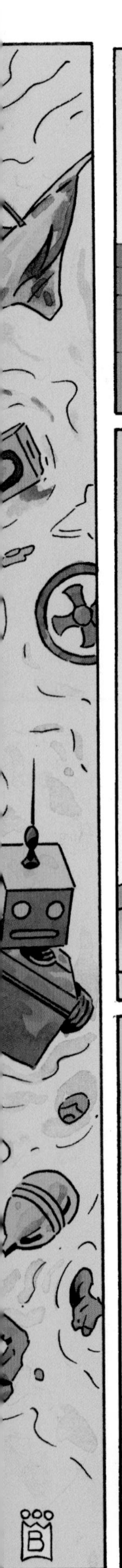

YOU'RE GOING TO TEACH ME ABOUT MAGIC?

NOW?

OH-- RIGHT.

YOU ALREADY DID TELL US ALL ABOUT HOW THE REALLY OLD MAGIC WORKED.

FROM ONE OF GRANDPAW'S BOOKS--THE ONE WHERE HE GOT MAD WHEN YOU TOOK IT.
I REMEMBER.

AND NOW YOU NEED ME TO REMEMBER WHAT YOU READ TO US?
FIND THE THING IN ALL OF TOYLAND THAT *ISN'T* A TOY?

AND *FIX* IT?

WHY? WHAT GOOD'LL *THAT* DO?

BECAUSE I'VE GOT TOO MUCH *ELSE* TO THINK ABOUT, IF YOU MUST KNOW.
HOW TO RESCUE OUR SISTER, FOR ONE!

OH.

WILL IT HURT?

NEXT: THE FISHER KING

IT'S A DANGEROUS TIME.
BUT THIS MAY BE OUR CHANCE AT LONG LAST.

THERESE IS POWERFUL.
AND NOW THAT SHE ISN'T IN IMMEDIATE DANGER OF STARVING TO DEATH, SHE MAY HAVE TIME ENOUGH TO RESTORE US.
PERHAPS.
EVEN A TIGER'S CARCASS WON'T LAST FOREVER.

IT DOESN'T HAVE TO LAST FOREVER. JUST LONG ENOUGH.
CONSIDER THIS THOUGH, MR. IVES. SHE'S BECOMING BESTIAL. SAVAGE.

SO?
WHO CARES WHAT BECOMES OF HER? ULTIMATELY, SHE'S DISPOSABLE, LIKE THE OTHERS. WE HAVE TO HARDEN OUR HEARTS AND THINK OF THE GREATER GOOD.
THE PLAN IS, OUR EXPOSURE TO HER IS SUPPOSED TO PURIFY US. BUT IT SEEMS MORE LIKE HER EXPOSURE TO US IS DIMINISHING HER.

HMMMM.
SOMETHING TO CONSIDER, MR. WELLSTUFFED.
SOMETHING TO CONSIDER.

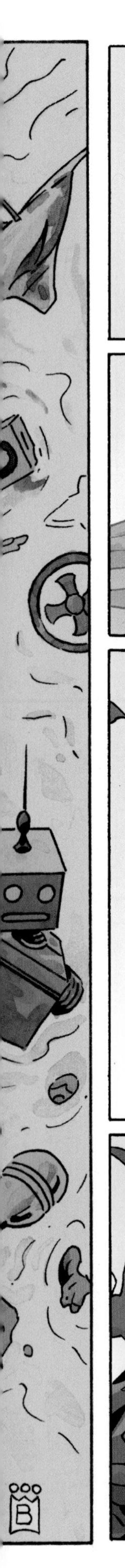

ONCE UPON A TIME THERE WAS A DISTANT SHORE.

SO?
YOU'VE BEEN QUIET FOR A LONG TIME.

IS THAT ALL? DON'T YOU HAVE NO MORE TO TELL ME?

OR AM I TOO DUMB TO FIGURE OUT THE REST ON MY OWN?

WE'RE HERE, DARIEN!
HUH?

WE'D NEVER DESERT YOU IN THIS CRITICAL TIME.
BUT WE THOUGHT YOU COULD USE A REST.

GIVE YOU TIME TO PREPARE FOR THE REALLY HARD PART.
WOW.
YOU CHANGED.

BEACH TOYS
Chapter 7 of CUBS in TOYLAND
In which we examine the nature of the old ways, let things play out more or less as they must...
THE SWORD OR THE CUP.
BOTH ARE NEEDED FOR THE OLD MAGIC.
ONE TO SPILL THE BLOOD, ONE TO CATCH IT.
...and finally, let that inevitable other shoe drop.
AMBROSE?
ALL THE BOOKS AND LEGENDS SAY THE FISHER KING HAS TO MAKE A PERILOUS CHOICE BETWEEN ONE OR THE OTHER.
BUT WHAT IF THAT'S NOT THE CASE?
BILL WILLINGHAM writer/creator
MARK BUCKINGHAM pencils
STEVE LEIALOHA inks
LEE LOUGHRIDGE colors
TODD KLEIN letters
GREGORY LOCKARD asst. ed.
SHELLY BOND editor

WHAT IF THE REAL CHOICE IS TO TAKE UP BOTH, OR NEITHER?
THAT MAKES MORE SENSE TO ME. TO CHOOSE NOTHING IS INDECISION, THE TRUE ENEMY OF DARING.
BUT YOU GOT SO OLD!
DO YOU KNOW WHAT I THINK?
THE CUP WILL SAVE ME, WHICH MEANS THE BLADE MUST BE FOR YOU.
LOOK!
MOMMY?
DADDY?
EVERYONE ELSE IS TOO FAR AWAY TO HELP.
YOU'RE THE ONLY ONE WHO CAN, NOBLE SON.

I MADE MY SACRIFICE.
ME TOO.
DON'T BE A BABY. EITHER LEARN TO COOK...
...OR GET OUT OF THE KITCHEN.
THE CUP IS FOR THE GIRL AND THE KNIFE IS FOR THE BOY.
THAT'S SO OBVIOUS.
SORRY, KIDDO, BUT IT WAS ALWAYS A STORY OF SACRIFICE.
ONE CAN LIVE, OR BOTH WILL SURELY...
IT'S YOUR JOB, SON.
PACK LEADER HAS RESPONSI-BILITIES.
PLEASE STOP.
I'D TAKE THE HIT MYSELF.
PLEASE.
BUT I'M NOT THERE.
UUGGHHN...

IS THIS IT?
IS THIS MY WHOLE LIFE NOW?
NOTHING TO DO?
ONLY AWFUL THINGS TO EAT?
THERE, THERE, MAJESTY.
BETTER THINGS AWAIT US. A GREAT UNDER-TAKING.
MAY IT BE.
GOOD NEWS, YOUR HIGHNESS!
HMMM?
WE SCOURED THE BEACH AND FOUND MORE WOOD FOR THE COOK FIRE.
BEHOLD!
OH!

WAIT.
HAND ME THOSE, NAN.
THESE LOOK FAMILIAR.
THEY SEEM TO--
OH NO.
OH NO!
I **KNOW** THESE TOYS.
THEY'RE MY BROTHER'S.
HE SHOULDN'T **BE** HERE!
HE'LL SPOIL EVERYTHING!
THERE'S NOT ENOUGH **FOOD** FOR BOTH OF US!

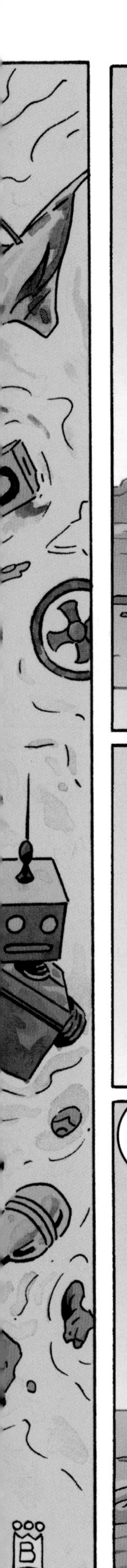

YOU CAN'T MAKE ME DO THAT.

YOU CAN'T!
I'M JUST A LITTLE KID.

IT'S ONLY THE GROWNUPS' JOB TO SAVE THE DAY.
AND THEY DON'T SURRENDER TO DO IT. NOT IN THE WOLF FAMILY. THEY FIND A WAY TO WIN.
DAD ALWAYS SAID SO, A MILLION BILLION TIMES.

DID YOU THINK OF THAT, AMBROSE? HUH? DID'JA?
ALL I HAVE TO DO IS FIND ANOTHER WAY.

MAYBE FIND ENOUGH STUFF TO BUILD A RAFT.
THAT COULD WORK.

IT COULD.

HEY THERE.

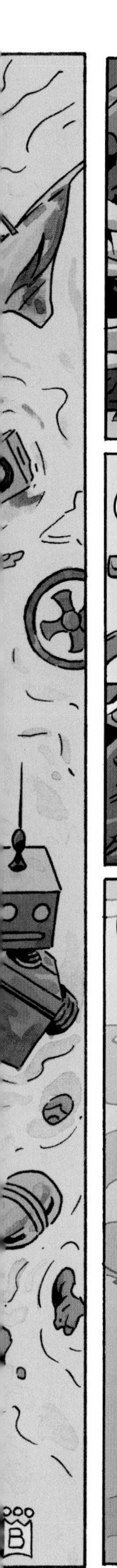

LOOK AT YOU.

A POOR, LOST PUPPY, JUST LIKE ME.
LOST YOUR EYES, HUH?

THAT'S OKAY, WE'RE ALL A LITTLE BANGED UP ON "TEAM DARE."
YOU CAN STILL HELP.

SEE? BETTER WITH SOME CUSHIONING.

NOW ALL WE GOTTA DO IS BUILD A RAFT. GRAB THERESE FROM THE BAD TOYS AND GET FAR AWAY, BEFORE WE BOTH STARVE.
WE'VE GOT A SECRET WEAPON, THOUGH.

I BET WE ONLY HAVE TO GET A LITTLE BIT AWAY FROM THIS STINKY PLACE BEFORE BOTH THERESE AND I CAN FLY AGAIN.
THEN WE'RE HOME SAFE IN NO--
HEY!
A MIGHTY MINI POOL TABLE! I WANTED ONE OF THESE FOR EVER AND EVER!

THIS GIVES ME A BIG IDEA!
HA! SO MUCH FOR YOU, MR. SMARTYPANTS! YOU DON'T KNOW EVERYTHING!
I FIGURED IT ALL OUT ON MY OWN.
IN TIME...
I'LL BET THAT WAS THE REAL TEST ALL ALONG.
TO COME UP WITH A BETTER WAY TO SAVE BOTH OF US.
SEE? I PAID ATTENTION TO THE STORIES, TOO, NO MATTER WHAT AMBROSE SAID.
AND THERE'S ALWAYS A TRICKY WAY TO GET AWAY IN THE END. THAT'S A RULE IN EVERY BOOK.
FIRST I CATCH A FISH SO THERESE AND I DON'T CROAK.

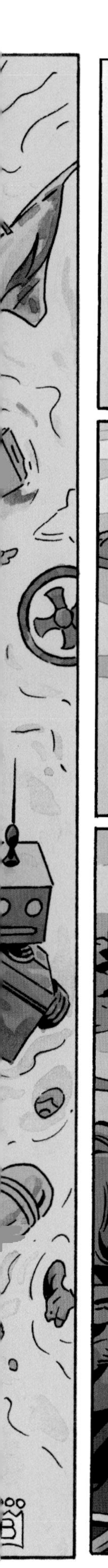

CRAP PIES. THE PLASTIC WORM ISN'T WORKING.
BUT THAT'S OKAY.

WE AREN'T BEATEN YET, BUDDY.

WE STILL HAVE THE STICK, WHICH MAKES A REALLY COOL SPEAR.
I'LL BET AMBROSE DIDN'T THINK OF THIS BECAUSE YOU CAN'T LEARN IT IN A BOOK. YOU HAVE TO WATCH REAL INDIANS ON TV SHOWS!

SHHHHH.
COME ON.
A LITTLE CLOSER.

HERE WE GO!

HA!
I'M STILL THE BEST HUNTER IN THE PACK!

OH.

RUBBER.

VERY FUNNY.

THAT'S JUST *CHEATING!*
I WON! I *DID!*
I FOUND A DIFFERENT WAY, FAIR AND SQUARE, BUT YOU--!

I DON'T *WANT* TO DIE.
PLEASE!
NOT YET.
I'M STILL A LITTLE KID.

CAN'T I *GROW UP* JUST A LITTLE MORE, FIRST?

I NEVER EVEN GOT TO *DO* ANYTHING YET.

PLEASE?

MINUTES, OR PERHAPS HOURS PASS.
OKAY.
YOU WIN.

I'LL DO IT YOUR WAY.
THE PACK LEADER HAS THE RESPONSIBILITY, RIGHT?

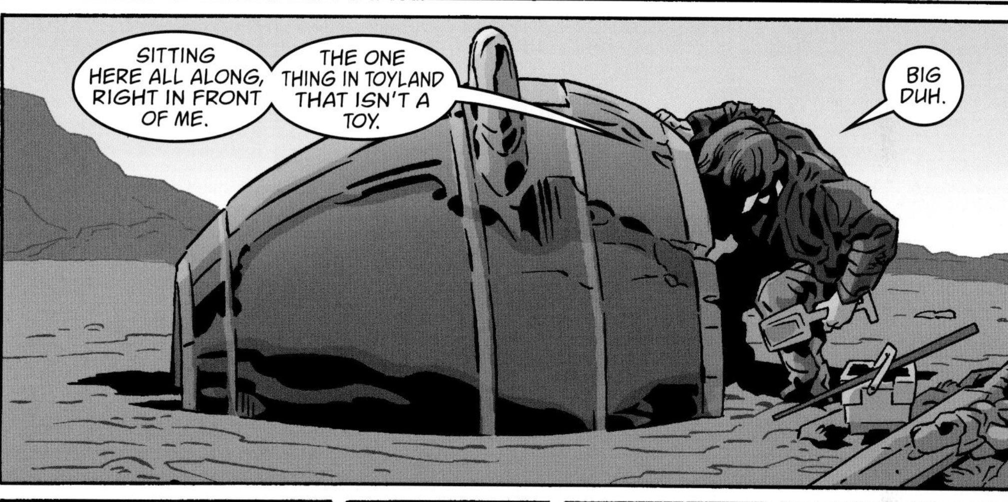
SITTING HERE ALL ALONG, RIGHT IN FRONT OF ME.
THE ONE THING IN TOYLAND THAT ISN'T A TOY.
BIG DUH.

EXCEPT I THOUGHT MAYBE YOU MEANT ME.
I UNDER-STAND NOW. WE NEEDED BOTH THE SWORD AND THE CUP.

I FOUND THE SWORD.

AND NOW I CLEAN OUT THE CUP.

CAN'T HAVE PRISSY THERESE GETTING SAND IN HER DINNER.

JUST SET
THIS THING UPRIGHT
AND--

HHHNNNNN!

CRAP.

HOW CAN
I DO IT, IF IT'S
TOO--?
OH.

SANDCASTLE
BUCKET.

FINE.
I'LL DO IT
THAT WAY,
THEN.
DID I
FIGURE THAT
OUT ON MY OWN,
OR DID YOU PUT
THAT IN MY
HEAD TOO?

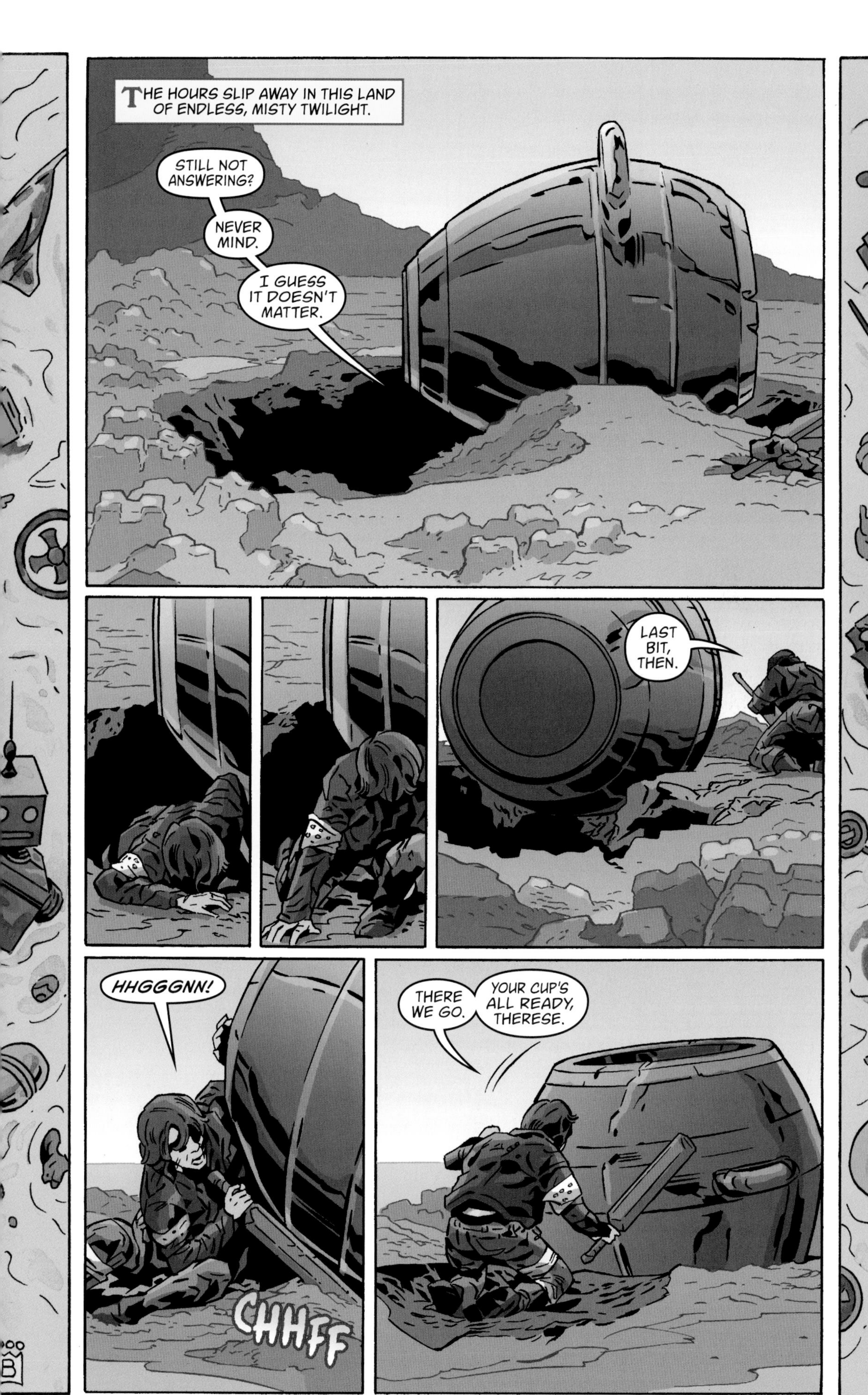
THE HOURS SLIP AWAY IN THIS LAND OF ENDLESS, MISTY TWILIGHT.
STILL NOT ANSWERING?
NEVER MIND.
I GUESS IT DOESN'T MATTER.
LAST BIT, THEN.
HHGGGNN!
CHHFF
THERE WE GO.
YOUR CUP'S ALL READY, THERESE.

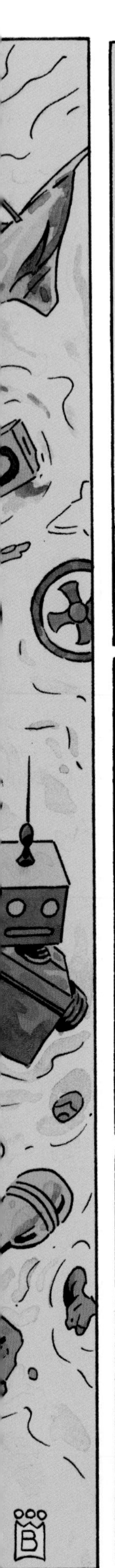

TELL ME ONE THING, BEFORE I FINISH.
WILL ANYONE EVER KNOW?

WILL THEY FIND OUT I DID THE RIGHT THING?

IN THE END I LOOKED OUT FOR HER, THE WAY THE PACK LEADER SHOULD.
RIGHT?

YES.
I'M READY.

NEXT:
THE RETURN

OH NO!
COME ON.
WHY WOULD HE--?
WHY?
YOUR MAJESTY?
COULD YOU SLOW DOWN, PLEASE?
THESE STEPS CAN BE TRICKY!
IF YOU WERE TO--
HURRY UP, NOW.
GO AWAY!
LEAVE ME ALONE, MR. IVES!
I NEED TO SEE FOR MYSELF!
GATHER CLOSE AND I'LL TELL YOU A STORY.
IT'S A TRUE STORY IN WHICH I PLAYED A PART--THOUGH NOT THE BIGGEST OR MOST VITAL, I CONFESS.

TOY REPAIR
Chapter 8 of CUBS in TOYLAND
In which we surrender to the harsh lessons of even the most magical of lives (though we shouldn't say that's the same as being defeated by them).
BILL WILLINGHAM writer/creator
MARK BUCKINGHAM pencils
STEVE LEIALOHA inks
LEE LOUGHRIDGE colors
TODD KLEIN letters
GREGORY LOCKARD asst. ed.
SHELLY BOND editor
ONCE UPON A TIME A BRAVE BUT SPOILED LITTLE GIRL HAD A GREAT ADVENTURE.
WHAT?
I DON'T UNDERSTAND.
GRASS?
LEAVES GROWING?
BUT EVERYTHING'S DEAD IN TOYLAND.

WHERE ARE YOU?
THIS LOOKS LIKE--
SNIFF
YES, THIS IS **DEFINITELY** YOUR JACKET.
DARE?
QUIT HIDING! I KNOW YOU'RE HERE!
MAYBE YOU'RE--
OH, THAT SMELL IS **LOVELY!**
AND FULL TO THE TOP WITH--WHAT?
HMMM?
TASTES LIKE...
CHICKEN AND GRAVY?
WONDROUS DAY!

MORE!
NOW IT'S DIFFERENT! IT'S-- UHM--

LAMB?

ON A DISTANT SHORE THERE WAS A MAGIC CAULDRON, WHICH HADN'T BEEN MAGICAL FOR MANY LIFETIMES.
MMMMMMM!
NOT UNTIL THE LITTLE GIRL'S BROTHER RESTORED IT, AT A TERRIBLE COST.
HE'S GONE.

HELLO?
ALL GONE NOW.

ALL GONE.

HE SPOKE!
AMAZING!
ARE YOU TALKING ABOUT MY BROTHER?
A BOY ABOUT MY AGE?
HIS NAME IS DARIEN.
DARE!
REX WAS ONE OF THOSE WHO'D GIVEN UP AGES AGO. HE WAS LEFT OUT ON THE SHORE, BECAUSE THE LIFE HAD FADED OUT OF HIM.
I DON'T KNOW ABOUT THIS BOY YOU'RE LOOKING FOR.
BUT THE FISHER KING WAS HERE, ALL RIGHT.
IT FINALLY BEGINS!
MAY IT BE!

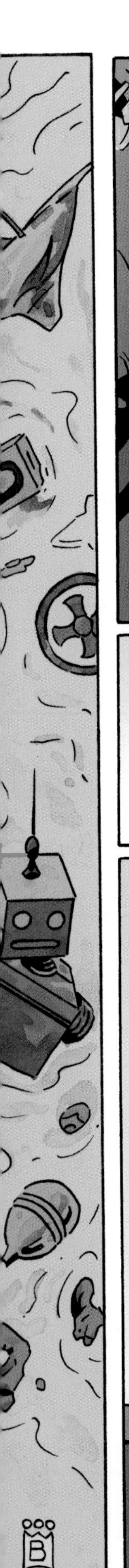

THE WHO?
MAKE SENSE!
SHE'S STARTING TO RESTORE THE DISCARDIA!

I WAS HIS COMPANION--AT THE END.
HELPED HIM IN HIS FINAL QUEST.

PUT SOME SPARK RIGHT BACK INTO ME, HE DID.
HE'S GONE.

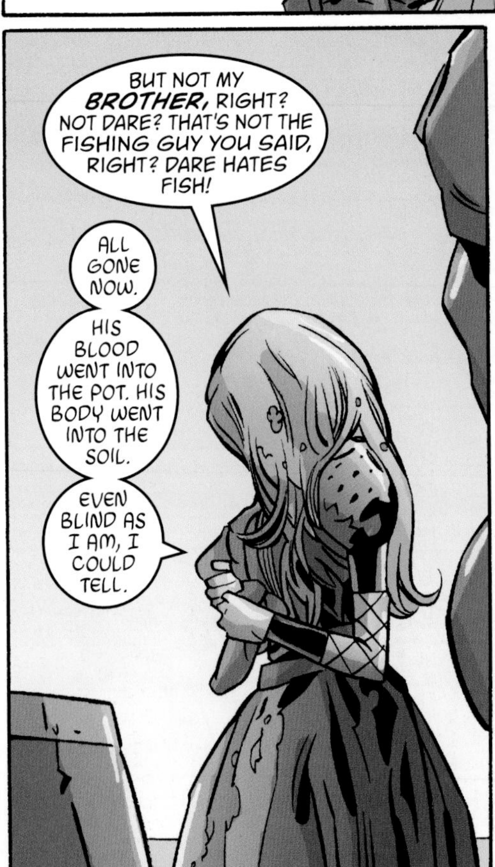

BUT NOT MY BROTHER, RIGHT? NOT DARE? THAT'S NOT THE FISHING GUY YOU SAID, RIGHT? DARE HATES FISH!
ALL GONE NOW.
HIS BLOOD WENT INTO THE POT. HIS BODY WENT INTO THE SOIL.
EVEN BLIND AS I AM, I COULD TELL.

AND SO IT GOES.
THE STORY VARIES A BIT, FROM ONE TELLING TO THE NEXT, BUT THERE'S ALWAYS A LAME KING, A BLIND DOG FOLLOWING, THE CUP AND SWORD, AND EVENTUALLY THE MAGIC CAULDRON.
PLEASE?
SAY IT WASN'T HIM, OKAY?

THE OLDEST MAGIC ONLY **WORKED** WITH A LOT OF SPILLED BLOOD.
I DON'T UNDER-STAND.

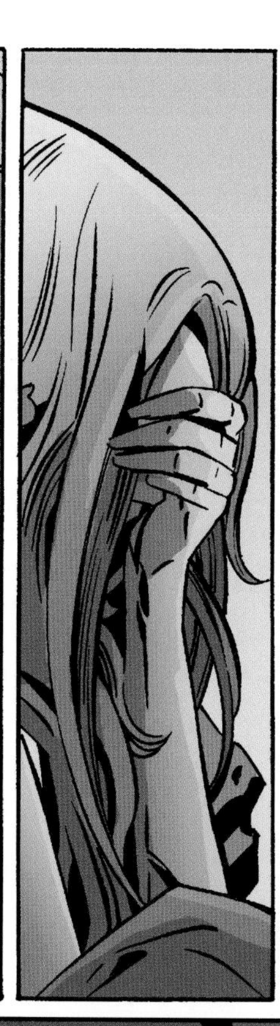

IT TURNED OUT THE BOY'S BLOOD WAS TRULY POTENT STUFF.
ALL THE SONS AND DAUGHTERS OF SNOW WHITE AND HER WOLF WERE POWERFUL. TWO MAGIC BLOODLINES MIXED TO BECOME **MORE** THAN THEIR PARTS.
WHEN IS THE QUEEN GOING TO RE-STORE US?

HAD THEY BEEN RAISED **DIFFERENT,** THEY COULD HAVE BECOME THE GODS AND MONSTERS OF A LONG AND DARK AGE.
SHE GOT A GOOD START ON REX, AND THEN JUST STOPPED.
HUSH NOW.

IT WILL CONTINUE IN HER TIME.

I'M **CONVINCED** OF IT NOW. SHE'S THE ONE.
SHE CAME TO THE WONDROUS SHORE AND NEVER DIED.
WE ONLY NEED TO BE PATIENT FOR A **LITTLE** WHILE LONGER.

FUNNY THING ABOUT DEATH AND KINSHIP.
IT'S A NEW DISH EVERY DAY, YOUR MAJESTY.
IT NEVER RUNS OUT. AND ALWAYS MAGICALLY FRESH AND HOT.
NO NEED TO BURN ANY MORE TOYS, NO-SIREE.

THERESE NEVER MUCH LIKED DARIEN IN LIFE, BUT MOURNED HIM A GOOD LONG TIME AFTER HE PASSED.
CHICKEN AND DUMPLINGS TODAY, IN A LOVELY GRAVY.
WOULD YOU LIKE US TO PICK OUT THE PEAS FOR YOU?

NO THANKS. IT'S FINE AS IT IS.

LATER AND LATER STILL...
IF I'D WAITED JUST A DAY OR TWO LONGER, MR. MOUNT-BATTEN WOULDN'T HAVE...
HE MIGHT STILL BE ALIVE.

DIDN'T HAVE TO EAT MUCH OF HIM, THOUGH.
GOT MOST OF HIM INTO HIS GRAVE, SO THAT'S SOMETHING, AT LEAST.

FINALLY, AFTER A LONG TIME INDEED, THE GIRL ROUSED HERSELF.
OKAY, THAT'S ENOUGH PINING OVER THE DEAD FOR NOW.
WE'VE A KINGDOM TO REBUILD.
TIME TO PUT MY BROTHER'S SACRIFICE TO WORK.

PLEASE GO AND FIND MR. STEAMPUDDLE. TELL HIM IT'S TIME TO GROW LARGE AGAIN AND READY HIMSELF FOR AN OCEAN VOYAGE.
GET READY FOR A LOT OF THEM, IN FACT.
HE'S ABOUT TO BE A VERY BUSY BOAT.
THAT WON'T WORK, YOUR MAJESTY. THE GREAT PRETEND ISN'T A BOTTOMLESS WELL OF POWER. WE HAVE TO HUSBAND IT CAREFULLY.
STEAMPUDDLE COULD ONLY TRAVEL TO AND FROM THE WONDROUS SHORE WHEN WE NEEDED A NEW KING OR QUEEN.
ONLY THEN.
WE'RE BOUND BY UNBREAKABLE RULES AND TRADI-TIONS.
THAT WAS BEFORE.
I THINK YOU'LL FIND THINGS ARE DIFFERENT NOW.
I'M THE QUEEN OF TOYLAND. THE LAND AND THE QUEEN ARE ONE. I COMMAND THE MANY POWERS OF THE GREAT PRETEND.

I DID FROM THE VERY BEGINNING-- FROM MY FIRST STEP ONTO THESE SHORES--BUT DIDN'T KNOW IT UNTIL RECENTLY.
TOO MUCH OF A SPOILED BRAT TO REALIZE IT, I SUPPOSE.
IN ANY CASE, YOU'RE ABOUT TO SEE HOW WELL THOSE POWERS DANCE ON THE END OF MY STRINGS.
NOW HERE'S THE GOOD NEWS AND THE BAD NEWS.
IT'S TIME FOR YOUR RESTORATION TO BEGIN, BUT I'M NOT JUST GOING TO WAVE MY HAND AND MAKE YOU WHOLE AGAIN.
I'M NOT SURE I COULD, BUT EVEN IF I COULD, I WOULDN'T.

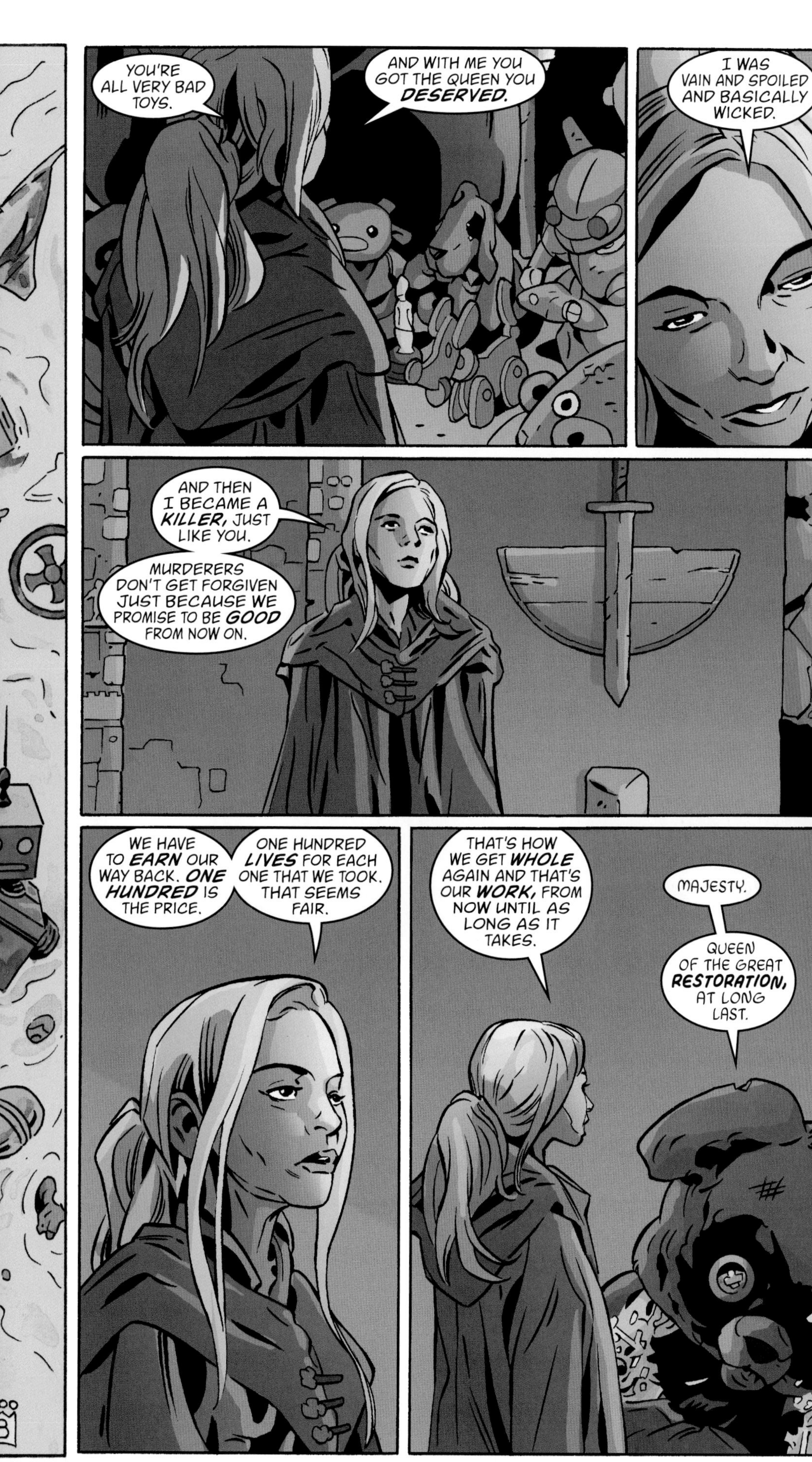
YOU'RE ALL VERY BAD TOYS.
AND WITH ME YOU GOT THE QUEEN YOU DESERVED.
I WAS VAIN AND SPOILED AND BASICALLY WICKED.
AND THEN I BECAME A KILLER, JUST LIKE YOU.
MURDERERS DON'T GET FORGIVEN JUST BECAUSE WE PROMISE TO BE GOOD FROM NOW ON.
WE HAVE TO EARN OUR WAY BACK. ONE HUNDRED IS THE PRICE.
ONE HUNDRED LIVES FOR EACH ONE THAT WE TOOK. THAT SEEMS FAIR.
THAT'S HOW WE GET WHOLE AGAIN AND THAT'S OUR WORK, FROM NOW UNTIL AS LONG AS IT TAKES.
MAJESTY.
QUEEN OF THE GREAT RESTORATION, AT LONG LAST.

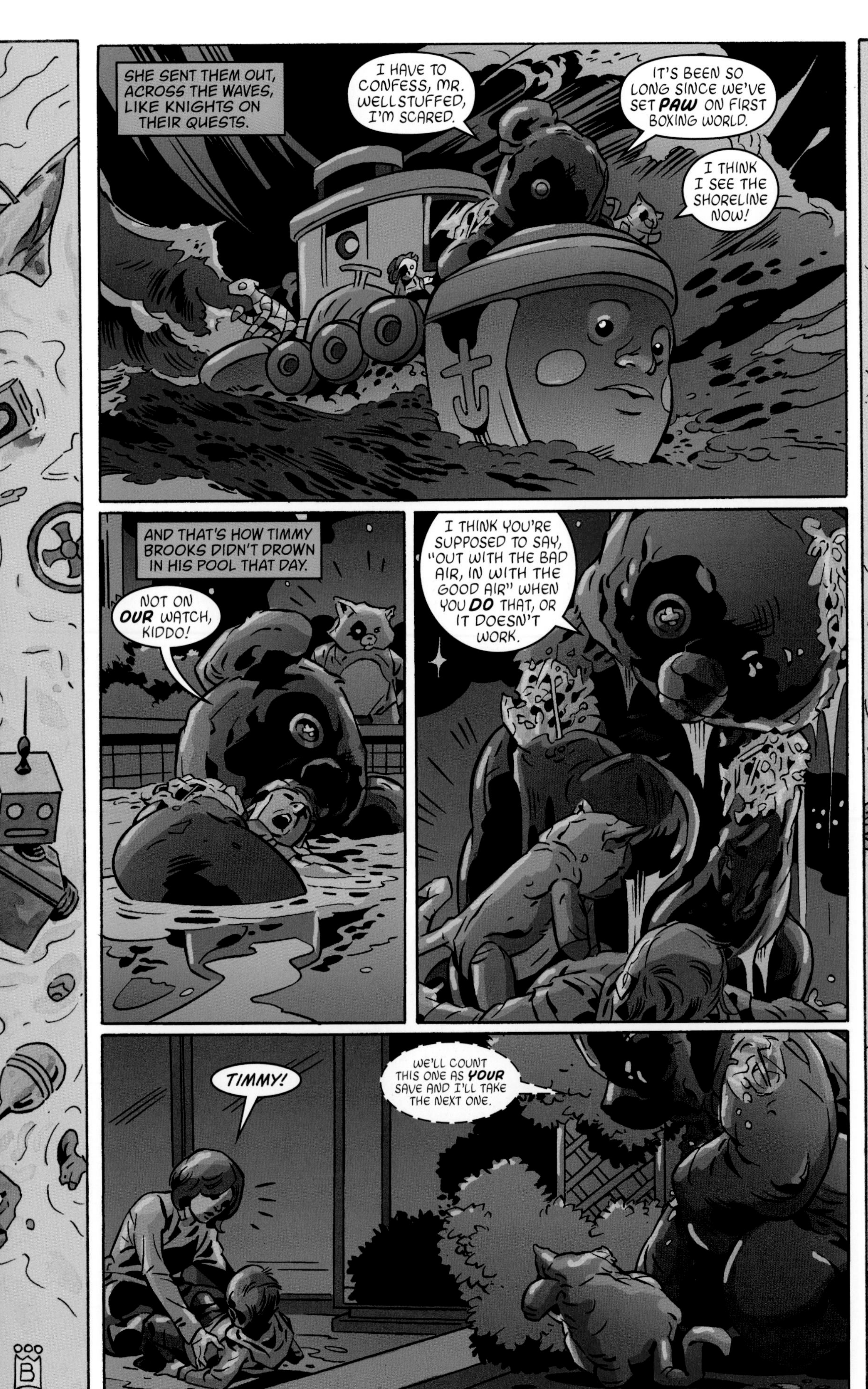
SHE SENT THEM OUT, ACROSS THE WAVES, LIKE KNIGHTS ON THEIR QUESTS.
I HAVE TO CONFESS, MR. WELLSTUFFED, I'M SCARED.
IT'S BEEN SO LONG SINCE WE'VE SET PAW ON FIRST BOXING WORLD.
I THINK I SEE THE SHORELINE NOW!
AND THAT'S HOW TIMMY BROOKS DIDN'T DROWN IN HIS POOL THAT DAY.
NOT ON OUR WATCH, KIDDO!
I THINK YOU'RE SUPPOSED TO SAY, "OUT WITH THE BAD AIR, IN WITH THE GOOD AIR" WHEN YOU DO THAT, OR IT DOESN'T WORK.
TIMMY!
WE'LL COUNT THIS ONE AS YOUR SAVE AND I'LL TAKE THE NEXT ONE.

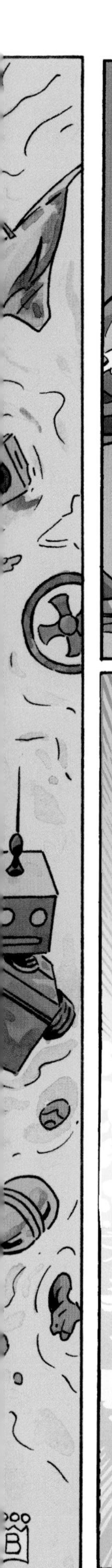

THAT'S HOW BABY MARJORY TURPIN DIDN'T CHOKE ON THE BUILDING BLOCK.
SQUEEZE HER AGAIN!
POP THAT SUCKER LOOSE!

HUZZAH!

BACK AND FORTH THEY WENT, RETURNING OFTEN OVER THE YEARS TO RE-PORT THEIR SUCCESSES TO THE QUEEN, BEFORE BEING SENT OUT AGAIN.
LOOK AT THAT.

MY ARM IS NEARLY BRAND NEW AGAIN.
YOU'RE WELL ON YOUR WAY TO LOOKING FRESH FROM THE BOX AGAIN, MR. IVES.

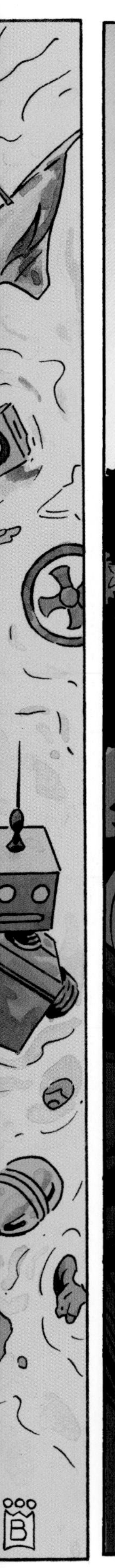

TOYLAND BECAME A ***BETTER*** PLACE OVER THOSE MANY YEARS. BLUE DAY AND VELVET NIGHT RETURNED TO REPLACE THE ENDLESS MISERY OF GRAY MIST.

THE LAND AND ITS QUEEN WERE ONE.

FEELS SQUISHY UNDER MY FELT.

HEY, GILLY, I CAN SEE YOUR ***HOUSE*** FROM HERE.

I'M THE TRAIN THEY CALL THE CHOO CHOO OF CHATTANOOGA...
PLEASANT DAY, MA'AM, DON'T YOU THINK?
SURE.
I SUPPOSE.
THERESE REMAINED IN TOYLAND. EVERY DAY SHE ATE FROM THE MAGIC CAULDRON, WHICH NEVER RAN OUT OF DELIGHTFUL FOOD, EACH MEAL DIFFERENT FROM THE LAST.
AND EACH BITE TASTED LIKE ASHES IN HER MOUTH.

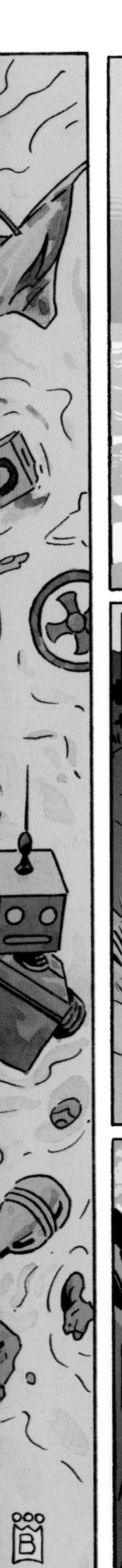

EPILOGUE
IN TIME, WHEN MOST OF HER SUBJECTS HAD BEEN RESTORED, AND THOUSANDS OF CHILDREN HAD BEEN SAVED, THERESE RETURNED TO THE MUNDY WORLD.

WAIT HERE, PLEASE, MR. STEAM-PUDDLE. I WON'T BE LONG.

I WAS THE ONE TOY SHE COULD NEVER *FIX*. NOT REALLY A PART OF HER KINGDOM, I GUESS. NOT COVERED BY HER AUTHORITY.
AFTER DYING IN TOYLAND, I NEVER *MOVED* AGAIN IN THE MUNDY. I WAS NEVER ABLE TO TELL THE PARENTS WHAT HAPPENED TO THEIR LOST CHILDREN.

I'M SO SORRY.

COME ALONG, REX.

ONE DAY THERESE DELIVERED THE NEWS I COULDN'T.
MOM?
!
I DON'T KNOW IF YOU RECOGNIZE ME. THE YEARS PASSED DIFFERENTLY WHERE I...
I'M THERESE.
I'VE COME TO TELL YOU WHAT HAPPENED TO DARE-- HOW HE SAVED ME.
WHERE'S DAD?

THE END

"Strike me if you can, witch, for I'm hungry and intend to eat!"

MANY YEARS FROM NOW...
I'LL BE IN AFTER A BIT, LOVE. JUST WANT TO JOT A LINE OR TWO WHILE THEY'RE IN MY MIND.
OKAY, BUT NOT TOO LONG. YOU HAVE TO TAKE BRAGGER TO SCHOOL IN THE MORNING, BECAUSE I'VE GOT THAT THING WITH MISTER TOOMEY.
I'LL BE GOOD.
PROMISE.
SLEEPING ON THE STAIRS AGAIN, FLANDERS?
BE THE DEATH OF ME SOMEDAY.
HOW?
TRIP ON ME AND YOU'D JUST FLY THE REST OF THE WAY. SAFE AS HOUSES.

A History of Fables in America, the Mundy World and Beyond by A. Wolf Volume 7
Once more I take up my pen with an urge to leave off briefly from the main narrative and diverge (if I may be forgiven the poetic excess) onto one of the paths less taken.
I'm inspired to write of the Great Wolf, and one of his lesser-known tales—lesser known, but not lacking in terrible import for his life and the destiny of nearly every Fable he later encountered.
In those days...

The Destiny Game
Part One of Two
written and created by Bill Willingham
guest art by Gene Ha
guest colors by Art Lyon
letters by Todd Klein
special thanks to Zander Cannon
assistant editor Gregory Lockard
editor Shelly Bond
In those days the Big Bad Wolf was the greatest monster to prowl the deep and dark woods known as the Black Forest.
He feared nothing, and nothing it seemed could harm or even bother him, except perhaps for too much rain on too cold a morning.
GIVE IT UP, CHILD!
YOU'VE NO HOPE OF OUTRUNNING ME, AND I'M TOO COLD AND WET TO LOVE A LONG CHASE TODAY!
DASHING INTO A TINY HUT WON'T SAVE YOU!
I COULD SCATTER IT WITH A SINGLE PUFF!

INSTEAD I'LL CRASH IT AROUND YOUR--!
WHAT?!
SORCERY!

BEST TURN AND FLEE, DIRE WOLF, FOR YOU'VE CHASED ME TOO FAR.
I'M NOT THE HELPLESS LITTLE GIRL YOU PERCEIVED IN THE WOODS, AND HERE YOU'VE STUMBLED INTO MY PLACE OF POWER.
LOOK AROUND YOU.
GODS AND MONSTERS AND GREAT PRINCIPALITIES, WHO'VE FALLEN PREY TO MY WORKINGS, NOW DECORATE MY CHAMBERS AS STATUES AND COAT RACKS.
FLEE NOW, I ADJURE YOU, LEST YOU SHARE THEIR STONY ETERNITY.

STRIKE ME IF YOU CAN, WITCH, FOR I'M HUNGRY AND INTEND TO EAT!
I THOUGHT SO. THOSE WHO CAN REALLY DO WHAT THEY PROMISE DON'T FIRST PAUSE TO PROMISE WHAT THEY CAN DO.
NO!
SQUEAL YOUR LAST HURRIED PRAYER, FOR HERE IT COMES!
PLEASE! I'M SO YOUNG!
I'M AFRAID TO DIE BEFORE I'VE YET LIVED!
I'VE FULFILLED NO DREAMS, ACCOMPLISHED NO GREAT DEEDS, AND NOT YET FELT A LOVER'S TOUCH. THAT'S PALTRY COIN TO TAKE INTO THE NEXT LIFE.
I BEG OF YOU, GREAT AND TERRIBLE BEAST.
SHOW MERCY!

I'VE NONE IN ME, GIRL.
THEN SHOW SELF-INTEREST INSTEAD, FOR I'VE A BARGAIN TO STRIKE.

EH?
WHAT CAN YOU POSSIBLY OFFER IN RETURN FOR YOUR LIFE?
YOUR DESTINY.

I LIED ABOUT THIS CHAMBER BEING MY PLACE OF POWER. IT'S NOT MY HOME, NOR DO I REALLY HOLD POWERS OF CONJURATION OR TRANSFORMATION.

I THOUGHT TO FOOL YOU, FOR MY LIFE WAS AT STAKE. BUT LOOK AT ME NOW WITH THE TRUE SIGHT I BELIEVE YOU TO POSSESS. YOU KNOW I'M NOT LYING THIS TIME.
I CAN DO IT.

NAME YOUR BARGAIN THEN, GIRL, AND TELL IT TRUE THIS TIME.
SWEAR AN OATH NOT TO HARM ME AND I'LL TELL YOU YOUR FATE.
OH?

YOU'D MAKE SCANT VITTLES, THAT MUCH IS TRUE. AND I'VE STRIVED ALL MY DAYS TO MAKE MYSELF STRONG ENOUGH TO PUT MY OWN FATHER'S THROAT UNDER MY FANGS.
YOU CAN TELL ME IF I'M EVER TO ACHIEVE HIS DESTRUC-TION?

LET ME UP, PLEASE.
PAW PRINTS ALL OVER MY DRESS.
NEED DO, GREAT WOLF, IS SWEAR YOUR OATH WITH STRONG WORDS.
I'VE NEVER FORSWORN MYSELF YET, CHILD, NOR WILL I.
In those days there were harrowing consequences for oathbreakers.
Giant cauldrons in Hell where one would boil for eternity and be eaten from time to time. Rivers of scythes. All sorts of ugly punishments.

NOW, MY FATE, GIRL. TELL IT DIRECT, WITHOUT THE PRACTITIONER'S USUAL OBSCURE NONSENSE AND CRYPTIC MUMBO JUMBO.
BLUNT AND UNDECORATED?
FINE.

HERE IT IS, THEN.
THREE DAYS FROM NOW YOU DIE, TORN TO PIECES BY A TERRIBLE BEAST, AS BIG AND BAD AS YOURSELF.

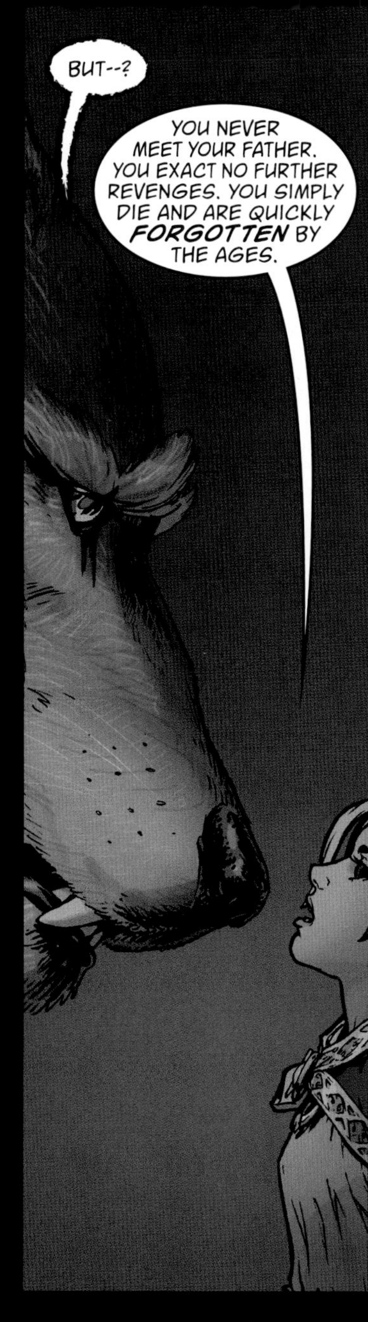
BUT--?
YOU NEVER MEET YOUR FATHER. YOU EXACT NO FURTHER REVENGES. YOU SIMPLY DIE AND ARE QUICKLY FORGOTTEN BY THE AGES.

THAT'S IT?
THAT'S IT. NO MERCY. NO REPRIEVE.
NOW PLEASE BE ON YOUR WAY.

The Wolf was stricken to his core. True to his word though, he went on his way, leaving the girl unmolested.

YOU CAN STOP HIDING IN THE SHADOWS, MAGUS ATLANTES.
THE MONSTER IS GONE AND ALL DANGER HAS PASSED.
I WASN'T HIDING IN FEAR, MADAM, MERELY ACTING WITH DISCRETION.
I'VE NO DESIRE FOR ANYONE, MAN OR BEAST, TO KNOW I'M KEEPING CLANDESTINE RENDEZVOUS WITH WOMEN FROM THE DEEP REALMS.
BUT MY SWORD ARM IS FIT AND, AS EVER, I'VE MANY SPELLS OF ILLUSION, DIVERSION OR DESTRUCTION AT THE READY.
HAD IT BECOME NECESSARY, I WOULD HAVE STEPPED IN AND SLAIN THE BEAST FOR YOU.
GOOD THING I WAS ABLE TO BARGAIN WITH THE MONSTER, FOR I FEAR HE MIGHT HAVE PROVED TOO POWERFUL FOR THE TWO OF US COMBINED.
STILL, IT'S OF NO MATTER NOW. SHALL WE CONCLUDE OUR OWN BARGAIN?
LET'S DO SO. I SEE YOU'VE BROUGHT THE BOOK. MAY I SEE IT?
OF COURSE.

THE BOOK OF FATES. WITH THIS I CAN ADD A HUNDRED NEW DESTINIES TO MY CACHE.
WOULD THAT I HAD THE ABILITY TO MAKE FULL USE OF ITS TREASURES AS YOU CAN. IT WAS STILL OF SOME UTILITY TO ME AND I'M RELUCTANT TO PART WITH IT.
AND SURRENDER THIS PLACE TOO, MAGUS. IT'S ALSO PART OF THE PRICE.
YES, THIS GRAND CHAMBER AND ITS PASSAGEWAYS ARE ALSO YOURS, LADY.
I'VE RECENTLY COMPLETED MY CASTLE OF ILLUSIONS AND HAVE NO FURTHER NEED OF THIS PARTICULAR HIDEY-HOLE.
I'VE MET YOUR PRICE, AS YOU CAN SEE. NOW I'LL HAVE MY PAYMENT.
OF COURSE, SORCERER, OF COURSE. YOUR FATE, THEN, IS THIS.
YOU WILL NOT AGE AND YOU'LL CONTINUE TO GROW IN STRENGTH AND POWER AS THE CENTURIES ACCUMULATE.
IN TIME YOU WILL MEET THE MOST BEAUTIFUL WOMAN IN MANY WORLDS, AND KNOW THAT SHE IS THE LOVE OF YOUR LIFE.

HER SKIN AS PALE AS NEW FALLEN SNOW. HER HAIR AS DARK AS A RAVEN'S SECRET HEART. HER LIPS A RED FLOWER THAT WILL EVENTUALLY PART TO CONFESS HER LOVE FOR YOU.
SHE'LL BE STRONG IN WILD MAGIC, THIS ONE, ADDING HER POWERS TO YOURS AND IN TIME BEARING YOU SEVEN CHILDREN.
YOUR SONS AND DAUGHTERS WILL GO ON TO BECOME THE GODS AND MONSTERS THAT LAY WASTE TO WORLDS.

PERFECT. EVERYTHING I ASKED FOR AND MORE.
I TOLD YOU THIS FATE WAS BETTER THAN ALL OTHERS THAT HAVE EVER PASSED INTO MY CLASP. ANY **WONDER** THEN THAT I HELD OUT FOR A DEAR PRICE?

AND THE DOWN-SIDE? WHAT **DOOMS** ARE ALSO INCLUDED IN MY NEW DESTINY?
IT DEPENDS ON WHAT YOU CONSIDER AN UNACCEPTABLE OUTCOME.
YOU'LL OUTLIVE ALL YOUR CHILDREN, BUT ONLY AFTER YOU'VE DIED SEVEN TIMES.

WHAT DOES **THAT** MEAN?

I DON'T KNOW.
INTRIGUING THOUGH, ISN'T IT?

NOW, I TRUST YOU'LL REMAIN FOR A DAY OR TWO TO DETAIL THE WONDERS AND INTRICACIES OF MY NEW STRONGHOLD?
AND TO MOVE MY OWN THINGS OUT, YES.

In those days a turtle could be a magical queen, and the teacup on her back could be a vast kingdom.
OH DEAR.
OH NO, I DIDN'T MEAN TO--
WHAT I MEANT TO SAY, GREAT MONSTER OF THE WOODS, IS THAT I'D NO INTENTION OF BOTHERING YOU WITH MY UNWORTHY INTRUSION INTO YOUR TERRITORY.
PURELY AN ACCIDENT THAT I HAPPENED TO COME THIS WAY.
AND PERHAPS I MIGHT POINT OUT I'D MAKE A SPARE AND TINY MEAL? HARDLY WORTH A SINGLE SNAP AND GOBBLE?
DON'T WORRY, TURTLE.
YOU'RE SAFE.

I'VE LOST MY APPETITE TODAY.
PERHAPS FOR ALL TIME.
OH?
YOU SEEM DEPRESSED, SIR.
I AM.
DEVASTATED, IN FACT.
AND WHAT DIRE EVENTS COULD BRING THE GREAT AND TERRIBLE LORD OF WOLVES TO SUCH A STATE OF MISERY?
ONLY THE MOST IGNOBLE OUTCOME OF A LIFE, STARTED IN TRAGEDY, AND BUILT IN INCREMENTS OF RAGE AND FURY.
NOW ABOUT TO COME TO AN ABRUPT END, BEFORE ANY OF MY LOFTY GOALS WERE ACCOMPLISHED!
AND WHAT LOFTY GOALS WERE THOSE, IF THE FOREST'S MOST HUMBLE OF CREATURES MAY BE SO BOLD AS TO INQUIRE?
STANDARD STUFF, REALLY.
HUNT AND KILL MY FATHER.

MAYBE DEVOUR HIM TOO, BUT I WASN'T QUITE DECIDED ON THAT.
EATING YOUR OWN DAD COULD GET WEIRD.
CERTAINLY, ADDING HIS MEAT TO MINE MIGHT BE CONSTRUED AS TOO CLOSE A FATHER-SON RELATIONSHIP, AND I WANT NO INHERITANCE FROM HIM.
SO I PROBABLY WOULD HAVE JUST TORN HIM LIMB FROM LIMB--MAYBE PISSED ON HIS ENTRAILS A BIT--AND LEFT IT AT THAT.
A WISE CHOICE, ALL THINGS CONSIDERED.
IN ANY CASE, ALL THAT IS DONE NOW. OVER.
I'M DOOMED TO DIE TOMORROW.
DEAR ME. OF WHAT MALADY, MAY I ASK?
TORN APART BY A MONSTER OF MY EQUAL.
OH, I'LL TRY TO RALLY ENOUGH TO GIVE A GOOD ACCOUNTING OF MYSELF, BUT IT WON'T MATTER.

MY FATE IS SEALED.
YOUR FATE DO YOU SAY, AUGUST SIR?

YES. MY FATE WAS REVEALED TO ME ONLY YESTERDAY. TOMORROW I AM DOOMED TO DIE.
REVEALED, YOU SAY? IT WOULDN'T HAVE BEEN DELIVERED TO YOU VIA THE PRONOUNCEMENT OF THE GREEN WOMAN, WOULD IT?

SOME-TIMES LIVES IN PONDS?
I DON'T KNOW WHERE SHE LIVES, BUT I FOUND HER IN A GREAT CAVE OF CONSID-ERABLE ENCHANTMENT. SHE WAS GREEN, THOUGH.
NOT GOBLIN-SKIN GREEN. NOT A WART OR CANKER ON HER. SMOOTH GREEN SKIN SHE HAD. BAD NEWS HANDED TO ME BY A PRETTY GIRL.

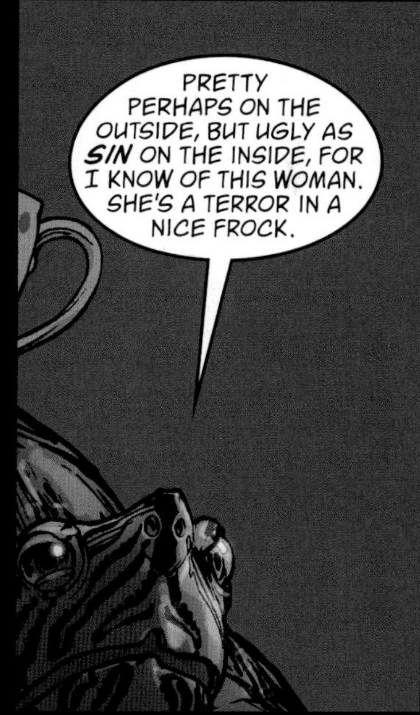

PRETTY PERHAPS ON THE OUTSIDE, BUT UGLY AS SIN ON THE INSIDE, FOR I KNOW OF THIS WOMAN. SHE'S A TERROR IN A NICE FROCK.

NO MATTER. ONE CANNOT ESCAPE HIS OWN FATE.
BUT THAT'S JUST THE THING, SIR. IT MAY NOT HAVE BEEN YOUR FATE, FOR SHE IS POWERFUL INDEED, CONNIVING AT ALL TIMES, AND OFTEN WHIMSICAL.
YOU SEE, SHE DOESN'T REVEAL FATES, SHE ASSIGNS THEM.
AND CAN UNASSIGN THEM.

NEXT: A RECKONING

In those days it might not have been common for a Wolf of remarkable stature to have a conversation with a teacup-wearing turtle.
But it did happen at least once.
THE SMALL GREEN WOMAN ASSIGNS FATES?
THE HELL YOU SAY!
I'VE NEVER HEARD OF SUCH A THING!
IT'S AMAZING TO BE SURE, BUT TRUE.
The Destiny Game Part Two of Two
written and created by Bill Willingham
guest art by Gene Ha
guest colors by Art Lyon
letters by Todd Klein
special thanks to Zander Cannon and Andrew Pepoy
asst. editor Gregory Lockard
editor Shelly Bond

HERS IS THE POWER TO CHOOSE FROM AMONG DIVERSE DESTINIES AND DISTRIBUTE WHAT SHE WILL TO WHOM SHE WILL.
RUMOR HAS IT SHE ALWAYS DOES SO TO HER OWN ADVANTAGE, FOR LOVE OF NOTHING OUTSIDE HERSELF HAS EVER TOUCHED HER.

HOW DOES SHE DO IT? HOW CAN SHE?
I'M NOT SURE, FOR I WAS NEVER AS GIFTED IN THE ELEGANT ARTS AS WAS MY FORMER HUSBAND.

I SUSPECT, IN PART, SHE'S SOME-THING OF A PERSONAL COURIER SERVING THE FATES, MAKING SURE THE MORE IMPORTANT DESTINIES GET DELIVERED TO THE CORRECT SUBJECTS.
SEVEN DESTINIES THIS TIME MERIT SPECIAL ATTENTION.
DELIVER THEM FAITHFULLY.
CHOOSE YOUR SUBJECTS CAREFULLY.
I WILL, AS ALWAYS, VENERABLE HOSTS.

THREE INVOKE CATACLYSMS OF WAR.
THREE INCITE ACTS OF MERCY THAT WILL CHANGE THE COURSE OF NATIONS.
THE REMAINING DESTINY BRINGS ABOUT A LOVE AFFAIR THAT WILL BE THE RUIN OF FOUR KING-DOMS.
PERHAPS SHE SKIMS OFF SOME OF THE REALLY GOOD ONES FOR HERSELF.
AH, WITH THIS ONE I CAN EXTRACT A DEAR REWARD FROM KING RAEDWALD, WHO WANTS SO MUCH FOR HIS NEWBORN DAUGHTER.
THEN AGAIN, HER ODD ACTIONS COULD BE PART OF THEIR INSCRUTABLE DESIGNS.

BUT I BELIEVE SHE ALSO STRIKES BARGAINS WITH THE VARIOUS LORDS AND LADIES OF SCYTHE AND HARROW, FOR MANY IN THIS LIFE DIE WITH THEIR DESTINIES UNFULFILLED.
WHAT HAPPENED HERE?
A GREAT BEAST SPILLED HIS RAGE OUT ON THESE FIELDS. THESE WARRIORS IN THEIR TENS AND IN THEIR HUNDREDS SOUGHT TO OPPOSE HIM.
THEY FAILED, BUT SOME DIED WELL IN THE STRUGGLE.
WE'RE CHOOSING THOSE TO BE ENLARGED IN THE LIFE TO FOLLOW.

THE BRAVEST WILL FEAST WITH US TONIGHT, IN THE GREAT HALL.
YOU KNOW WHY I'M HERE?
YES, WE WERE INSTRUCTED YOU HAVE LEAVE TO PASS AMONG THESE MEN, LIKE THE RAVENS DO, TO PLUCK OUT YOUR SCAVENGER'S MEAL.
NOT ENTIRELY ACCURATE, BUT CREDIT'S DUE FOR POETRY.
LET'S SEE. LET'S SEE.
OH, THIS BOY WOULD HAVE BECOME A GLASS BLOWER OF SOME NOTE, HAD HE LIVED.
SHE GATHERS THOSE UNSPENT FATES AND KEEPS THEM FROM WITHERING, BY STORING THEM IN SOMETHING SHE CALLS HER CLASP.
I CAN USE THAT.
AND THIS ONE WOULD'VE HANGED FOR A THIEF WITHIN A YEAR. ALWAYS GOOD TO HAVE AN EXTRA PUNISHMENT TO DOLE OUT. I'LL TAKE HIS FATE TOO.
AND THIS ONE--

WHATEVER THE FACTS, THE UNDENIABLE TRUTH IS, HER POWERS ARE PRESCRIPTIVE, RATHER THAN DESCRIPTIVE.
SHE'S ABLE TO KEEP MANY DESTINIES AT A TIME AND GIFT THEM TO WHOMSOEVER SHE PLEASES.
SO SHE CAN REMOVE THIS DOOM SHE'S PLACED ON ME?
WHO KNOWS? BUT IT WOULDN'T SURPRISE ME IF THE ONE WHO PUT IT THERE CAN TAKE IT AWAY AGAIN.
WORTH FINDING OUT, DON'T YOU THINK?
YOU HAVE MY GRATITUDE, TURTLE.
THEREFORE I WON'T DEVOUR YOU, THOUGH IT WOULD PLEASE ME TO DO SO.
MY APPETITE IS RESTORED, ALL AT ONCE, AND I DO SO LIKE CRUNCHY TURTLE TREATS.
AND ONE WITH AN ENTIRE CIVILIZATION ON HER BACK, WHICH I COULD GOBBLE WITH A SINGLE BITE, IS ALMOST TOO TEMPTING TO PASS UP.
BUT, FOR GOOD OR ILL, I PAY MY DEBTS.
YOU'RE SAFE!

PHEW.
YOU UNDERSTAND, DON'T YOU, THAT THE REPRIEVE ONLY COVERS ***THIS*** TIME?
NEXT TIME WE MEET, BY DESIGN OR HAPPENSTANCE, YOU'RE BACK ON THE MENU.
I UNDER-STAND.
I AM THE ***UNREPENTANT*** LORD OF MONSTERS, AFTER ALL.
YES, I PICKED UP ON THAT.
GOOD.
AS LONG AS WE'RE CLEAR.

In those days the Lord of Wolves could run swifter than any creature of the land—faster, in fact, than most things could fly.
He could run all out for thirty nights and thirty days without rest.
A simple dash of only one day and night was almost effortless.
On the third day after he discovered the place for the first time, the wolf was back outside the Green Woman's new stronghold.

YOU!
YOU?
HELP!
HELP, MAGUS! THE BEAST IS UPON ME!
ONE CHANCE, GIRL. UNDO MY FATE, OR I RIP YOUR FACE OFF WITH MY NEXT BREATH.
I CAN'T! I'VE NO POWER TO RESCIND DESTINIES ALREADY GIVEN!

TOO BAD THEN.
YOU'RE DEAD NOW.
WAIT!
WAIT!
SPEAK QUICKLY.
THERE'S ONE THING I CAN DO!
I CAN'T TAKE BACK WHAT I'VE GIVEN YOU, BUT--!
YOU ALREADY SAID THAT.
BY THE AUTHORITY OF THE DEEP REALM, WHOSE REPRESENTATIVE I AM IN THE DRY PARTS OF THE WORLDS, I IRREVOCABLY TRADE YOUR DOOM WITH THE MUCH BETTER FATE OF MAGUS ATLANTES!
THAT'S IT, WOLF LORD. IT'S DONE.
JUST LIKE THAT?
NO RHYMING?
NO ORNATE MUMBO JUMBO?
NONE OF THAT NONSENSE IS NEEDED. I'M A GREAT POWER, NOT A SIMPLE CONJURER WHO NEEDS TO FOCUS HER INEPT MIND.

BUT I CAN TRADE YOUR FATE WITH ANOTHER!
A MAN WITH AN IMMORTAL FATE IS HERE NOW!
SPARE ME ONCE MORE AND I'LL SWAP YOUR DOOM FOR HIS!
WHEN?
NOW! I CAN DO IT RIGHT NOW! FROM HERE!
BE ABOUT IT THEN, OR MEASURE YOUR LIFE IN A FEW HEARTBEATS.
TRAITOROUS WITCH.
NO!
I WON'T LET YOU DO THIS TO ME!
WE HAD A DEAL!

BACK UP, LITTLE GIRL. STAY OUT OF THIS, AND BE FORGOTTEN.
INTERFERE, AND I'LL RECALL WHAT YOU TRIED TO DO.
THINK YOU'RE THE FIRST MONSTER I'VE HAD TO KILL?
I'M NOT AN INSIPID LITTLE GODDESS, RIPE WITH ALL MANNER OF POWER TO MANIPULATE, INTERFERE AND MEDDLE, BUT ENTIRELY UNFIT TO DEFEND HERSELF.
I'M A TRAINED KILLER. A COMBAT SORCERER OF THE FIRST ORDER.
JOY.
TRAINED IN THE WEYNAKANA RIVER SCHOOL!
NEVER HEARD OF IT.

PRETTY SURE I KILLED AND **GUTTED** HIM TWO YEARS BACK.

DRAGGED HIS STEAMING **ENTRAILS** AROUND THE BASE OF ALL SIX OF HIS INFAMOUS TOWERS OF BEDAZZLE-MENT.

THAT WAS HIM, RIGHT?

SAME GUY?

In those days the Great Wolf killed many monsters, summoned from distant worlds.
IMPOSSIBLE!
WAIT YOUR TURN, BOY!
GET TO YOU NEXT.

The wolf was doomed to die in three days, ripped apart by a monster.
NO!
THIS WASN'T WHAT I WAS PROMISED!
But on the third day, it was a great sorcerer who'd received that terrible fate.
It was Atlantes of the Castle of Illusions who was ripped apart by a beast exactly as big and bad as the wolf.
IT'S NOT FAIR!
TOO BAD.
NO ONE CAN ESCAPE HIS FATE.

In the ages to come the Green Woman of the Lake grew more dutiful in her fate-making. Less whimsical.
Perhaps her misadventure with the wolf and the sorcerer scared greater maturity into her.
TAKE UP EXCALIBUR, ARTHUR PENDRAGON, AND BECOME THE RIGHTFUL KING.
Many centuries would pass before she saw the wolf again, and that was a tumultuous day too, but perhaps a story for another time.
The wolf went on to live out the better fate he'd fought and killed to obtain that day, though he never knew the details ahead of him.
He learned the details of his life only as they occurred, and was content to live out his years that way.

CLICK
GET YOUR WRITING DONE?
ALL DONE.
I THINK I'LL GO SEE MY DAD TOMORROW.
GOOD IDEA. YOU TWO DON'T SPEAK AS OFTEN AS YOU SHOULD.
SPEAKING CAN BE OVERRATED. DONE READING?
YES. I'M DONE READING. YOU'RE DONE WRITING. WE'RE BOTH DONE *SPEAKING* FOR THE NIGHT. WHAT'S LEFT?
SCOOT OVER.
The End

FABLETOWN

"Don't blame the student for the failings of the teacher."

Back to the main narrative then. The fall of my father, Bigby Wolf, started, appropriately enough, in the fall.
YOU DON'T MIND LENDING IT, BRIAR?
NOT AT ALL. IT'S IN A GOOD CAUSE.
Riding in Cars with Gods
Chapter One of Snow White
Bill Willingham: writer-creator
Mark Buckingham: pencils
Steve Leialoha: inks
Lee Loughridge: colors
Todd Klein: letters
Gregory Lockard: asst. ed.
Shelly Bond: editor
AND IT CAN GO ANYWHERE AT ALL? ANY WORLD?
AS WELL AS THE SPACES BETWEEN WORLDS. IT SEEMS TO CARRY ITS OWN ENVIRONMENT WITH IT.
More specifically, it started on the day Castle Dark was officially rechristened Fabletown — which also happened to be the terrifying day my dad finally learned how to drive.

JUST REMEMBER, THE DEAL IS SHE HAS TO SERVE ONE THOUSAND TIMES BEFORE SHE REVERTS TO THE EVIL DESTROYER WITCH, HADEON.
KEEP A CAREFUL COUNT OF EVERY TIME YOU START HER UP. IF YOU LOSE COUNT, ASK HER. SHE HAS TO ANSWER CORRECTLY.

I'VE TURNED THE ENGINE OVER EXACTLY NINETEEN TIMES GETTING HERE FROM THE OLD IMPERIAL HOME-WORLD.
NO MATTER HOW LONG YOU'RE GONE, JUST MAKE SURE YOU GET BACK HOME BEFORE THE NINE HUNDRED AND NINETY-NINTH USE.

AND THEN WE'LL DRIVE HER RIGHT TO THE WRECKING YARD AND DROP HER INTO ONE OF THOSE CAR-CRUSHING THINGS.
WHAT KIND OF GAS DOES SHE USE? PREMIUM, I'D GUESS, HUH?

THAT'S THE ICKY PART.
BLOOD.
SHE RUNS ON BLOOD. THE MORE INNOCENT, THE BETTER THE MILEAGE.

IT WAS BOTH SURPRISING AND DISTURBING TO FIND THE NUMBER OF GAS STATIONS ON THE WAY BACK HERE THAT WERE ALREADY SET UP TO PROVIDE THAT SORT OF FUEL.

I REPACKED YOUR BAGS FOR THE TRIP.
TYPICALLY, YOU HADN'T PACKED NEARLY ENOUGH.
SNOW. STINKY.

I'M NOT STINKY ANYMORE-- uh--MEANING I'M NOT **NAMED** STINKY.
I KNOW YOU'VE BEEN OUT OF CIRCULATION FOR A WHILE, BUT YOU NEED TO CATCH UP ON A **LOT** OF STUFF, MISSY ROSE.

BRIAR ROSE.
IT'S SO WONDERFUL TO SEE YOU MADE IT HOME, AT LONG LAST.
WELCOME BACK.

I CAN'T THANK YOU **ENOUGH** FOR LETTING US USE YOUR MAGIC CAR TO SEARCH FOR OUR MISSING CHILDREN.
NOT AT ALL. AS I WAS TELLING BIGBY, IT'S WORTH IT TO HAVE A VERY **BAD** THING BEING USED TO DO SOMETHING SO VERY **RIGHT.**

IT'S YOURS FOR AS LONG AS YOU NEED IT.
WE SHOULD BE GOING SOON. SNOW, ANY LUCK ON FINDING A CO-DRIVER TO GO WITH ME?

THAT'S ME. I'M GOING WITH YOU.

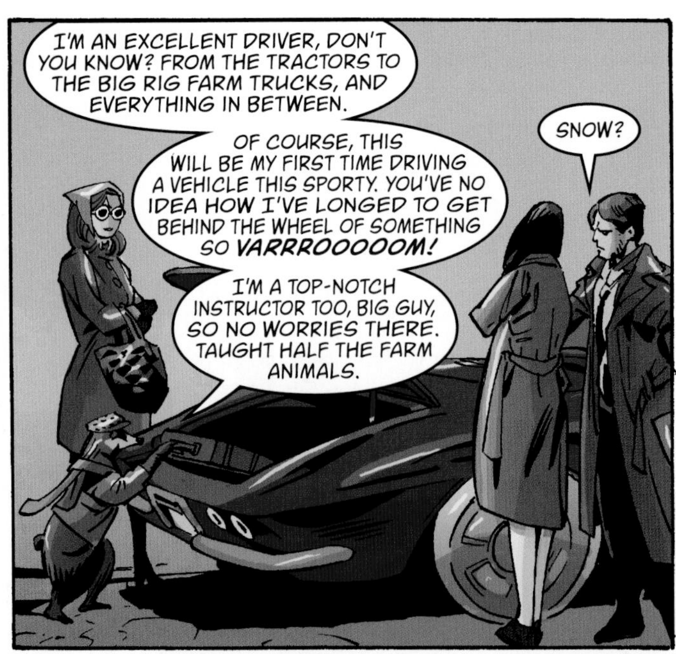
I'M AN EXCELLENT DRIVER, DON'T YOU KNOW? FROM THE TRACTORS TO THE BIG RIG FARM TRUCKS, AND EVERYTHING IN BETWEEN.
OF COURSE, THIS WILL BE MY FIRST TIME DRIVING A VEHICLE THIS SPORTY. YOU'VE NO IDEA HOW I'VE LONGED TO GET BEHIND THE WHEEL OF SOMETHING SO VARRROOOOOM!
I'M A TOP-NOTCH INSTRUCTOR TOO, BIG GUY, SO NO WORRIES THERE. TAUGHT HALF THE FARM ANIMALS.
SNOW?

BAG'S ALL PACKED. FAREWELLS MADE. I'M READY TO GO, AS SOON AS YOU ARE.

I'LL MAKE MYSELF A WEE BIT BIGGER HERE, TO SEE OVER THE DASH.

WHO'S GOT THE KEYS?
HE WAS THE BEST I COULD DO.

TAKE CARE, BOTH OF YOU.
AND BRING MY BABIES HOME.

WAHOOOOOOO! ROAD TRIP!
HANG ON, PAL! IMMA BOUTTA PUT THE PEDAL TO THE METAL!

It was about the same time (though it's hard to pin down, since time runs differently in some of the worlds we know) that Beast's Blue Fairy problems were about to come due.
TIME'S RUNNING OUT, SHERIFF.
I KNOW.

BY MY CALCULATIONS, SHE ARRIVES TOMORROW, OR THE NEXT DAY AT THE LATEST. AND GEPPETTO'S NOT WILLING TO SURRENDER TO HER.
I KNOW.
GOT A PLAN YET?
WORKING ON IT.

WHAT'S THAT YOU'RE READING? FAIRY LAW?
LOOKING FOR A PRECEDENT OR A LOOPHOLE--ANYTHING AT ALL THAT KEEPS HER FROM TAKING ME AWAY FOR SEVEN HUNDRED AND SEVENTY-SEVEN YEARS.

ANY LUCK?
ONE POSSIBILITY THAT HAS NO CHANCE OF WORKING.
SO WHAT ARE YOU GOING TO DO?

TRY IT ANYWAY.
DESPERATE TIMES CALL FOR DESPERATE MEASURES, RIGHT?

Briar Rose's magic car easily carried Brock and my father from one world to another, almost faster than my sister Winter could do the same trick.
ROAD TRIP RULES, RIGHT, BIGBY? NO TELLING TALES OF WHATEVER ADVENTURES AND SHENANIGANS WE GET INTO?
I'LL MAKE THE FIRST DEPOSIT INTO THE TRUST BANK BY ADMITTING SOMETHING YOU CAN NEVER REPEAT.

I DON'T MIND THE NAME STINKY. IN FACT I SORT OF LIKE IT. BUT A CHURCH LEADER NEEDS DIGNITY.
DO TELL.
AND HERE'S ANOTHER ADMISSION. I DIDN'T JUST ACCI-DENTALLY FALL DOWN MISSY SKUNK'S HOLE THAT NIGHT.

I WAS DRUNK. SHE WAS LOOKING GOOD, AND...WELL... Y'KNOW HOW THINGS ARE. YOU MARRIED OUTSIDE YOUR SPECIES.
THE HEART WANTS WHAT THE HEART WANTS, AM I RIGHT? AND A HOT BABE'S FROTHY LOINS WANT WHAT A HOT BABE'S FROTHY LOINS WANT.

THIS ISN'T A ROAD TRIP, BADGER. IT'S A SEARCH FOR MY TWO MISSING CUBS.
NOW LET'S START THE DRIVING LESSONS. I WANT TO BE ABLE TO CONTINUE THE QUEST ON MY OWN AFTER I STRANGLE YOU FOR TOO MUCH CHATTER.

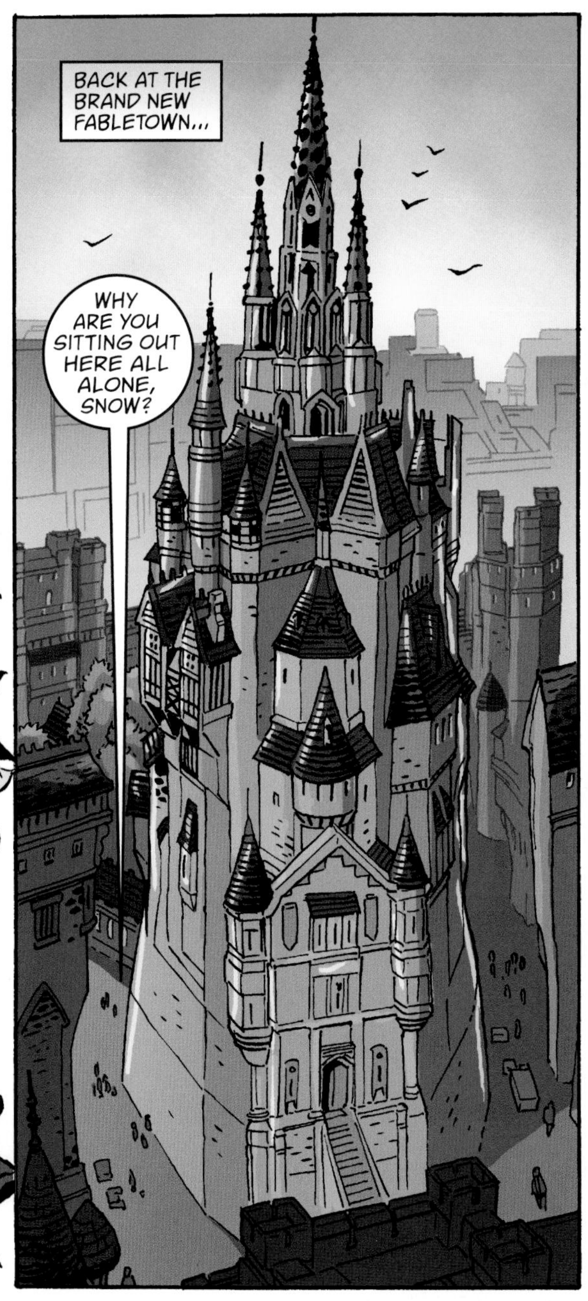
BACK AT THE BRAND NEW FABLETOWN...
WHY ARE YOU SITTING OUT HERE ALL ALONE, SNOW?

I'M WAITING FOR THE SUPPLY TRUCK TO HEAD BACK TO THE FARM.
ROSE RED IS WATCHING MY BABIES NOW, BUT I NEED TO GET BACK TO THEM.
THOSE WHO ARE LEFT.

THEY NEED THEIR MOMMY.
WELL, YOU CAN'T SIT OUT HERE ALL ALONE.
SCOOT.
MAKE SOME ROOM.

SO MUCH HAS HAPPENED WHILE I'VE BEEN ASLEEP, I HAVEN'T YET BEEN ABLE TO CATCH UP ON A *FRACTION* OF IT.
TRAGEDY UPON TRAGEDY. ALL MANNER OF BAD BUSINESS.

BLUE AND CHARMING DEAD IN THE WAR, OR DIRECTLY BECAUSE OF IT. FABLETOWN DESTROYED AND REPLACED BY-- WELL, THIS.
TOTENKINDER DEAD ONCE AND THEN MAYBE NOT DEAD BUT YOUNGER AND MARRIED. COULD HAVE KNOCKED ME OVER WITH A FEATHER WHEN I HEARD THAT.

AND TWO MISSING KIDS. DON'T FORGET THAT.
NO, OF COURSE NOT. I'M NOT TRYING TO DIMINISH WHAT YOU'RE GOING THROUGH.

BIGBY WILL FIND THEM. THAT NEW CAR OF MINE IS AMAZING. IT CAN GO ANYWHERE.
IF I WERE LOST AND IN NEED OF RESCUE, BIGBY'S THE ONE PERSON IN ALL OF THE ENDLESS WORLDS I'D WANT LOOKING FOR ME.

I NEED TO BE HOME, IN CASE THEY'RE TRYING TO REACH ME THERE.
THEN HOME YOU SHALL BE. IT'S STUPID WAITING AROUND FOR THAT DIRTY OLD DELIVERY TRUCK WHEN I CAN JUST GIVE YOU MY CAR.

EXCEPT THAT YOU ALREADY GAVE IT TO BIGBY.
RIGHT, SO I'LL BUY A NEW ONE. I ONLY NEED TO SCRAPE TOGETHER ENOUGH CASH TO BUY A SINGLE LOTTERY TICKET AND I'LL BE RICH AGAIN BY THIS EVENING.
AS LONG AS I'M ETERNALLY BLESSED WITH WEALTH, I CAN'T THINK OF A BETTER USE FOR IT.

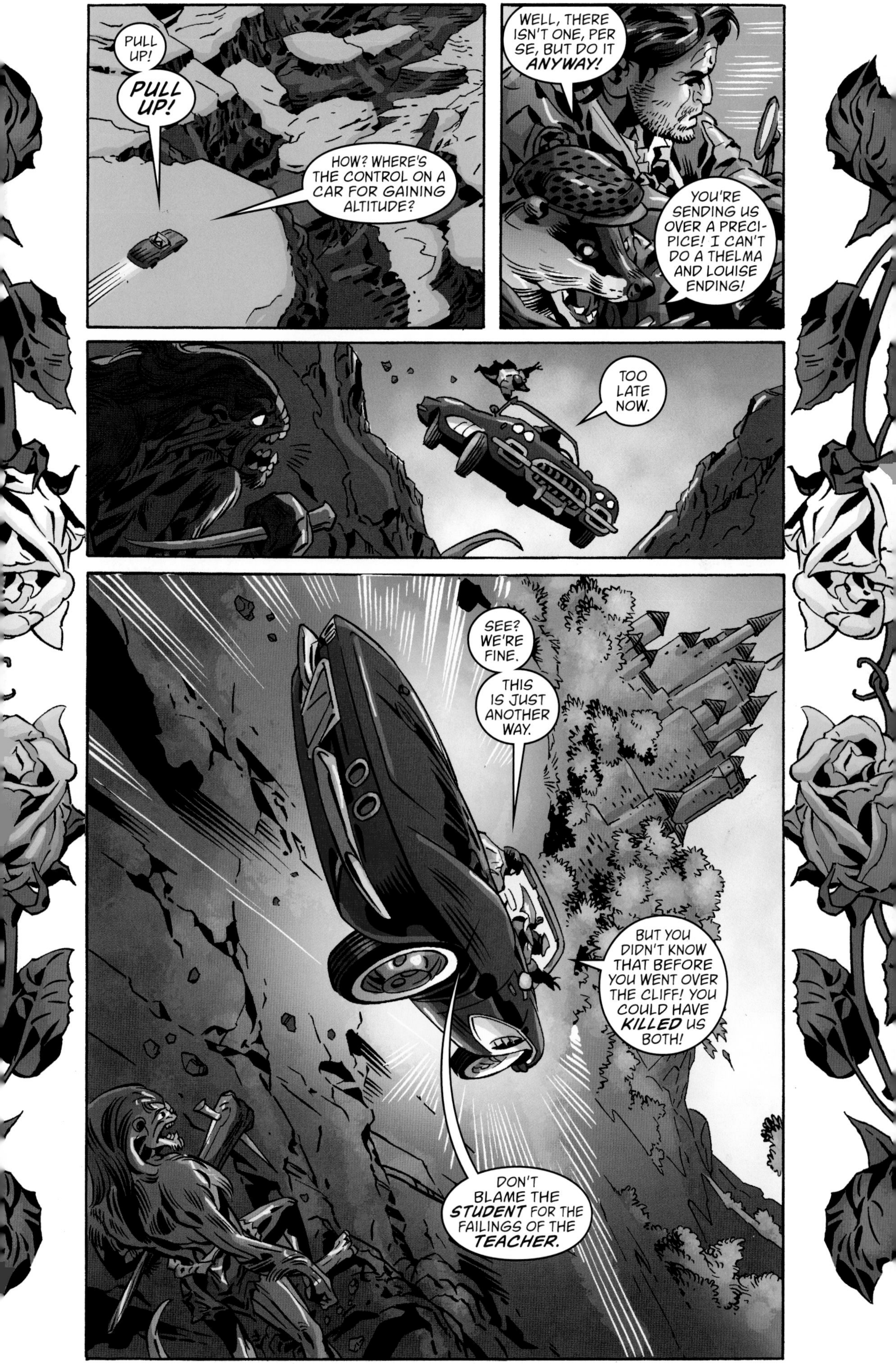

PULL UP!
PULL UP!
HOW? WHERE'S THE CONTROL ON A CAR FOR GAINING ALTITUDE?

WELL, THERE ISN'T ONE, PER SE, BUT DO IT *ANYWAY!*
YOU'RE SENDING US OVER A PRECI-PICE! I CAN'T DO A THELMA AND LOUISE ENDING!

TOO LATE NOW.

SEE? WE'RE FINE.
THIS IS JUST ANOTHER WAY.
BUT YOU DIDN'T KNOW THAT BEFORE YOU WENT OVER THE CLIFF! YOU COULD HAVE *KILLED* US BOTH!
DON'T BLAME THE *STUDENT* FOR THE FAILINGS OF THE *TEACHER.*

I'M BEGINNING TO GET IT BACK.
THE OLD SKILLS.

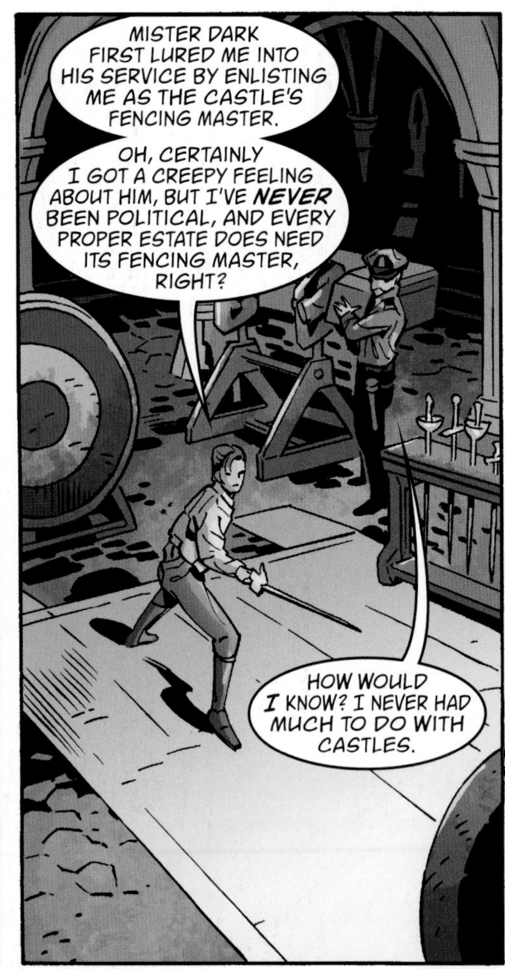
MISTER DARK FIRST LURED ME INTO HIS SERVICE BY ENLISTING ME AS THE CASTLE'S FENCING MASTER.
OH, CERTAINLY I GOT A CREEPY FEELING ABOUT HIM, BUT I'VE **NEVER** BEEN POLITICAL, AND EVERY PROPER ESTATE DOES NEED ITS FENCING MASTER, RIGHT?
HOW WOULD *I* KNOW? I NEVER HAD MUCH TO DO WITH CASTLES.

I WAS BASICALLY A BRIDGE TROLL UNTIL I CROSSED OVER TO THE MUNDY WORLD.
WELL, TRUST ME, SQUIRE GRIMBLE. IT WOULD BE A **SCANDAL** NOT TO HAVE ONE.

I NEED MORE THAN THIS, THOUGH.
A THOUSAND PRACTICE LUNGES A DAY ARE HELPING ME GET MY LEGS AND WRIST BACK, BUT IT'S NOT ENOUGH.

I NEED AN OPPONENT-- ONE WORTHY OF MY METTLE.
WHO'S THE BEST SWORDSMAN IN FABLETOWN?

THAT WOULD HAVE BEEN PRINCE CHARMING--NO QUESTION OF IT. BUT HE DIED IN THE WAR.
I'D THINK BLUEBEARD WAS NEXT BEST, BUT HE DIED TOO.

BOY BLUE COULD HOLD HIS OWN, ESPECIALLY WITH THE VORPAL SWORD, BUT--
LET ME GUESS. HE'S DEAD?

YUP.
ARE ALL THE HEROES OF FABLE-TOWN DEAD? ARE YOU PEOPLE THAT UNLUCKY?
NEVER MIND. LET'S NOT GET DISTRACTED FROM OUR PURPOSE. WHO'S THE BEST LIVING SWORDS-MAN IN THE COMMUNITY?

YOU GOT ME THERE.
CINDERELLA MAYBE?

A WOMAN?
BLUEBEARD'S TOP STUDENT FOR A WHILE.
I CAN'T FIGHT A WOMAN! NOT EVEN IN PRACTICE.

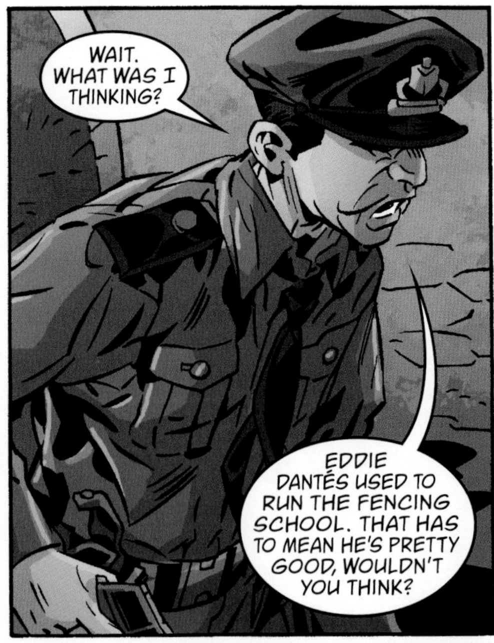
WAIT. WHAT WAS I THINKING?
EDDIE DANTÉS USED TO RUN THE FENCING SCHOOL. THAT HAS TO MEAN HE'S PRETTY GOOD, WOULDN'T YOU THINK?

WANT ME TO FIND HIM?
WOULD YOU, PLEASE?
SURE. NO PROBLEM.

BUT MAYBE FIRST, YOU SHOULD EXPLAIN A THING OR TWO.
HOW IS IT YOU HAPPEN TO HAVE A SWORD THAT CAN MAGICALLY **CHANGE** FROM ONE TYPE OF SWORD TO ANOTHER, AT LEAST THREE TIMES WHILE I'VE BEEN WATCHING YOU?

I HAVE NO IDEA. I SIMPLY SELECTED ONE FROM THE RACKS TO PRACTICE. I ASSUMED IT WAS SOME SORT OF CLEVER MAGICAL TRAINING BLADE.
A TOOL TO GET A MAN USED TO FIGHTING WITH DIFFERENT WEAPONS, WITH VARYING WEIGHTS AND BALANCES AND SUCH.

NO, MR. HOLT, YOU DIDN'T JUST GRAB IT FROM THE RACK. I PERSONALLY UNPACKED EVERY WEAPON WE BROUGHT DOWN TO THE CITY.
AND BEFORE THAT, I INVENTORIED EVERY BLADE THAT WAS ALREADY HERE.

THAT THING WASN'T AMONG THEM.
FOLKS DON'T THINK I NOTICE MUCH, BUT I DO. I NOTICE EVERY-THING.

I NOTICED A SUPPOSEDLY STARVING SLAVE EAT HIS FIRST MEAL IN MONTHS WITH CALM MODERATION.
A SUPPOSEDLY WEAKENED MAN WHO WORKED HIS WAY UP TO A THOUSAND FENCING LUNGES A DAY, WITHIN DAYS RATHER THAN WEEKS OR MONTHS.

NEED I GO ON?
BRAVO. YOU FOUND ME OUT.
CARE TO TELL ME WHAT YOUR GAME IS?

NOT JUST YET.

WHAT DID YOU--?
--NEVER EVEN HAD TIME TO--
I KNOW. ASTOUNDING, ISN'T IT?

THOSE UNSCHOOLED IN THIS MOST ELEGANT OF MARTIAL ARTS SELDOM REALIZE HOW MUCH DISTANCE A MASTER SWORDSMAN CAN CROSS IN A SINGLE LUNGE.

ENTIRELY MY FAULT YOU CAUGHT ON TO ME.

I SHOULDN'T HAVE DRAWN MY OWN SPECIAL BLADE FROM ITS ETHEREAL SCABBARD--NOT UNTIL I WAS PREPARED TO USE IT IN **EARNEST**--BUT I COULDN'T RESIST.

I MISSED PRACTICING WITH IT.

NOW, SHOULD I **CRUSH** YOU AND END YOUR SAD, TINY LIFE?

NO. YOU'VE NO VOICE LEFT. NO WAY TO FURTHER INTERFERE WITH MY DESIGNS AND SCHEMA.
AFTER ALL, THE NOBILITY HAVE AN OBLIGATION TO SHOW MERCY TO THE **WRETCHED** CLASSES, NON?

YOU'RE COMING ALONG NICELY, PAL.
MAY EVEN BE A NATURAL AT THIS.

OF COURSE, PILOTING A CAR THAT CAN GO ANYWHERE IS A FAR CRY FROM DRIVING A BIG TRACTOR, FOR EXAMPLE, THAT HAS TO STAY IN A VERY NARROW FURROW.
OR RISK DESTROYING THE CROPS, Y'KNOW?

AM I RIGHT?
ARE YOU EVEN LISTENING TO ME?

YEAH, HANGING ON EVERY WORD.
FURROW. CROPS. TRACTOR.

SO THEN, WHAT'S OUR STRATEGY HERE? WHAT'S OUR GAME PLAN?
WE GOING TO STOP AT TOUGH PLACES AND QUESTION THE LOCALS? SEE IF THEY'VE SEEN YOUR KIDS COMING THROUGH? MAYBE HAVE TO GET ROUGH AND BEAT THE TRUTH OUT OF THEM?

IF IT COMES TO THAT.
BUT FIRST I'M GOING TO DRIVE HERE AND THERE UNTIL I PICK UP THEIR SCENT.
SERIOUSLY?

ISN'T THAT A BIT OF A LONG SHOT?
IF MY CUBS HAVE BEEN ANYWHERE CLOSE TO WHEREVER WE MIGHT HAPPEN TO PASS, I'LL PICK UP THEIR SCENT. COUNT ON IT.

SO THAT'S SOME REAL GOD OF WOLVES STUFF, HUH? BIG TIME SUPER-SMELLING POWERS?
CALL IT WHAT YOU WANT.

THE GOD OF WOLVES AND THE GOD OF BADGERS ON THE ROAD TOGETHER, ON A NOBLE MISSION. MAYBE EVEN A SACRED QUEST.
IN THE MEANTIME WE'LL PROBABLY GET INVOLVED WITH PEOPLE'S LIVES, SOLVE THEIR PROBLEMS-- THAT SORT OF THING.

SURE. YOU DO THAT, WHILE I CONTINUE THE SEARCH.
I CAN TRY TO REMEMBER TO PICK YOU UP ON THE WAY BACK.

TRUE, OUR GOLD SUPPLIES ARE FLUSH NOW, BECAUSE WE WERE ABLE TO RECOVER MOST OF WHAT WE USED IN OUR ATTEMPT TO BOX MISTER DARK.
BUT IT DOESN'T **COMPARE** TO WHAT HE HAD IN ALL OF BLUEBEARD'S TREASURE ROOMS.

AND SINCE IT'S THE NATURE OF MONEY TO BE SPENT, ***ESPECIALLY*** WHEN ONE IS TRYING TO REBUILD A GOVERNMENT AND A COMMUNITY FROM THE GROUND UP...
WELL, LET ME TELL ***YOU,*** MISS DUGLAS, IT CAN DISAPPEAR FASTER THAN ONE MIGHT EXPECT.

CALL ME LEIGH.
MISS DUGLAS IS SO ***FORMAL.***

AND I WANT TO BE ***ANYTHING*** BUT FORMAL WITH YOU, YOUR HONOR. OH DEAR. YOU'VE GOT A LITTLE DROP OF GRAVY ON YOUR CHIN. LET ME GET THAT FOR YOU.
UH...
OH... UH...

ALL BETTER.
OF COURSE. OF COURSE, BUT...
THAT IS TO SAY...

BY THE WAY, IN CASE YOU MISSED IT, THAT WAS JUST A *HUGE* HINT THAT THIS MIGHT BE A GOOD TIME TO TELL ME *YOUR* FIRST NAME.
OH! RIGHT! OF COURSE THAT'S *EXACTLY* WHAT THAT WOULD BE, WOULDN'T IT?

ROBERON.
MY NAME IS ROBERON. *ROBER* FOR SHORT.
BUT NO ONE'S CALLED ME BY MY GIVEN NAME FOR SO LONG.

MY WIFE USED TO CALL ME HER ROBBER BARON... Y'KNOW, AS A PET NAME, BACK WHEN I WAS STILL A BARON AND DOUR OLD HUGO MARSHBEARD WAS KING.

LOOK AT ME. I'M BABBLING.
YOU'RE DOING FINE. AND I ONLY MEANT, SINCE WE'VE BEEN WORKING *SO* CLOSELY TOGETHER TO REESTABLISH FABLETOWN, AND ARE LIKELY TO CONTINUE DOING SO...

RIGHT!
YES!
OF COURSE!
SPEAKING OF WHICH, WE SHOULD GET BACK *DOWNSTAIRS* AND SEE TO THE UNLOADING OF... WHATEVER'S BEING UNLOADED.

GOOD NEWS, SNOW.
THE LOTTERY JUST ANNOUNCED MY TICKET AS THE **WINNER.** THAT WAS GOOD ENOUGH TO HAVE THE MERCEDES DEALER DELIVER A NEW CAR LICKETY SPLIT.

WE'LL HAVE YOU ON YOUR WAY IN **NO** TIME.
UHM... **THANKS,** OF COURSE, BRIAR, BUT THE FARM TRUCK WOULD HAVE BEEN FINE. IT'S NEARLY READY TO GO.

POO ON THAT CREAKY OLD RATTLETRAP. WE NEED TO GET YOU HOME RIGHT NOW.
OH, **SNOW!**
GOOD, YOU'RE STILL HERE!

AS LONG AS YOU ARE--WELL, YOU ALREADY KNOW MISS DUGLAS, BUT I DON'T BELIEVE YOU'VE BEEN INTRO-DUCED TO OUR **OTHER** MIRACULOUS CASTLE RESCUE.
OH NO.
ON THE CONTRARY, YOUR HONOR. SNOW AND I GO **WAY** BACK.

WAY BACK **INDEED.**

BRANDISH!
YOUR TRUEST LOVE, MIRACULOUSLY RESTORED TO YOU AFTER AGES OF FORCED SEPARATION.
WHAT?!
SNOW?
THE HELL YOU SAY!
NOW THAT I'VE CONFIRMED IT IS INDEED HER, MY LITTLE LOST SNOW, I CAN REVEAL A SMALL SUBTERFUGE.
MY TRUE SELF IS NONE OTHER THAN PRINCE BRANDISH OF CASTLE LANCEDORE, PROTECTOR OF THE GOLDEN REALM, MARSHAL OF THE WEST...
...AND THE FIRST AND ONE TRUE HUSBAND TO SNOW WHITE.

NEXT: *YIKES!*

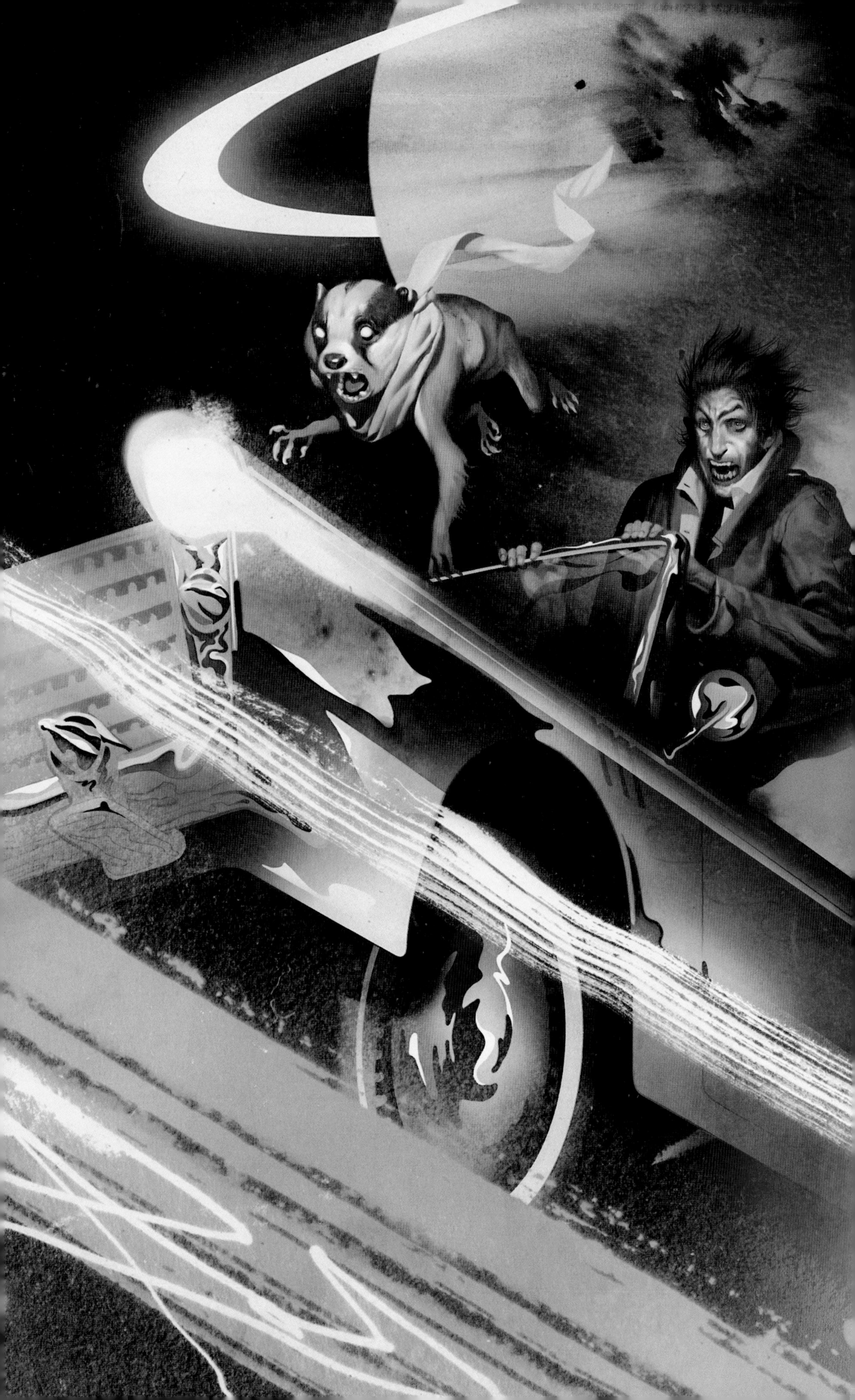

"The vow is the deed, Snow. You should know that much."

Fabletown by the Book
Chapter Two of Snow White
Bill Willingham: writer-creator
Mark Buckingham: pencils
Steve Leialoha and
Andrew Pepoy: inks
Lee Loughridge: colors
Todd Klein: letters
Gregory Lockard: asst. ed.
Shelly Bond: editor
At about the same time my mom was being surprised by that bad man in the new Fabletown, something else was taking shape in a different world that would turn out to have an impact on all our lives — perhaps mine most of all.
I DON'T KNOW HOW LONG I'LL BE GONE, BUT DON'T TAKE THAT AS AN INVITATION TO DESTROY THE PLACE.
MR. KALILULOLY IS IN CHARGE WHILE I'M AWAY. MIND HIM AS YOU WOULD ME.
AND DO TAKE NOTE, IF THE LINENS START A WAR WITH THE TABLEWARE AGAIN, OR VICE VERSA, I'LL HAVE DONE WITH THE LOT OF YOU THIS TIME.
MY PATIENCE WITH YOUR CHILDISH FEUDS IS EXHAUSTED. PUT AWAY YOUR ANCIENT GRIEVANCES OR I'LL WRITE A PERMANENT END TO THEM.
MARK ME ON THAT.

AND BE NICE TO OUR GUEST.
WE WILL, MA'AM. **PROMISE** WE WILL.

SUCH A BOTHER, THESE TEDIUMS AND CHORES.

I FEEL TERRIBLE, DASHING TO RUN AN **ERRAND** AFTER YOU'VE ONLY JUST ARRIVED TO VISIT, MY SWEET, BUT IT CAN'T BE HELPED.
YOU KNOW MORE THAN MOST, WE'RE ALL SLAVES TO THE CALENDAR.
PLEASE STAY. ENJOY THE HOSPITALITY OF MY AIRS AND MY **ACRES** WHILE I'M GONE, AND **OH** HOW WE'LL CATCH UP ON MY RETURN.

TUCK IN, SQUIRE WYRMHOUSE. LOOK OUT FOR YOURSELF, AND **PLEASE** PROTECT THOSE WITHIN YOU.
YOUR WILL AND ONLY YOUR WILL, MADAM.

FABLETOWN CASTLE, NEW YORK...
NO NEED TO WORRY. THIS IS JUST A MISTAKE.
IF YOU'LL EXCUSE US FOR A MOMENT, I CAN SETTLE THIS WITH MISTER--WITH THE PRINCE.

ALONE AT LAST.
STOP IT.
PLEASE.

STOP WHAT, DEAR?
PAWING AT ME. AND DON'T CALL ME THAT. I NEED TO EXPLAIN SOME-THING--

A MAN CAN TOUCH HIS WIFE.
IT'S MY RIGHT.

AND MORE.

OH MY.

SHOULD WE DO SOMETHING?
NOT YET.
SNOW CAN GENERALLY TAKE CARE OF HERSELF.

THAT MUCH IS TRUE. LOOKING AFTER HER OWN INTERESTS IS WHAT SHE DOES BEST.

WAIT!

STOP IT!
STOP THIS RIGHT NOW!

WHY?
RATHER I MEAN TO SAY, WHY SHOULD I?
I'VE BEEN WAITING CENTURIES TO TAKE A HUSBAND'S PRIVILEGES.

YOU'RE NOT MY HUSBAND!
OF COURSE I AM, SNOWFLAKE.

WE BETROTHED OURSELVES TO EACH OTHER LONG AGO.
I WAS A CHILD!
AND WE WERE NEVER MARRIED.

WE NEVER HAD THE CEREMONY, I'LL GRANT YOU THAT MUCH. YOU CAN HAVE THE WEDDING OF YOUR DREAMS, IF THAT'S YOUR HEART'S DESIRE.
BUT A CEREMONY IS MEANINGLESS IN THE HIGH LAW OF OUR LAND. THE PROMISE IS ALL THAT MATTERS.

THE VOW IS THE DEED, SNOW.
YOU SHOULD KNOW THAT MUCH.

"ALL OF THE SORCERIES AT MY FATHER'S COMMAND COULDN'T UNDO THE SIMPLE AND INNOCENT WORDS WE SPOKE ON THAT FATEFUL DAY."
I WON'T HAVE IT!
I'VE MORTGAGED HALF MY KINGDOM TO KEEP US IN FAVOR WITH THE NEW EMPEROR--TO KEEP US IN POWER!
MARRY STRATEGICALLY NOW AND WE CAN RULE THIS ENTIRE WORLD.
I WON'T HAVE YOU THROW AWAY ALL MY WORK BY MOONING OVER A RAGAMUFFIN FOREST GIRL WHO DIED DECADES AGO!
I DON'T BELIEVE SHE IS DEAD, FATHER. I'D FEEL IT IF SHE WERE.
THERE WAS POWER IN HER AND I MEAN TO HAVE IT.
I INTEND TO GIVE IT TO MY SONS.

WORDS OF GREAT POTENCY.
VAST AND TERRIBLE POWERS WERE PUT INTO MOTION THEN.
LET GO!
ENOUGH OF THIS. I'M GOING TO INTERVENE.

TRY AND HE'LL KILL YOU.
BEST LET THIS PLAY OUT.

YOU LET IT PLAY, LADY. I DON'T KNOW YOU AND I DON'T LET STRANGERS BOSS ME AROUND.
I'M STEPPING IN.

MISTER MAYOR?
RIGHT WITH YOU, BRIAR ROSE.

EXCUSE ME, MR. HOLT, OR WHATEVER YOUR NAME IS!

NO, I DON'T THINK SO.
I DON'T EXCUSE YOU, OLD MAN.
HEY!

YOU MIND YOUR PLACE TOO, GIRL.
WHAT THE HELL?

DON'T!
SHUSH NOW. THAT'S A GOOD GIRL.

DON'T DO THIS! THERE'S STILL TIME TO--
I'M NOT DOING ANYTHING, MY LOVE. JUST TAKING YOU SOMEWHERE WE CAN TALK WITHOUT SO MANY INTER-RUPTIONS.

While my mother was getting into the biggest trouble of her life (if you don't count all the assassination attempts, invasions, personal betrayals and abandonments), my dad was much too far away to be of any help to her.
NO, MY DAUGHTER THERESE DIDN'T PASS THIS WAY, BUT I KNOW MY SON DARE DID.

HIS SCENT IS FAINT, BUT HE DEFINITELY TOUCHED DOWN NEAR HERE, EVEN IF ONLY FOR A MOMENT.

PICTURE ME AS A CHILD.
SAME HAIR COLOR. MORE ROUNDED AND INNOCENT VERSIONS OF MY FEATURES.
NO ONE THAT LOOKED ANYTHING LIKE YOU PASSED THROUGH HERE, STRANGER. I'D SWEAR ON IT.
IF YOU GIVE YOUR HEART, LIFE AND GOOD WORKS TO BLUE, SOMEDAY HE'LL COME IN HIS POWER AND GLORY TO SMITE THE OVERLORDS AND SET YOU FREE.
WHAT OVERLORDS? WE'RE A REPRESENTATIVE LITOCRACY. PASS THE READING TEST, NO MATTER WHAT AGE, AND YOU CAN VOTE.

At that moment, or as close as I can pin the timeline down...
WAKE UP, ROBER.
ARE YOU OKAY?

NO, I AM DECIDEDLY NOT OKAY.
I FEEL LIKE I'VE BEEN WALLOPED BY A BEAR.
I TRIED TO WARN YOU.

HOW'S BRIAR?
I'LL LIVE, I GUESS.

WHY DIDN'T YOU LEAVE HIM BE?
COULDN'T YOU SEE THE POWER HE HAD--THE IMMENSE MAGICAL ENERGIES CRACKLING AROUND HIM LIKE FIRE?

NO, I COULDN'T.
WHICH BEGS THE QUESTION, HOW CAN YOU SEE SUCH THINGS, MISS DUGLAS?

THERE WE ARE, MY DOVE. SAFE AND SOUND, TUCKED IN BEHIND A STOUT DOOR.
GOOD LUCK ANYONE BREAKING *THIS* ONE DOWN BEFORE WE'VE HAD A CHANCE TO FINISH OUR TALK.

DO YOU LIKE MY SUITE OF ROOMS? LAVISH, ISN'T IT?
THE GOOD PEOPLE OF FABLETOWN WERE QUITE GENEROUS IN REWARDING MY SMALL PART IN KEEPING LEIGH DUGLAS *ALIVE* DURING HER ORDEALS.
BRANDISH, YOU HAVE TO *LISTEN* TO ME.

OF COURSE I WILL, DARLING. A HUSBAND AND WIFE *NEED* TO LISTEN TO EACH OTHER-- TO RELY CHIEFLY ON EACH OTHER.
WE'RE NOT MARRIED. WE *CAN'T* BE. I'M ALREADY MARRIED TO *BIGBY WOLF.*

I'LL ENTREAT YOU TO KINDLY NEVER MENTION THAT ANIMAL'S NAME AGAIN IN MY PRESENCE. I'M FULL *AWARE* OF WHAT YOU AND THE FOREST CREATURE HAVE DONE.
HONESTLY, DEAR, WHEN I PICTURE IN MY MIND'S EYE YOU AND THAT *THING* TOGETHER, YOU LYING UNDER HIM, WRITHING AND GRUNTING YOUR UNNATURAL LUSTS--

WELL, IT'S ENOUGH TO TEMPT A GENTLEMAN TO ACT ALARMINGLY *UN-GENTLY* INDEED.
BUT I'M RESOLVED TO *FORGIVE* YOU YOUR WILD AND WICKED WAYS. WHAT EVILS YOU GOT UP TO, LACKING MY SUP-PORT AND GUIDANCE, ARE A THING OF THE PAST.

A SLATE WIPED CLEAN. YOU'RE WELCOME.
PLEASE, I BEG OF YOU, LET ME SPEAK.

WHO'S STOPPING YOU, SNOWFLAKE? GO AHEAD. AIR WHATEVER'S ON YOUR PRETTY LITTLE MIND.
DESPITE THE WAY YOU'VE ACTED TODAY, I WANT TO TRY TO SAVE YOUR LIFE BY TALKING YOU OUT OF WHATEVER IT IS YOU HAVE PLANNED.

THERE'S STILL TIME TO TURN BACK. NO ONE'S DIED YET. NO ONE NEEDS TO.
NOT TRUE, MY SWEET. BIGBY HAS TO DIE. I CAN FORGIVE YOU ENTERING INTO A FALSE AND ILLEGAL MARRIAGE, BUT NOT HIM FOR TAKING ADVANTAGE OF A PROMISED WOMAN.

SOONER OR LATER, HE'LL HEAR OF MY RETURN AND COME RUNNING TO YOUR SIDE, LIKE THE LOYAL DOG HE IS.
I'LL DISPATCH HIM QUICKLY, AS A FAVOR TO YOU.

AND OF COURSE YOUR SO-CALLED CUBS WILL HAVE TO GO AS WELL. AS IS ONLY PROPER IN A FAIR AND CIVILIZED LAND, YOUR ONLY CHILDREN MUST BE MY CHILDREN.

THE HELL--?!

SHUSH, CHILD. DON'T FRET.
WHAT MUST BE MUST BE.
WOMEN ARE EMOTIONAL BEINGS AND CAN'T UNDERSTAND THE HARSH MATTERS OF MEN.
THAT'S WHY THE GODS PUT MEN AT THE HEAD OF THE FAMILY.

SURE, YOU'LL BE UPSET AT FIRST, BUT HAPPIER IN THE LONG RUN, WHEN I GIVE YOU A BUSHEL OF NEW SONS AND DAUGHTERS TO REPLACE THE ABOMINATIONS YOU'VE WHELPED.

IT'S A CLEANSING ACT. WE'LL SCRUB THAT FILTH FROM YOUR CORRUPTED WOMB AND REFILL IT WITH CLEAN HUMAN BABIES.
YOU--

YOU'RE MAD.

PERTURBED AT BEST.
WHO WOULDN'T BE, GIVEN THE CIRCUM-STANCES?

I hadn't seen the Kingdom of Haven by that point. It was still ruled back then by the janitor-turned-king I was named after.
HOW'YA DOING, OLD DUFFER?
I'LL THANK YOU NOT TO TALK TO ME IN THAT GUISE.
REYNARD, ISN'T IT? I HAPPEN TO KNOW YOU'VE BECOME CAPABLE OF ASSUMING HUMAN FORM.
SPEAKING TO A MAN OF MY STATION WHILST IN THE SEMBLANCE OF A BEAST, WHEN YOU HAVE OTHER OPTIONS, IS A GRAVE INSULT.
GOOD FOR YOU, GEPPETTO.
YOU LOST AN ENTIRE EMPIRE DUE ENTIRELY TO YOUR OWN LACK OF IMAGINATION. YOU SQUANDERED THE LIVES OF MILLIONS--PERHAPS BILLIONS.
YOU'RE REDUCED TO A SAD OLD NOTHING OF A MAN.
AND YET YOU'RE STILL IMPRESSED WITH YOURSELF.
KUDOS FOR YOUR OVER-ABUNDANCE OF SELF-ESTEEM IN THE FACE OF A RIDICULOUS AMOUNT OF SELF- INFLICTED CALAMITY.

DO YOU HAVE SOME PURPOSE IN TALKING TO ME, RASCAL? I'M A BUSY MAN.
I WAS JUST CURIOUS AS TO THE POTTED PLANT. YOU'VE BEEN CARRYING THAT THING AROUND LIKE IT WAS A FRAGILE TREASURE EVER SINCE YOU CAME BACK TO HAVEN.

I WAS WORRIED YOU MIGHT BE GOING JUST A WEE BIT 'ROUND THE BEND.
YOU'VE MADE YOUR INSIPID OBSERVATION, SANS AN ACTUAL QUESTION. NOW I'LL THANK YOU TO MOVE ALONG.

NARCISSIST.
CUR.

HEY!
GEPPETTO!
HOLD IT RIGHT THERE! DON'T WALK AWAY FROM ME!

WHAT ARE YOU DOING OUTSIDE-- TODAY, OF ALL DAYS?
GET BACK IN THE CASTLE AND LOCK YOURSELF IN YOUR ROOM, LIKE I TOLD YOU TO!

THIS PLANT NEEDS SOME FRESH AIR AND WATER. I TOOK IT OUT FOR BOTH. AND SINCE WHEN DO I TAKE ORDERS FROM YOU, BEAST?
SINCE I WENT WAY OUT ON A LIMB TO SAVE YOUR BONY ASS FROM THE BLUE FAIRY, WHO MIGHT ARRIVE ANY SECOND. SHE CAN'T SEE YOU HERE OR WE'RE BOTH COOKED.

ALSO SINCE I'M SHERIFF OF THE WHOLE DAMNED KINGDOM NOW.
YOU?
ME. OFFICIALLY APPOINTED BY HIS HIGHNESS, AMBROSE THE FIRST, LAST WEEK.

IS THAT FLY-EATING MORON MORE DAFT THAN EVEN I SUSPECTED?
HEY, WATCH IT, PAL. YOU JUST SPOKE TREASON.

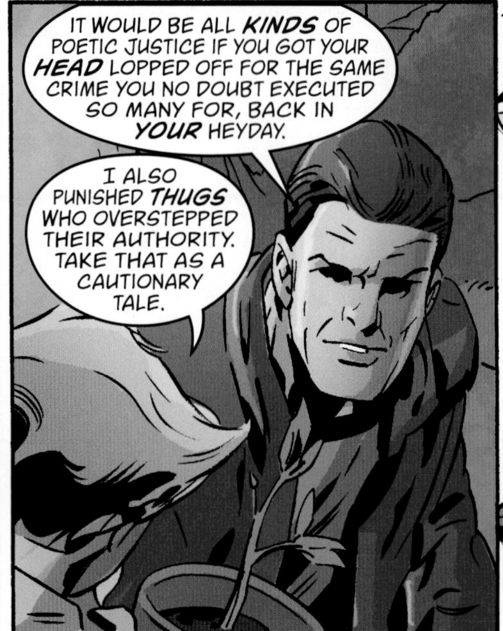
IT WOULD BE ALL KINDS OF POETIC JUSTICE IF YOU GOT YOUR HEAD LOPPED OFF FOR THE SAME CRIME YOU NO DOUBT EXECUTED SO MANY FOR, BACK IN YOUR HEYDAY.
I ALSO PUNISHED THUGS WHO OVERSTEPPED THEIR AUTHORITY. TAKE THAT AS A CAUTIONARY TALE.

NO, YOU TAKE IT. TAKE YOURSELF AND YOUR VANITY AND YOUR LITTLE PET PLANT BACK INTO THE CASTLE, RIGHT NOW.

OR I'LL HAVE A COUPLE OF MY THUGS COME OUT HERE AND DO UNTO YOU WITH CHAINS AND DRAGGING AND AN INSPIRED FIST OR TWO WHAT YOU CAN'T SEEM TO FIGURE OUT HOW TO DO WITH YOUR OWN TWO LEGS.

SO, WHAT'S GOING TO HAPPEN HERE?

ARE YOU GOING TO RAPE ME? IF THAT'S YOUR NOTION, THEN LET ME TRY ONE LAST TIME TO TALK YOU OUT OF IT.
BY DOING SO, YOU'D COMMIT SUICIDE, JUST AS SURELY AS IF YOU DRAGGED A KNIFE ACROSS YOUR THROAT.

MY HUSBAND WILL--
FLY TO YOUR SIDE AND AVENGE YOU BY TEARING ME LIMB FROM LIMB. YES, I KNOW HE'S A SAVAGE MONSTER. I'VE HEARD EVERY SCARY STORY.

BUT DON'T COUNT ME OUT. I'VE DISPATCHED BIGGER THAN HIM IN MY TIME. AND I ALWAYS HAVE A TRICK OR TWO UP MY SLEEVE.
THAT ISN'T WHAT I WAS GOING TO SAY.

I'M SORRY, MY LITTLE FOREST PRINCESS. I INTERRUPTED YOU. HOW BOORISH OF ME. DO PLEASE CONTINUE.
WHAT I WAS GOING TO SAY IS, MY HUSBAND WILL BE CROSS WITH ME WHEN HE FINDS OUT I DIDN'T LEAVE ANYTHING ALIVE ON WHICH TO SATE HIS FURY.

TOUCH ME AGAIN AND YOU'VE SIGNED YOUR OWN DEATH WARRANT, BECAUSE I'LL KILL YOU MYSELF, JUST AS SURELY AS NIGHT FOLLOWS DAY.
BELIEVE THAT AS YOU'VE NEVER BELIEVED ANYTHING ELSE.

PRETTY SPEECH.

YOU NEEDN'T WORRY, THOUGH. I HAVE NO INTENTION OF TAKING MY RIGHTS WITH YOU, UNTIL YOU ASK ME TO--WHICH YOU WILL.
TRUST ME ON THAT MUCH. YOU'LL COME PANTING FOR ME SOONER THAN YOU THINK.

BEFORE ANY OF THAT, YOU'LL HAVE TO WASH THE DOG'S STINK OFF YOU.
THOROUGHLY.

I WON'T RISK GETTING WHATEVER FLEAS AND OTHER PESTILENCES HE'S INFESTED YOU WITH.
YOU'LL FIND A VERY MODERN SHOWER IN THE BATHING ROOM. GET TO IT.

I wish I could have been there that day, that long-ago day in a remote corner of Haven.
WHAT ARE WE DOING WAY OUT HERE?

That lovely and terrible day when my fate flew in on powdered blue wings.
I'M DOING A JOB. I HAVE NO IDEA WHAT YOU'RE DOING HERE, REYNARD.
I CAME TO WATCH THE SHOW. THIS IS BLUE FAIRY DAY, RIGHT?
POSSIBLY.

I'M CURIOUS TO SEE WHAT YOU'LL DO. HOW YOU'RE GOING TO GET OUT OF BEING TAKEN AWAY AS A SLAVE FOR, HOW MANY CENTURIES IS IT?
A LOT.

YEAH, AND IF YOU DON'T HAVE SOMETHING REALLY CLEVER UP YOUR SLEEVE, I FIGURE SOMEONE SHOULD SEE THE ENSLAVEMENT TAKE PLACE AND BE ABLE TO TELL THE TALE.
HOW GENEROUS OF YOU.

HERE SHE COMES.

I SEE GEPPETTO ISN'T HERE TO FACE MY WRATH.
THEN YOUR FREEDOM IS FORFEIT IN HIS *PLACE,* YOUNG MAN, ACCORDING TO OUR AGREEMENT. I TRUST YOU'VE SAID YOUR FAREWELLS.

NOPE. NO FAREWELLS, MA'AM.
NO NEED TO, SINCE I'M NOT *GOING* ANYWHERE.
YOU SEE, I HAVE FULFILLED THE BARGAIN. GEPPETTO ACTUALLY *IS* HERE, BY ALL LEGAL DEFINITIONS.

OH SO? UNDER THE SUZERAINTY OF *WHAT* LAWS? I HAVE NO TRUCK WITH THE LAWS OF MAN IN ANY WORLD.
HOW FORTUNATE THEN THAT IT'S NOT THE LAWS OF MAN, BUT *FAIRY* LAW OF WHICH I SPEAK.

SPECIFICALLY THE LAWS GOVERNING COURTSHIP AND THE UNION OF HIGH PERSONAGES.
GEPPETTO ISN'T HERE BECAUSE HE CAN'T BE. AS THE HOPEFUL *SUITOR,* IT WOULD BE THE HEIGHT OF GAUCHERIE FOR HIM TO PLEAD HIS OWN CASE.

THEREFORE I STAND HERE AS HIS SWORN REPRESENTATIVE, IN HIS PLACE, AS IF HE *WERE* IN FACT HERE IN PERSON.
SO, READY TO TALK *MARRIAGE,* MADAM?
?

NEXT: UNSUITABLE SUITORS (OR: THE SHIPPING NEWS)

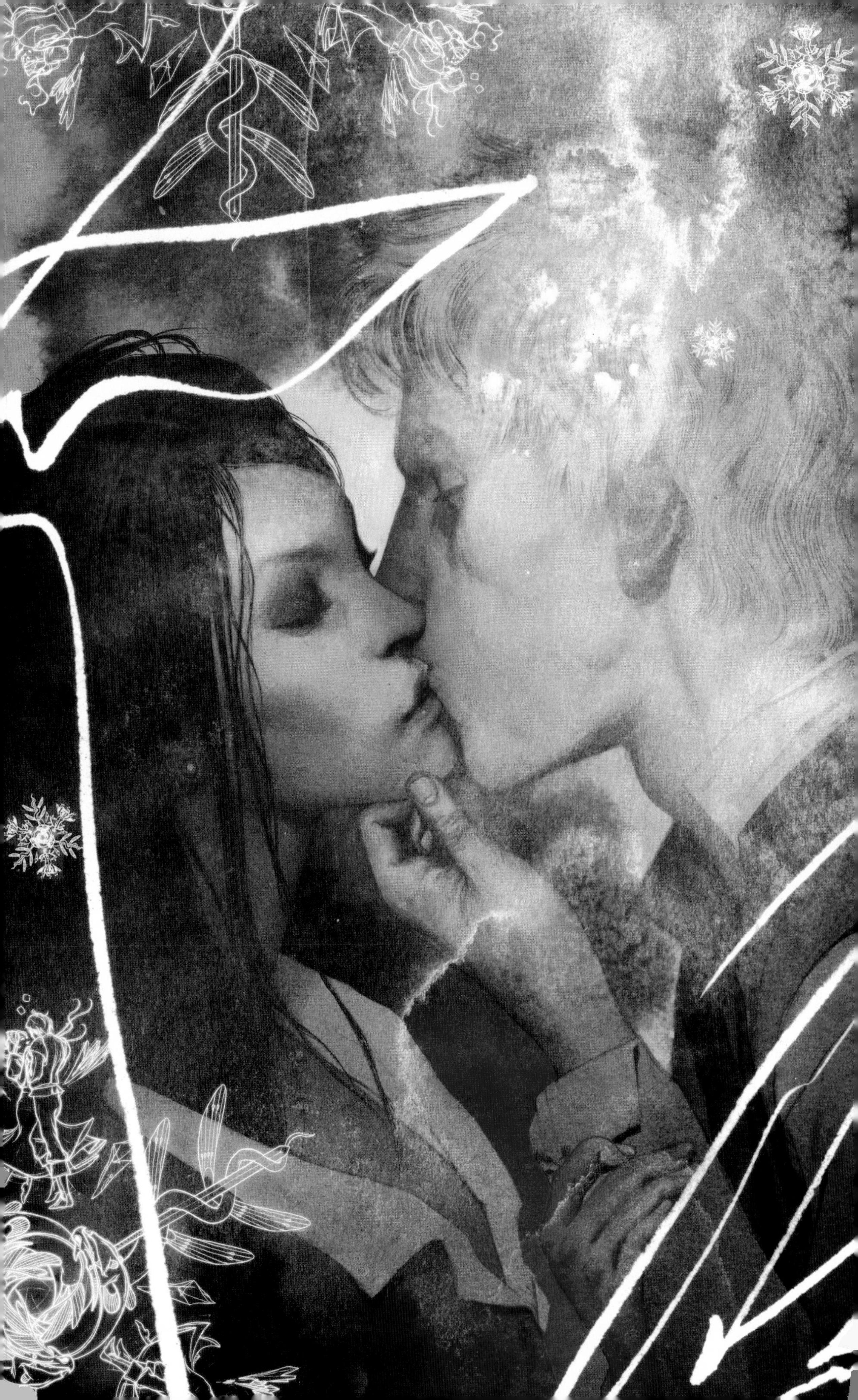

"Carefully note the part where the sanctity of traditional marriage is affirmed."

On an otherwise unspectacular hillside, in the modest kingdom of Haven, a man and an alien being in the semblance of a woman wrestled over their fates, not realizing it was actually mine being decided that day.
MARRIAGE?
TO WHOM?
TO GEPPETTO, OF COURSE. THAT'S WHY HE'S NOT HERE, SINCE IT WOULD BE GROSSLY UNSUITABLE FOR THE SUITOR TO PLEAD HIS OWN CASE TO HIS INTENDED.
WE'RE NOT BARBARIANS, AFTER ALL.
WOW.
NEVER SAW THAT COMING.
THE SHIPPING NEWS
Chapter Three of Snow White
Bill Willingham: writer-creator Mark Buckingham: pencils
Steve Leialoha: inks (1-5, 7, 17-20) Lee Loughridge: colors Gregory Lockard: assoc. ed.
Andrew Pepoy: inks (6, 8-16) Todd Klein: letters Shelly Bond: editor

HE WANTS TO MARRY ME?
WHY?

NOW, NOW, AUGUST LADY, YOU KNOW, SINCE I'VE STATED MY PRINCIPAL'S INTENTIONS, IT'S EQUALLY UNSUITABLE TO CONTINUE DEALING DIRECTLY WITH YOU, BECAUSE YOU ARE THE OBJECT OF HIS AMOROUS CAMPAIGN.

YOU MAY ANSWER IF THE MATCH IS OF NO INTEREST TO YOU. OTHER-WISE YOU MUST DEPART AND SEND YOUR SWORN REPRESENTATIVE TO ACT FOR YOU.
IT'S IMPORTANT THAT ALL THINGS BE HANDLED IN THE CORRECT MANNER, RIGHT?

OH.
UHM.
I GUESS I SHOULD--

I'LL SEND SOMEONE TO ACT FOR ME.
VERY GOOD, MADAM. MY PRINCIPAL WILL BE MOST PLEASED TO HEAR THE PROMISING NEWS.

BUT NOW PROPRIETY DICTATES WE MUTUALLY RETIRE, AND YOU TAKE YOURSELF TO A RESPECTABLE REMOVE.
UHM...OF COURSE. RIGHT AWAY.
WE LOOK FORWARD TO RECEIVING YOUR AMBASSADOR OF THE HEART WITH EVERY ANTICIPATION OF A DELIGHTFUL AND PRODUCTIVE NEGOTIATION.
RIGHT AWAY.
FAREWELL, MOST ALLURING CELESTIAL LADY.
AGAIN, I SAY, WOW.
BRAVO.
MY HAT'S OFF TO YOU, SIR.
HOW DID YOU EVER GET SOUR OLD GEPPETTO TO AGREE TO THIS?
I HAVEN'T. NOT YET. BUT NOW I'VE BOUGHT A LOT OF TIME TO FIGURE OUT HOW TO CONVINCE, TRICK OR FORCE HIM TO GO ALONG WITH IT.
NO WAY!
ACCORDING TO MY RESEARCH, NEITHER PARTY IS ALLOWED TO SPEAK TO THE OTHER FOR AS LONG AS THE NEGOTIATION TAKES PLACE.
AND FAIRY WEDDING NEGO-TIATIONS HAVE BEEN KNOWN TO DRAG ON FOR YEARS--CENTURIES, IN FACT.
AND I THOUGHT I WAS THE PRINCE OF SCHEMERS. YOU'RE LIKE A GOD TO ME.

MEANWHILE...
SHOULD WE BREAK IT DOWN?
HOW?

THIS DOOR'S SOLID OAK. WE'D NEED A BATTERING RAM.
OR A SHAPED CHARGE.
OR BIGBY. OR BEAST. WHERE ARE OUR BIG GUNS WHEN WE NEED THEM?

GRIMBLE IS BIG ENOUGH TO TAKE THIS DOOR DOWN, WHEN HE'S BEING ALL TROLLISH, AND HE MAY EVEN HAVE EXPLOSIVES. WHERE'S HE?
I HAVE NO IDEA. COME TO THINK OF IT, I HAVEN'T SEEN HIM SINCE THIS MORNING.

WHERE ARE THE THIRTEENTH FLOOR WITCHES, THEN?
MOVING BACK INTO THE NEW THIRTEENTH FLOOR.

WELL, ONE OF THEM COULD-- I DON'T KNOW--TURN THE DOOR INTO BUTTERFLIES OR SOMETHING.
SURE, BECAUSE THEY ALWAYS JUST HAPPEN TO HAVE A "TURN THE DOOR INTO BUTTERFLIES" SPELL ALL CONJURED UP AND READY TO FIRE.

YOU'RE NOT BEING HELPFUL, MRS. SPRATT.
NOT MY NAME ANYMORE!
HOLD ON. NO NEED TO SNIPE AT EACH OTHER.

I THINK I CAN PICK THIS, IF ONE OF YOU HAS A HAIRPIN, OR SOMETHING CLOSE.
YOOPS!
IF YOU PEOPLE WOULD STOP CLUCKING OUTSIDE MY DOOR AND READ YOUR OWN LAWS, YOU'D DISCOVER THERE'S NO CAUSE TO INTERFERE.

HERE. ONE OF THE TWO COPIES RECOVERED FROM THE MESS YOU SILLY PEOPLE MADE OF THE PREVIOUS ITERATION OF FABLETOWN.
CAREFULLY NOTE THE PART WHERE THE SANCTITY OF TRADITIONAL MARRIAGE IS AFFIRMED.

BUT YOU AREN'T MARRIED TO--
DON'T START THAT AGAIN. I JUST HAD AN EARFUL OF THE SAME NONSENSE FROM MY WIFE.

WE PLEDGED OURSELVES TO EACH OTHER BY STRONG OATHS IN THE OLD WAY. THAT'S A MARRIAGE, EVEN BY YOUR OWN STANDARDS.
THEREFORE SNOW WAS NEVER LEGALLY MARRIED TO PRINCE CHARMING OR THE WOLF. BOTH HAVE TO BE TREATED AS THOUGH THEY NEVER EXISTED.

THAT'S YOUR LAW. READ IT.
WELL, TRUE, BUT THEY WERE WRITTEN IN A DIFFERENT TIME. A DIFFERENT AGE.
THEN AMEND THEM.

BUT UNTIL YOU DO, GET AWAY FROM MY DOOR AND QUIT INTRUDING INTO THE PRIVATE BUSINESS OF A FAMILY.
WAIT!

CAN WE AT LEAST SEE IF SNOW'S OKAY?
NO.
WHAT PART OF "PRIVATE BUSINESS" ARE YOU UNABLE TO GRASP?

SLAM!

WELL, FUCK US, HUH?
CAN I GET AN "AMEN" ON THAT?

My dad was making progress by then, having visited thirty worlds in as many hours.
SOMETHING REALLY STRANGE HAPPENED HERE.

THIS IS THE THIRD WORLD DARE TOUCHED DOWN IN, BUT ONLY FOR A MOMENT.
HERE AND GONE IN AN INSTANT.

AT LEAST WE'RE ON THE RIGHT TRACK THEN, HUH?
THREE POINTS OF CONTACT GIVE US A LINE OF TRAVEL, RIGHT? WE SIMPLY NEED TO GO IN THAT DIRECTION.

THAT'S JUST IT. WE DON'T HAVE A LINE TO FOLLOW BECAUSE WORLDS DON'T LINE UP.

AT LEAST NOT IN ANY WAY THAT I'M CAPABLE OF SEEING.

SNOW?

HOW LONG ARE YOU GOING TO BE IN THERE, HONEY?
TAP TAP

I'M GOING TO THE BATHROOM!
IT TAKES AS LONG AS IT TAKES, SO BACK OFF!

SPLOOOSH!
OKAY, QUICKLY, WHILE THE WATER MASKS OUR VOICES...GHOST, ARE YOU THERE?

OF COURSE, MOMMY. I DON'T LIKE THE MEANY MAN YOU'RE WITH.
IS HE A BAD MAN?

YES, A VERY BAD MAN.
SHOULD I KILL HIM, THEN?
I'D VERY MUCH LIKE TO.

SPLOOOSH!
NO. DON'T DO ANYTHING.

WHY DO YOU KEEP FLUSHING THE TOILET?

ARE YOU OKAY IN THERE?
TIP TAP

I'M FINE! I JUST DROPPED TOO BIG A LOAD FOR THE DAINTY MODERN PLUMBING WE'RE STUCK WITH! VERY UNLADYLIKE!
NOW, BACK OFF, LIKE I SAID! DON'T YOU REALIZE WOMEN ARE EMBARRASSED ABOUT HAVING THEIR BATHROOM ACTIVITIES OVERHEARD?

I'D VERY MUCH LIKE YOU TO KILL THE BAD MAN FOR MOMMY, BUT HE MAY BE TOO POWERFUL.
HE HAS SOME BIG MAGIC AT HIS COMMAND.
I'M NOT AFRAID.
SPLOOOSH!

I KNOW, HONEY, BUT I AM. IF YOU GET KILLED, WHO WOULD THERE BE TO SAVE MOMMY BY RUNNING FOR HELP?
INSTEAD, CAN YOU FIND DADDY? HE'S FAR AWAY.
OF COURSE I CAN. I CAN ALWAYS FIND YOU AND DADDY, NO MATTER HOW FAR YOU GO.
GOOD. THEN GO FIND HIM AND TELL HIM TO COME HOME FAST. TELL HIM MOMMY'S IN TROUBLE.
SPLOOSH!
OKAY, MOMMY. SHOULD I GO NOW?
YES, RIGHT NOW! BE VERY FAST AND VERY HEROIC!
GO!
ALL BETTER NOW, DARLING?
NO. NOT EVEN CLOSE. WILL YOU LET ME GO NOW?
AS SOON AS YOU START ACTING RATIONALLY, MY ONE TRUE LOVE.

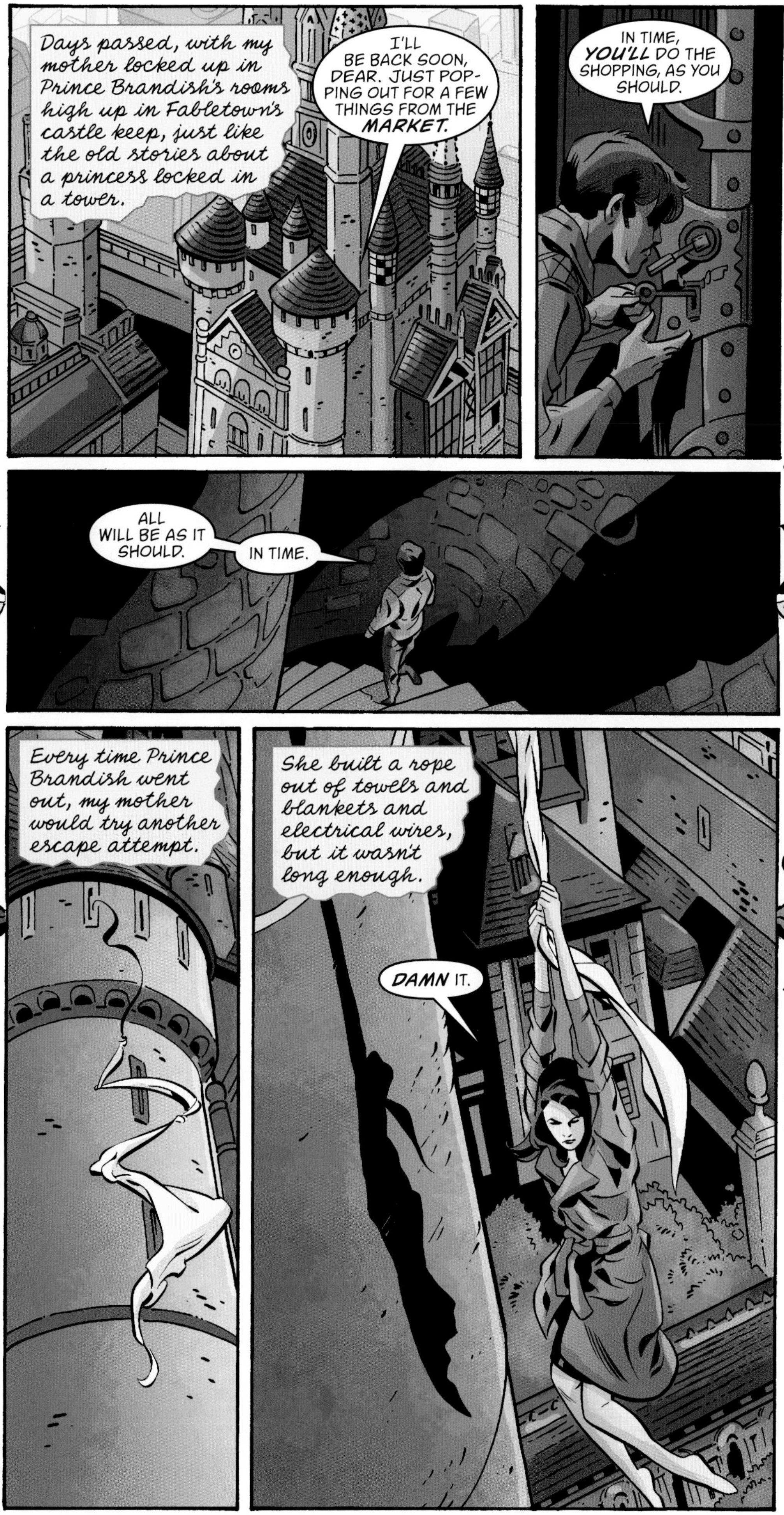

Days passed, with my mother locked up in Prince Brandish's rooms high up in Fabletown's castle keep, just like the old stories about a princess locked in a tower.

I'LL BE BACK SOON, DEAR. JUST POPPING OUT FOR A FEW THINGS FROM THE ***MARKET.***

IN TIME, ***YOU'LL*** DO THE SHOPPING, AS YOU SHOULD.

ALL WILL BE AS IT SHOULD.

IN TIME.

Every time Prince Brandish went out, my mother would try another escape attempt.

She built a rope out of towels and blankets and electrical wires, but it wasn't long enough.
DAMN IT.

She tried to talk others into helping her.
DON'T BE SO TIMID. JUST DANGLE A PISTOL FROM A STRING DOWN TO MY WINDOW FROM ABOVE, AND I'LL DO THE REST.

But that didn't work for reasons I still don't quite understand.
I'M SORRY, SNOW, BUT WE CAN'T INTERFERE. NOT YET.
THE GOOD NEWS IS WE'RE MAKING PROGRESS ON AMENDING VARIOUS APPLICABLE LAWS, BUT IT'S A SLOW PROCESS AT THE BEST OF TIMES.
CHANGING THE LAWS OF AGES CAN BE TOUGH SLED-DING.
THE BAD NEWS IS WE'RE STUCK ON WHETHER OR NOT WE CAN FAIRLY MAKE THE NEW LAWS RETRO-ACTIVE, SO AS TO BE ABLE TO HELP YOU WITH YOUR SPECIFIC DILEMMA.

FOR CRAP'S SAKE, YOUR HONOR, JUST HELP ME ESCAPE AND KILL THE MAN, AND YOU CAN TRY ME UNDER ANY SET OF LAWS YOU LIKE.

IT DOESN'T HELP TO GIVE IN TO DESPAIR, SNOW. WE'LL THINK OF SOMETHING. WE SPOKE TO ROSE AT THE FARM. YOU'LL BE PLEASED TO KNOW YOUR CHILDREN ARE FINE.
WELL--YOU KNOW--THE ONES WHO AREN'T CURRENTLY MISSING.

I even heard a rumor some of the witches planned their own rescue.
INTERESTING.
HE'S GOT SOME SOPHISTICATED MAGICAL **DEFENSES** SURROUNDING HIM.
OPENING SOON: THE NEW EDWARD BEAR'S CANDIES

WONDER WHERE HE CAME BY THEM. IT'S CERTAINLY SORCERER'S WORK, BUT LOOK AT THE CONSTRUCTION.
IT'S OVERLY COMPLEX AND DEFINITELY **FOREIGN.**

NOTE HOW ANY MORTAL ATTACK ON HIM WILL AUTOMATICALLY BE DEFLECTED TO HARM **SNOW.** THAT'S CLEVER.
IT CERTAINLY RULES OUT JUST BURNING HIM DOWN, LIKE THE **SCUM** HE IS.

I'LL HAVE TO TELL ROSE I CAN'T COMPLETE HER **FIRE** MISSION.
WHAT'S HIS POWER SOURCE?

AN OBJECT OF SOME KIND, ALWAYS NEAR HIM, BUT NOT ALWAYS **PRESENT** IN THIS FRAME OF EXISTENCE.
BRUTE FORCE WON'T WORK. WE'LL HAVE TO RETIRE FOR NOW AND PONDER FURTHER.

As the days wore on, my mother grew ever more desperate.
LOOK AT HIM, PETER. SO SMUG. BUT I COULD KILL HIM RIGHT NOW, BEFORE HE KNEW IT.
CAN'T DO IT, BO. THE THIRTEENTH FLOOR CREW PUT OUT THE WORD. HE'S OFFICIALLY UNTOUCHABLE.

...WEDDING BELLS, ON THE HILLSIDE...

...SOMETHING, SOMETHING THAT RHYMES WITH HILLSIDE...

HONEY, I'M HOME.

AH!
HAPPY TO SEE YOU TOO, SNOWDRIFT.
YOW, HOW THAT STINGS!
BUT LOOK AT YOUR OWN CHEEK, DARLING. THE INJURY YOU TRIED TO DO TO ME HAS CUT YOU INSTEAD.
AREN'T YOU GLAD I STOPPED YOU FROM GOING ALL THE WAY?

MY CUT WILL HEAL IMMEDIATELY. YOURS WON'T.
SORRY, BUT THAT'S HOW THE MAGIC WORKS.

AND IT LOOKS LIKE YOU BROKE OUR BATHROOM MIRROR TO MAKE YOUR WEAPON.
DON'T YOU KNOW THAT'S SEVEN YEARS' BAD LUCK, DEAR?
OW!

LET GO!
YOU'RE BREAKING MY ARM!
EXACTLY!

AAAAUUGHGHHH!
HOW ELSE WILL YOU LEARN?
NOW, PICK UP THE GROCERIES YOU MADE ME SPILL AND COOK MY SUPPER, YOU FOREST BRAT.

And a few days after that, in Haven...
...YOU MAKE BATH TIME SO MUCH FUN!

YOUR BATH HAS BEEN DRAWN, MAJESTY.
THANK YOU, MR. DAMPHOUSE.

PERFECT!
A BATH EVERY MORNING GETS YOU KISSED WITHOUT WARNING!

YOW!

THERE'S A GIRL IN MY BATH!
I KNOW YOU.
YOU CARRIED EXCALIBUR FOR A TIME AND THEN RETURNED IT TO ME, UNBLEMISHED BY DISHONOR AND UNRIGHTEOUSNESS. YOU'RE AMBROSE THE KING.
I'M THE LADY OF THE LAKE. YOU MAY CALL ME LAKE, FOR SIMPLICITY'S SAKE, IF YOU LIKE.
THE PEOPLE OF THESE TIMES DO MAKE SUCH A FETISH OF EXPRESSING COMPLEX THINGS IN SIMPLE WAYS.
UH... UHM...
And there, just like that, my future came calling.
I'M HERE AT THE BEHEST OF MY FRIEND THE BLUE FAIRY TO NEGOTIATE THE MATTER OF HER POSSIBLE ENGAGEMENT AND WEDDING TO THE DEPOSED EMPEROR.
IF YOU'D KINDLY CONDUCT ME TO MY COUNTERPART, WE CAN BEGIN.
UH-- UHM--

At about that time, back in the mundy world...
STAND ASIDE, MR. MAYOR. NOT YOU NOR ANYONE ELSE WILL KEEP ME FROM DOING WHAT YOU SHOULD'VE DONE DAYS AGO!
BUT WE'VE JUST PASSED THE VITAL NEW LAWS WE NEED. THE OFFICIAL WARRANTS AND INJUNCTIONS ARE BEING DRAWN UP EVEN AS WE SPEAK.
TOO LITTLE, TOO LATE, KING COLE.
SNOW! IF YOU CAN HEAR ME, HUNKER DOWN! I'M COMING IN, ALL GUNS BLAZING!
YOU'LL ONLY KILL HER IF YOU DO THIS.
NAW, DON'T TELL HIM, BUT I'M USING RUBBER BULLETS AND KNOCKOUT GAS. SNOW MIGHT NOT LIKE IT, BUT SHE WON'T DIE AND PRINCE SHITWHISTLE GOES OUT LIKE A LIGHT.
THEN WE THROW HIM IN A DARK, DANK CELL AND FIGURE OUT HOW TO DISMANTLE HIS DEFLECTION SPELLS.
THAT ACTUALLY MIGHT WORK. WE JUST NEED TO--
BOOM!

NEXT: SOMETHING TO DO WITH THE PARABLE ABOUT THE GLASS HOUSE AND THE STONES!

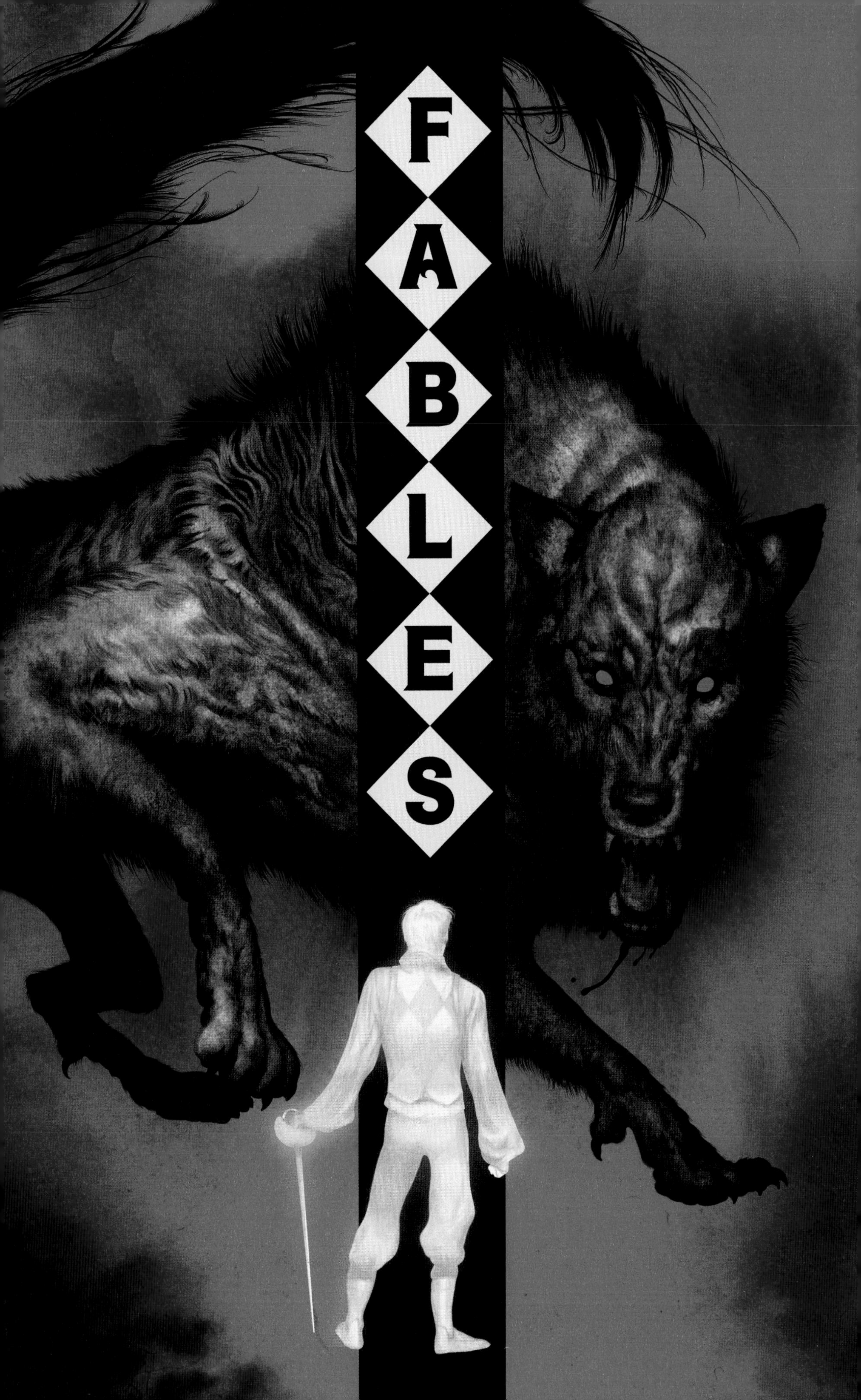
FABLES

"Greatness must be honored, no matter how dark and terrible the source of it."

MEANWHILE, IN THE BIGGEST COURTYARD OF FABLETOWN RESTORED...
AT LAST!
THE ANIMAL BRIDEGROOM IS HOME!

YOU MADE GOOD TIME, TOO.
YOUR SECRET AND INVISIBLE SON IS QUITE POWERFUL IN HIS OWN RIGHT, ABLE TO CROSS ENTIRE UNIVERSES IN A VERITABLE "BLINK."
HOW DOES THAT WORK?

IT'S AS IF DISTANCE DOESN'T ACTUALLY FIGURE INTO IT, AS LONG AS EITHER OF YOU IS AT JOURNEY'S END. BIG MAGIC THERE.
SNOW WILL GIVE ME EVEN MORE POWERFUL SONS AND DAUGHTERS OF MY OWN, ONCE I'M THROUGH WITH YOU.

WHERE'S MY WIFE?

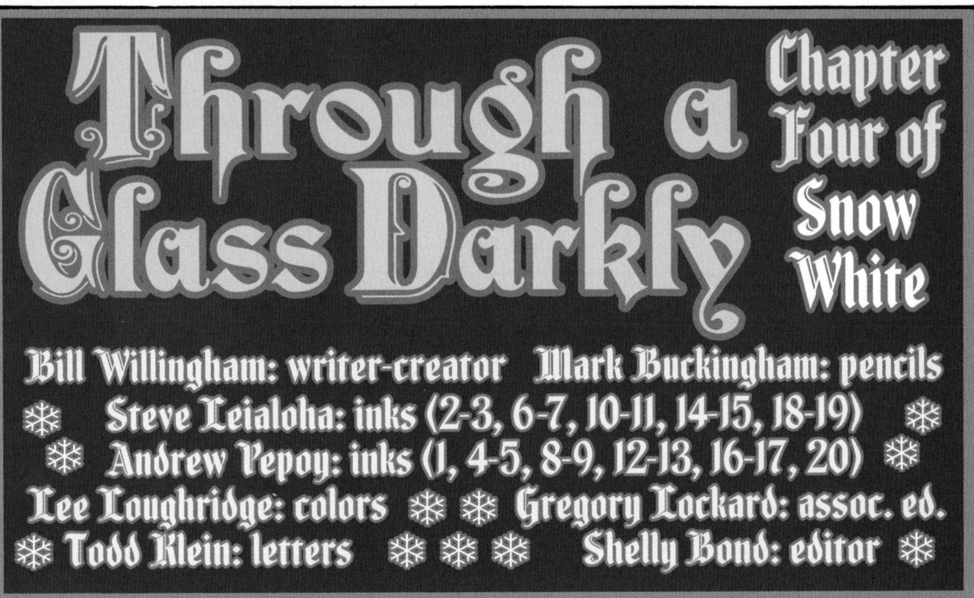
Through a Glass Darkly
Chapter Four of Snow White
Bill Willingham: writer-creator Mark Buckingham: pencils
Steve Leialoha: inks (2-3, 6-7, 10-11, 14-15, 18-19)
Andrew Pepoy: inks (1, 4-5, 8-9, 12-13, 16-17, 20)
Lee Loughridge: colors Gregory Lockard: assoc. ed.
Todd Klein: letters Shelly Bond: editor

My father, the Big Bad Wolf of nightmare and legend, fought Prince Brandish in a personal duel for the safety and honor of my mother, Snow White. Written like that, it sounds almost romantic— the stuff of high fantasy.
The truth, of course, wasn't so pretty. The actual fight isn't as easy to put down in words. I struggle to write the cold facts of the event even now, at so many years' remove.

SETTLE DOWN, ANIMAL. WE'LL *GET* TO THE HUFFING AND PUFFING, RENDING AND STABBING. ALL IN GOOD TIME.
A DUEL THIS IMPORTANT SHOULD HAVE A MODICUM OF *RITUAL* ATTACHED TO ITS OPENING--SOME REFINEMENT, IF YOU WILL.
TRY TO HAVE A SENSE OF MOMENT.
I'M GOING TO *KILL* YOU, BOY!
ONE WOULD CERTAINLY *ASSUME* AS MUCH, COMPARING US SIDE BY SIDE.
BUT I MAY SURPRISE YOU.

Many aspects of that fateful day were taken straight out of the old stories. The beautiful woman locked away in a tower by a monster.
BIGBY!
DON'T KILL HIM!
Until the handsome prince came to save her.
WHY NOT?
A VERMIN'S PURPOSE IS TO DIE.
Except it was the handsome prince who locked her away in this case, and the monster who came to save her.
BUT I MADE A SACRED VOW!
YOU'RE HOLDING YOURSELF TO THAT RIDICULOUS MARRIAGE PROMISE?
SEE? I KNEW SHE'D COME AROUND.

OF COURSE NOT. THAT'S HORSESHIT.
I MADE A SACRED VOW TO BE THE ONE TO END HIS MISERABLE LIFE, AND I MEAN TO KEEP IT!
LEAVE HIM TO ME!
SORRY.
CAN'T DO IT.
YOU AREN'T FORSWORN IF EVENTS INTERVENE BEFORE YOU CAN CARRY OUT YOUR OATH.
HE DIES NOW.
WELL, SOMEONE DIES NOW. I'LL GRANT THAT MUCH.
DAMMIT, BIGBY! YOU MAKE ME SO MAD SOME-TIMES!
GO ON, THEN! HAVE YOUR WAY! BUT MAKE IT QUICK!
SHE DIDN'T TELL HIM!

My mother didn't tell my dad that any harm he did to Brandish would also fall on her.
WOOOOOSH!
Aunt Rose said she could get stubbornly brave at times.
Lewis
NOD'S
YOW!
IMPRESSIVE, WOLF!

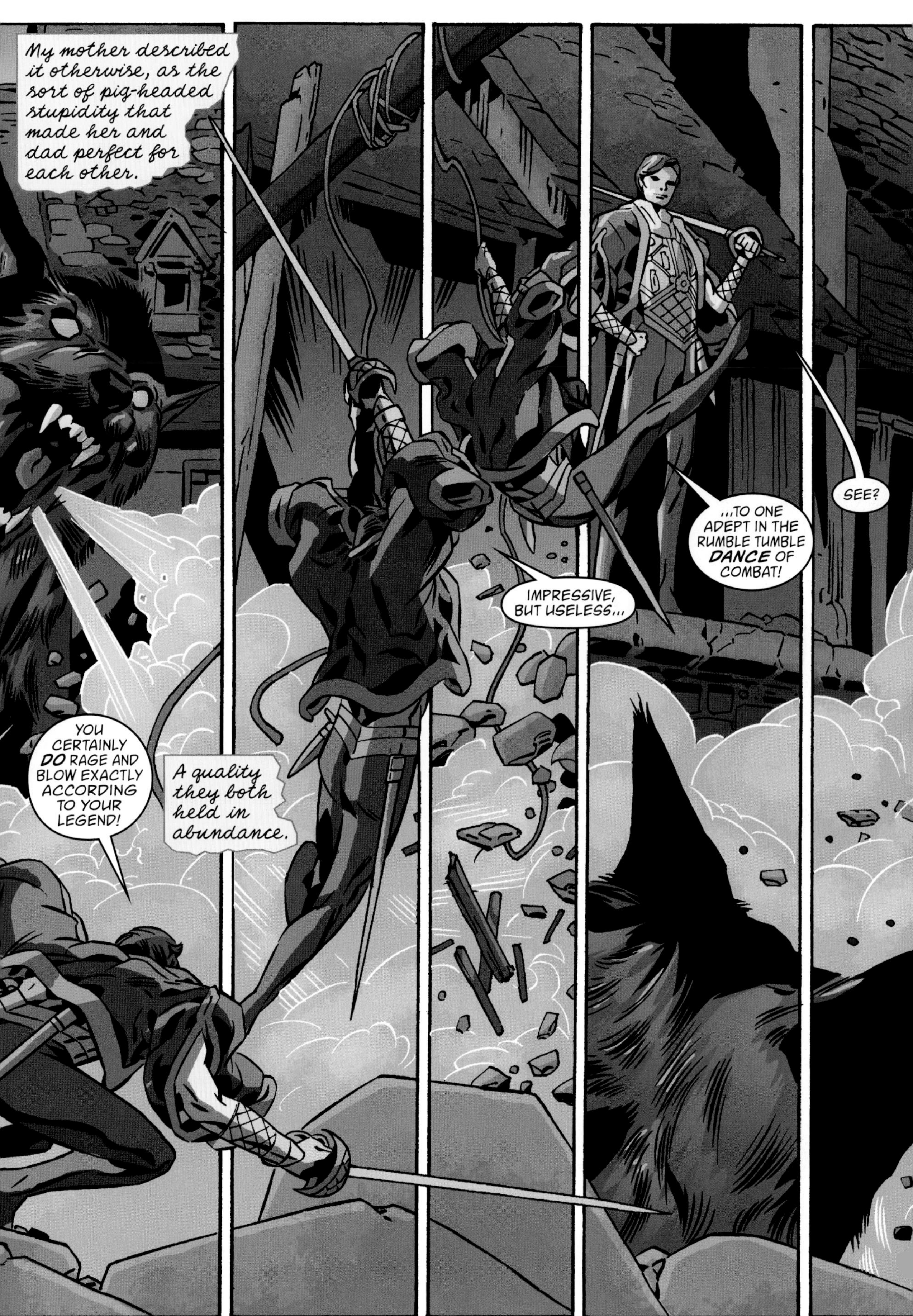
My mother described it otherwise, as the sort of pig-headed stupidity that made her and dad perfect for each other.
YOU CERTAINLY DO RAGE AND BLOW EXACTLY ACCORDING TO YOUR LEGEND!
A quality they both held in abundance.
IMPRESSIVE, BUT USELESS...
...TO ONE ADEPT IN THE RUMBLE TUMBLE DANCE OF COMBAT!
SEE?

The winds that hurled Brandish around the court-yard did the same to my mother, confined in her tower room.
OH!
OW!
MY ARM!
DAMMIT, BIGBY!
YOUR SISTER DIDN'T TELL HIM WHAT HAPPENS IF BIGBY HARMS BRANDISH!
NO, SHE WOULDN'T.
IDIOT.
BUT SNOW'S DOOMED!
NOT YET!
LISTEN UP, WITCHES! FIX THIS!

HOW?
HOW THE HELL SHOULD I KNOW? FIND A WAY! YOU'RE OUR MAGICAL GUNSLINGERS. BREAK THE SPELL THAT TRANSFERS INJURIES FROM BRANDISH TO SNOW!

GIVEN TIME I THINK I COULD DO IT. EVEN NOW I'M EXAMINING THE SPELL'S WARP AND WEAVE, WHICH IS REMARKABLE.
I THINK I COULD UNRAVEL IT IN A FEW DAYS.

WE DON'T HAVE A FEW DAYS. IN A MINUTE OR TWO BIGBY IS GOING TO CHOMP THE PIG PRINCE AND THEN SNOW'S GONE, TOO!
I HAVE AN IDEA. WHAT IF WE DON'T TRY TO BREAK THE SPELL, BUT ADD TO IT INSTEAD?
WHY?

I MIGHT BE ABLE TO BUILD IN A DELAY BETWEEN CAUSE AND EFFECT.
GIVE US SOME WIGGLE ROOM BETWEEN THE MOMENT WHEN THE WOLF KILLS THE MAN AND THE SAME HAPPENS TO SNOW.

YES!
WHATEVER THAT IS, DO THAT!

TOO SMALL TO PIN DOWN?
FINE!
I CAN BE SMALLER TOO!
AND JUST AS TOUGH!
DOESN'T HELP THOUGH, DOES IT?

YOU CAN'T HARM WHAT YOU CAN'T TOUCH.
AND NOW I'VE GOT THE MEASURE OF YOU, BIGBY.
YOU'LL NEVER LAY A PAW ON ME BUT THAT I ALLOW IT.
AND WHYSOEVER SHOULD I ALLOW IT?

While my father fought unknowingly to kill my mother, tense wedding negotiations were taking place in the Kingdom of Haven.
HOW WAS YOUR LUNCH, DEAR LADY?
THE FOOD WAS ODD, BUT I FOUND ITS ALIEN TASTE DELIGHTFUL.
THEY'RE CALLED CHILIDOGS, A SPECIAL CUISINE TREASURED BY OUR AUGUST KING, AND ONLY OFFERED TO HIS MOST FAVORED GUESTS.
ARE YOU READY TO RESUME, OR WOULD YOU LIKE TO REST FIRST? MY PRINCIPAL AND I ARE IN NO HURRY. BEST TO DO IT RIGHT, RATHER THAN FAST, NO?
WE CAN CONTINUE. WE WERE DISCUSSING THE DOWRY.
YES, AND I'M AFRAID I CAN'T COMPROMISE ON THIS POINT. YOUR PRINCIPAL'S DOWRY TO GEPPETTO MUST INCLUDE AT LEAST THREE MAGICAL TREASURES BEYOND PRICE.
I'VE TAKEN THE LIBERTY OF LISTING A FEW SUGGESTIONS.
A GOLDEN CHALICE CONTAINING THE TEARS OF THE NINE THOUSAND GODS OF LOST LEMURIA.
Dowry Suggestions
Golden chalice con
tears of the nine tho
s of Lost Lemuria
China cup pai
thrice-de

A CHINA CUP HAND-PAINTED BY THE THRICE-DEPARTED SHADE OF HONOROMI ONO ISU.
A COLLECTION OF--
Dowry Suggestions
1. Golden chalice containing
tears of the nine thousa
Gods of Lost Lemuria
2. China
thr
FORGIVE MY INTERRUPTION, LORD SHERIFF, BUT WHY IS A LOWLY ***WOODCARVER*** DESERVING OF SUCH IMPOSSIBLE RICHES?
BECAUSE, LADY OF THE DEPTHS, WOODCARVER THOUGH HE MAY HAVE BEEN, HE IS ***ANYTHING*** BUT LOWLY.
JUST TO NAME BUT ONE AMONG HIS MANY POMPS AND TITLES, HE WAS LORD OF THE BOXERS, WHO BOXED MORE THAN TEN THOUSAND VERY ***REAL*** GODS AND MONSTERS.
TELL ME, LAKE, HOW CLOSE DID THEY COME TO CATCHING ***YOU?***
I'LL CONFESS, I HAD TO GO DEEP TO ESCAPE THEM.
AND THERE WE ARE. GREATNESS MUST BE HONORED, NO MATTER ***HOW*** DARK AND TERRIBLE THE SOURCE OF IT.

MY ABSENT HAT IS OFF TO YOU, LORD OF FURY.
YOU ARE TRULY DEATH ON FOUR STOUT LEGS.
ONE GOOD BLOW OR BITE FROM YOU AND I SEE THAT I'M DOOMED BEYOND HOPE OF SURVIVAL.
SO, I'D BEST MAKE SURE YOU NEVER TOUCH ME.
MEANTIME, SEE HOW I PRICK AWAY AT YOU, HERE AND THERE.
LET THE MAGIC OF MY BLADE INVADE YOU BY INCRE-MENTS.

STAND STILL, BOUNCING BUG!
AH, BUT THAT'S THE ART OF IT, DON'T YOU SEE?
IT'S THE NEVER-CHANGING STORY OF MAN: A CONTEST OF SUPERIOR INTELLIGENCE, DEXTERITY, AND RAW TALENT HONED BY CENTURIES OF TRAINING, OVER BESTIAL RAGE.
AND I'LL WIN.
FOR CIVILIZED MAN WILL EVER TRIUMPH OVER THE MOST BRUTISH FORCES OF NATURE. THAT'S ALL OF HISTORY IN A NUTSHELL.
DEATH OF A THOUSAND SMALL CUTS.
AN OUTCOME NEVER IN DOUBT.

WELL, MRS. GREEN?
ARE YOU GETTING IT DONE?
I HAVE... SOMETHING.
A FEW LOOSE THREADS WHERE I CAN BEGIN TO ADD MY OWN WEAVE.

WHAT DOES THAT MEAN? QUIT SPEAKING GOBBLEDY-GOOK AND TELL ME SOME-THING REAL.

YOU AREN'T HELPING, ROSE RED.
THIS WOULD PROBABLY GO BETTER WITHOUT THE INTERRUPTIONS.
FINE!

YOU DO YOUR JOB AND I'LL DO MINE.
WHERE ARE YOU GOING?

TO FETCH MY SISTER.

NOW WHERE DID THEY DUMP THE...?
BINGO!
SNOW!
READY TO MAKE YOUR BIG ESCAPE?
ABOUT TIME YOU THOUGHT OF THIS. SO MUCH FOR TWINS READING EACH OTHER'S MINDS.
I GOT THERE EVENTUALLY. ALWAYS WAS A SLOW READER.
HOLY SHIT ON A BAGEL! WHAT HAPPENED TO YOUR ARM?
LONG STORY. I'LL TELL YOU ON THE WAY.

YOU'RE SLOWING DOWN, WOLF LORD.
MOVING IN FITS AND STARTS.
DO YOU FEEL IT?
YOUR BONES KNITTING?
YOUR SINEWS LOSING THEIR FLEX AND PUSH?
THE MAGIC OF BLADE AVICTRIX IS TAKING EFFECT.
THE SWORD THAT IS ACTUALLY A HUNDRED MAGIC WEAPONS CONQUERED AND ABSORBED OVER THE AGES INTO THE ONE WHICH RULES THEM ALL!
THIS IS PERHAPS MY FAVORITE ITERATION OF ALL. IT'S CALLED MARMIMAGO VASCULARIUS.

I USE IT ONLY RARELY, WHEN I WANT TO *DECORATE* MY PALACE WITH INTERESTING ART.

MEMENTOS OF MY *FAVORITE* BATTLES.

NEXT: THE BIG BREAKUP!

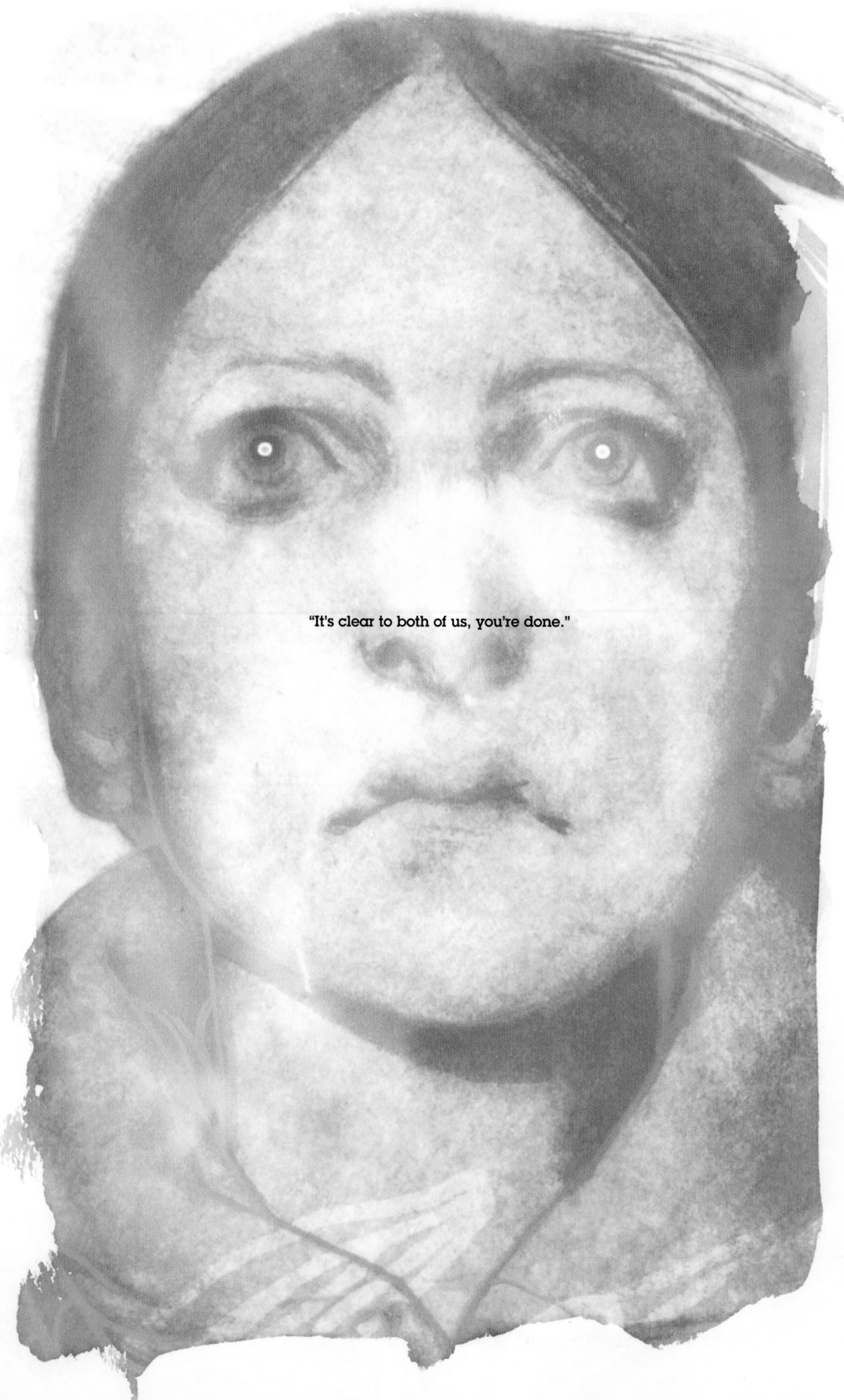
"It's clear to both of us, you're done."

Pardon me for going on so long about fate, but what's a personal journal for, if not to occasionally indulge oneself?
THIS WINE IS MARVELOUS.

It's been on my mind.
BLAME MY LOVELY WIFE. SHE'S TAKEN OVER THE KING'S WINE CELLARS WITH A PURPOSE.
SOMEONE HAD TO STEP IN AND PUT ORDER TO CHAOS. THE KING AND HIS...UHM...SOCIAL SECRETARY ARE BOTH GREAT OF HEART.

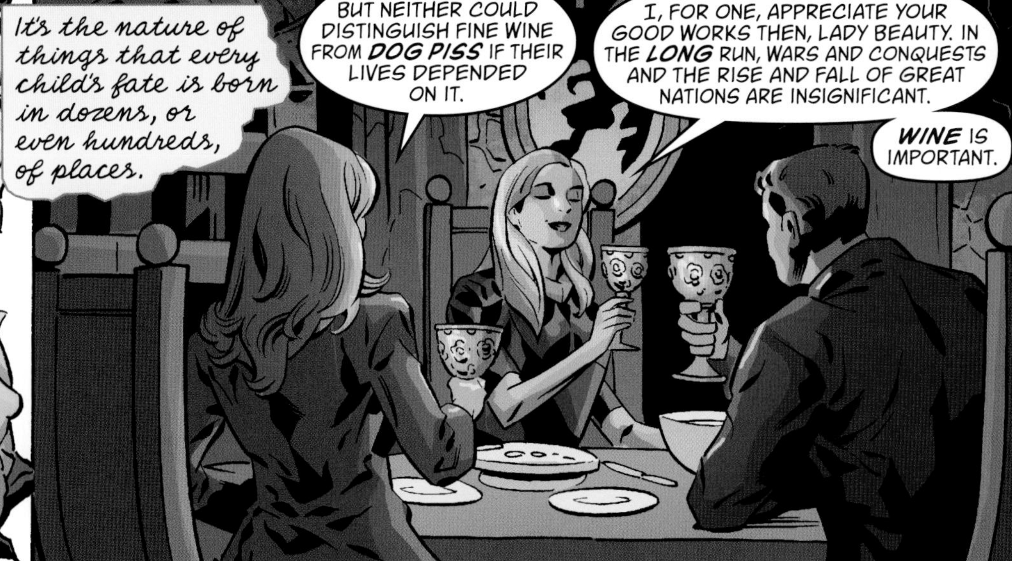
It's the nature of things that every child's fate is born in dozens, or even hundreds, of places.
BUT NEITHER COULD DISTINGUISH FINE WINE FROM DOG PISS IF THEIR LIVES DEPENDED ON IT.
I, FOR ONE, APPRECIATE YOUR GOOD WORKS THEN, LADY BEAUTY. IN THE LONG RUN, WARS AND CONQUESTS AND THE RISE AND FALL OF GREAT NATIONS ARE INSIGNIFICANT.
WINE IS IMPORTANT.

Snow Falling on Glass
Chapter Five of Snow White
Bill Willingham: writer-creator Mark Buckingham: pencils
Steve Leialoha: inks (pages 8-15, 19-20)
Andrew Pepoy: inks (pages 1-7, 16-18)
Lee Loughridge: colors Gregory Lockard: assoc. ed.
Todd Klein: letters Shelly Bond: editor

Scattered notes and asides, afterthoughts to other important matters of the moment, eventually to be collected.
DO YOU KNOW WHAT ELSE IS IMPORTANT?
TRUST.
On one day, for example, the course of my life was being decided in battle, in a Fabletown courtyard.
THE BLUE FAIRY TRUSTS ME TO ACT IN HER BEST INTEREST, IN THIS NEGOTIATION, TO MAKE SURE IT'S NOT SIMPLY A RUSE TO AVOID OTHER CERTAINTIES.
SHE BELIEVES I COULD PEEK AHEAD, IF I WANT, TO SEE IF A WEDDING IS INDEED FATED TO OCCUR.
It was being influenced and redirected on a distant shore of broken toys.
THAT WOULD BE CHEATING, THOUGH. I'M A GOOD PERSON NOW.
WELL, AT LEAST I'M A BETTER PERSON FOR THE TIME BEING. NOTHING'S EVER DECIDED FOREVER, RIGHT?
At the same time it was being scribbled in the margins of an intense wedding negotiation taking place in the Kingdom of Haven.
THE TIDE COMES IN. THE TIDE GOES OUT. WE'RE ALWAYS ON OUR WAY SOMEWHERE EVEN WHEN STANDING STILL.
SO, MISS LAKE, SHE SUSPECTS THIS NEGOTIATION IS A CHARADE?
At the time those momentous and terrible things were taking place, none knew they were also charting my life to come.
SHE DOES. AND I'LL FIND OUT, ONE WAY OR ANOTHER, AS I PROMISED HER I WOULD.
BUT ONLY IN THE NORMAL COURSE OF EVENTS. I'M ENJOYING THIS TOO MUCH TO PEER AHEAD.
My life in a nutshell: insignificant bits and pieces of other stories.
OH, DEAR. MY GLASS IS EMPTY.
SHALL WE OPEN ANOTHER BOTTLE?

FABLETOWN.
A TEMPORARY FIX WON'T DO. A BROKEN ARM IS NOTHING TO TRIFLE WITH.
I'M ACUTELY AWARE OF THAT, DOCTOR SWINEHEART, BUT DO IT MY WAY, REGARDLESS.
I'M THE GREATEST PHYSICIAN IN UNCOUNTABLE WORLDS. IN AN HOUR I COULD MEND A BROKEN ARM SO THAT NO ONE COULD TELL IT WAS EVER TRAUMATIZED.
AND, IF IT'S WITHIN MY POWER, YOU'LL HAVE THAT HOUR, DOCTOR, I PROMISE.
BUT NOT JUST YET.
THIS, AT LEAST, WILL NUMB THE PAIN SOME.
JUST WALK OUT THERE, SNOW, AND BLAST HIS HEAD OFF WITH A HAND-CANNON.
THE ASSHOLE DOESN'T DESERVE ANYTHING BETTER.

AND MAYBE BLOW MY HEAD OFF INSTEAD, IF THE WITCHES DON'T HAVE THE SPELL FIXED. WITH A FEW CUTS I CAN BETTER GAUGE IF IT'S WORKING.
BETTER THAN COMMITTING ALL TO ONE ROLL OF THE DICE. BESIDES, THE OCCASION DEMANDS BLADES.

FUCK OCCASION. SLAPPING A MAGAZINE IN AND CHAMBERING THE FIRST ROUND IS RITUAL ENOUGH.
SHOOT OUT HIS KNEECAPS FIRST, IF YOU'RE CONCERNED IT MAY STILL REBOUND ON YOU.

NO.
I'M ADAMANT ON THIS, ROSE.
YOU CAN BE SO GODDAMN PIG-HEADED AT TIMES!

POT, MEET KETTLE.
THEN LET'S USE MY ORIGINAL PLAN. YOU DISTRACT THE BASTARD WITH YOUR IMPORTANT SWORD DUEL RITUAL NONSENSE.
THEN I'LL LEAP OUT AND HOSE HIM DOWN WITH RUBBER BULLETS UNTIL HE'S OUT LIKE A LIGHT. MAYBE YOU ARE TOO, BUT SO WHAT?

YOU BOTH LIVE THROUGH IT, BUT HE'S THE ONE WHO WAKES UP IN CHAINS.
THAT'S A VERY GOOD PLAN. BUT HE CAN'T BE ALLOWED TO LIVE THROUGH THE DAY.

SO YOU KILL HIM, AND MAYBE YOU DIE TOO. AND YOU'RE OKAY WITH THAT?
YOU HAVE KIDS WHO'VE EXACTLY ONE PARENT LEFT. HAVE YOU THOUGHT OF THEM?

THEY'RE ALL I'M THINKING OF.
IF BRANDISH LIVES, HE PLANS TO KILL THEM, AND I BELIEVE HE'LL FIND A WAY TO DO IT, NO MATTER HOW CAREFULLY WE LOCK HIM AWAY.

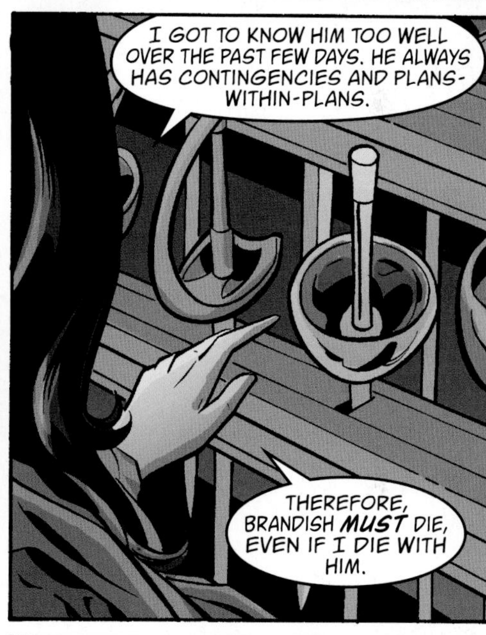
I GOT TO KNOW HIM TOO WELL OVER THE PAST FEW DAYS. HE ALWAYS HAS CONTINGENCIES AND PLANS-WITHIN-PLANS.
THEREFORE, BRANDISH MUST DIE, EVEN IF I DIE WITH HIM.

THEY'LL STILL HAVE YOU TO RAISE THEM UP RIGHT.
AND FIND MY MISSING ONES.
PROMISE ME, ROSE.
OF COURSE, BUT...

THIS ONE WILL DO.

THE ANCIENT TERROR OF THE NIGHT. THE GIANT WOLF OF THE HESSE, NOW A GLASS STATUE.
MARVELOUS.
HE WILL BE THE CENTERPIECE OF MY GREAT HALL.
BUT HE'S NOT A WOLF.
NOT REALLY.
OR AT LEAST NOT ONLY A WOLF.
IS THAT ENOUGH TO WORK WITH?

BIGBY'S FATHER COULD SURVIVE THIS. DOESN'T AUTOMATICALLY MEAN **BIGBY** CAN THOUGH.

HE WILL. TRANSFORMING HIMSELF FROM GLASS BACK INTO A CREATURE OF FLESH AND BONE SHOULD BE ***CHILD'S PLAY*** TO THE SON OF THE NORTH WIND.

WE'LL SEE.

HE'D **REJECTED** ALL OF HIS FATHER'S WAYS--THE POWERS OF THE NORTH WIND.
AND OF EVEN GREATER CONCERN IS THE WOLF'S **SPIRIT.**

THINKING HIMSELF ACTUALLY DEAD, WILL HIS SPIRIT HAVE ALREADY **MOVED ON,** ABANDONING THIS WORLD?
I'M LOOKING IN EVERY WAY I KNOW HOW, BUT I CAN'T FIND ANYONE HOME.

BRANDISH!
STEP UP AND DRAW STEEL, YOU SCURRILOUS COCKFACE!
SNOW!
HOW DID YOU GET OUT?
DOESN'T MATTER.
WHAT DOES MATTER IS THE UN-FINISHED BUSINESS BETWEEN US.
THIS BUSINESS OF UNFULFILLED VOWS.
NOW, NOW, MY LOVE. YOU'RE CLEARLY UPSET.
UNDERSTAND-ABLE, ALL THINGS CONSIDERED.

NO, NOT UPSET. THAT COMES LATER.
RESOLVED.

BIGBY NEVER LEARNED SWORDPLAY.
NEVER HAD TO.

I, HOWEVER, LEARNED IT FROM THE BEST WHO EVER TOOK UP A BLADE.
LET'S SEE IF THOSE LESSONS TOOK.
NOW, SNOW. SETTLE DOWN. THINK IT OVER.
THIS IS THE SERIOUS BUSINESS OF MEN--NOT FIT FOR THE DISTAFF SEX.

DID YOU DO IT? IS SNOW PROTECTED?
LET'S SEE.

YOU'RE INJURED.
FENCING LEFT-HANDED.
TRUE.
WITH THOSE DIS-ADVANTAGES, THIS WILL BE CLOSER TO A FAIR FIGHT.
PRINCE CHARMING MADE ME PRACTICE BOTH WAYS...
...DOMINANT HAND AND OTHERWISE.
WOW.
SNOW'S PRETTY GOOD!
SHE IS THAT, AND GIVING ME LOTS OF TIME AS A RESULT.

SO TELL ME, BRANDISH. I CAUGHT SOME OF YOUR BRAGGING DURING THE FIRST DUEL. ARE YOU AS EXPERT WITH THE SWORD AS YOU CLAIM?
ARE YOU AS GOOD AS ME?
OR WAS YOUR FANCY MAGIC SWORD A CRUTCH?
DID YOU SKIP A LOT OF THE HARD WORK OF PERFECTING AND POLISHING, KNOWING THAT YOUR WEAPON DOES MOST OF THE FIGHTING ON ITS OWN?
STOP IT!
I'M SERIOUS!
I THINK MAYBE YOU DID.
COME ON, SNOW WHITE. GIVE ME A FEW MINOR CUTS TO WORK WITH.
EACH ONE INSTANTLY TRANSFERRED TO YOU--BUT LET'S SEE IF WE CAN REDEFINE THE MEANING OF "INSTANT."

YOU'RE GOOD, I'LL GRANT YOU THAT MUCH.
ALL APPROPRIATE HONOR TO YOUR TEACHER.
BUT YOU'RE ALSO TIRING FASTER THAN I.
NOT SOON ENOUGH TO SAVE YOU.
LET'S BE REAL. THIS CAN ONLY END ONE WAY.
YOU'RE A STRONG WOMAN IN GOOD TRIM. BUT THAT HARDLY COMPARES TO A MAN'S STRENGTH AND STAMINA.
AREN'T YOU GOING TO LOOK LIKE AN IDIOT, IF THOSE END UP BEING YOUR LAST WORDS?
SHE IS SLOWING DOWN! SNOW DOES NEED TO END IT RIGHT NOW!
I HOPE NOT. I NEED ONE MORE SECOND.

OW!
THERE!
YOU CUT ME!
WITH FULL MALICE AND INTENT.
AND LOOK...
...IN NICKING YOU, I DID NOTHING TO MYSELF.
SO NOW WE CAN END THIS.
YOU DID IT!
DAMN RIGHT.

HERE.

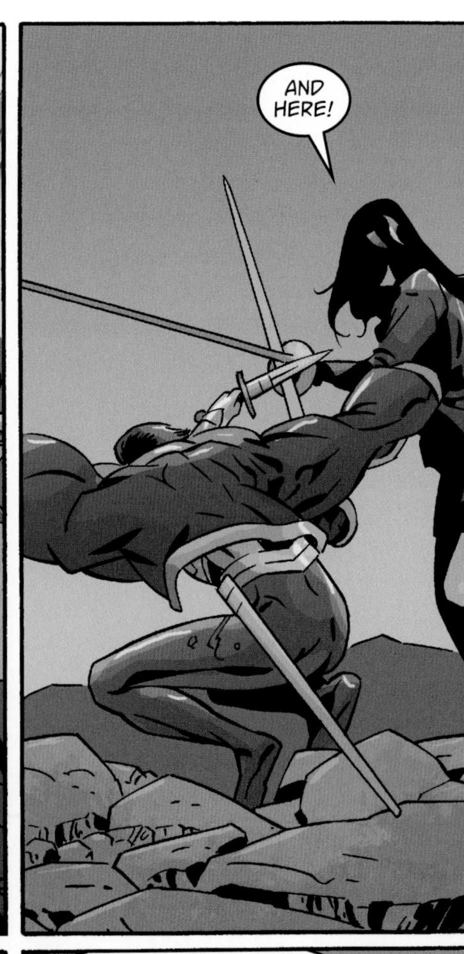
AND HERE!

AND HERE!

YOU'RE MISSING EVERY OTHER PARRY, IN A CONTEST WHERE YOU CAN ILL AFFORD TO MISS ONE.

IT'S CLEAR TO BOTH OF US, YOU'RE DONE.
BREATHE A LAST PRAYER, IF YOU HAVE ONE.
A FINAL CURSE IS ALL I HAVE TO GIVE.
I BEQUEATH YOU THE HOLLOWEST OF VICTORIES.
IN BEATING ME, YOU'VE LOST HIM.
FOREVER.

NO!
DID YOU THINK I COULDN'T OVERHEAR YOUR WITCHES' SCHEMES TO RESTORE HIM?
THEY COULD HAVE SAVED THEIR ENERGY, SPEAKING TELEPATHICALLY.
IT WAS THE SAME TO ME AS IF THEY'D SCREAMED EVERY WORD ALOUD.
TRY RESTORING YOUR WOLF NOW!

YOU DIDN'T SAVE YOURSELF DOING THAT.
NO, I SUPPOSE NOT.
WASN'T TRYING TO.
DO ME A KINDNESS IN THE NEXT LIFE.
SUFFER ENDLESSLY.
STRAIGHT THROUGH THE HEART.
TYPICAL.

And that's how my dad died.
OH, BIGBY.
How we got through the following years without him—well, that's another set of stories, which I suppose I'd best set about telling.
After all, that's the role in the little witch's wretched old prophecy that fell to me—to judge the rest, in my histories.
WHAT DO WE DO NOW?
SNOW?
DON'T WORRY. I'M NOT GOING TO LOSE IT.
I'LL CONTINUE TO BE STRONG FOR NOW. FOR THE ***CHILDREN.***
WE'LL GATHER WHAT WE ***CAN*** OF HIS PIECES FOR THE BURIAL.
A FORMAL FUNERAL IS IN ORDER.
WE'LL GATHER UP THE SHARDS ALL RIGHT, BUT NOT TO BURY.
OUR ORIGINAL PLAN IS STILL VIABLE, ***IF*** WE CAN PIECE HIM BACK TOGETHER.

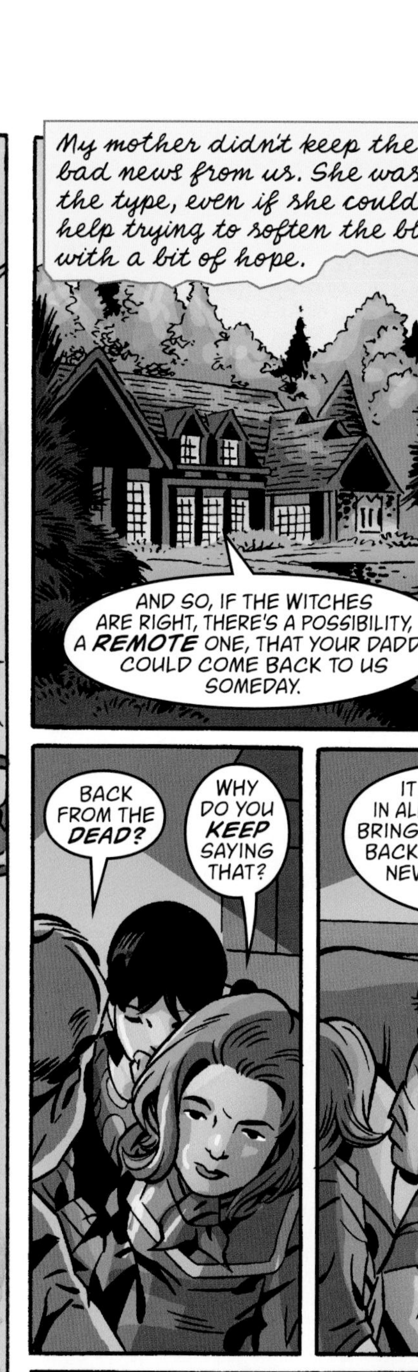
My mother didn't keep the bad news from us. She wasn't the type, even if she couldn't help trying to soften the blow with a bit of hope.
AND SO, IF THE WITCHES ARE RIGHT, THERE'S A POSSIBILITY, A REMOTE ONE, THAT YOUR DADDY COULD COME BACK TO US SOMEDAY.

BACK FROM THE DEAD?
IN A FEW DAYS THOUGH, I'LL HAVE TO CONTINUE THE SEARCH FOR YOUR BROTHER AND SISTER. AUNT ROSE WILL BE HERE, BUT YOU CAN'T BE HELLIONS ANY LONGER.
YOU'LL ALL HAVE TO BE A LITTLE MORE GROWN UP, FROM NOW ON.

BACK FROM THE DEAD?
WHY DO YOU KEEP SAYING THAT?

IT'S JUST THAT, IN ALL THE STORIES, BRINGING A LOVED ONE BACK FROM THE DEAD NEVER TURNS OUT WELL.

AND AREN'T WE THE PEOPLE IN THE STORIES?

KNOCK KNOCK
WHO COULD THAT BE?

IT'S TOO SOON FOR VISITORS TO COME CALLING TO PAY RESPECTS.

MOM?
!
I DON'T KNOW IF YOU RECOGNIZE ME. THE YEARS PASSED DIFFERENTLY WHERE I...
I'M THERESE.
I'VE COME HOME TO TELL YOU WHAT HAPPENED TO DARE--HOW HE SAVED ME.
WHERE'S DAD?

The End

Treasures from the Woodland Vaults

Designs, sketches and layouts by Mark Buckingham

20
11

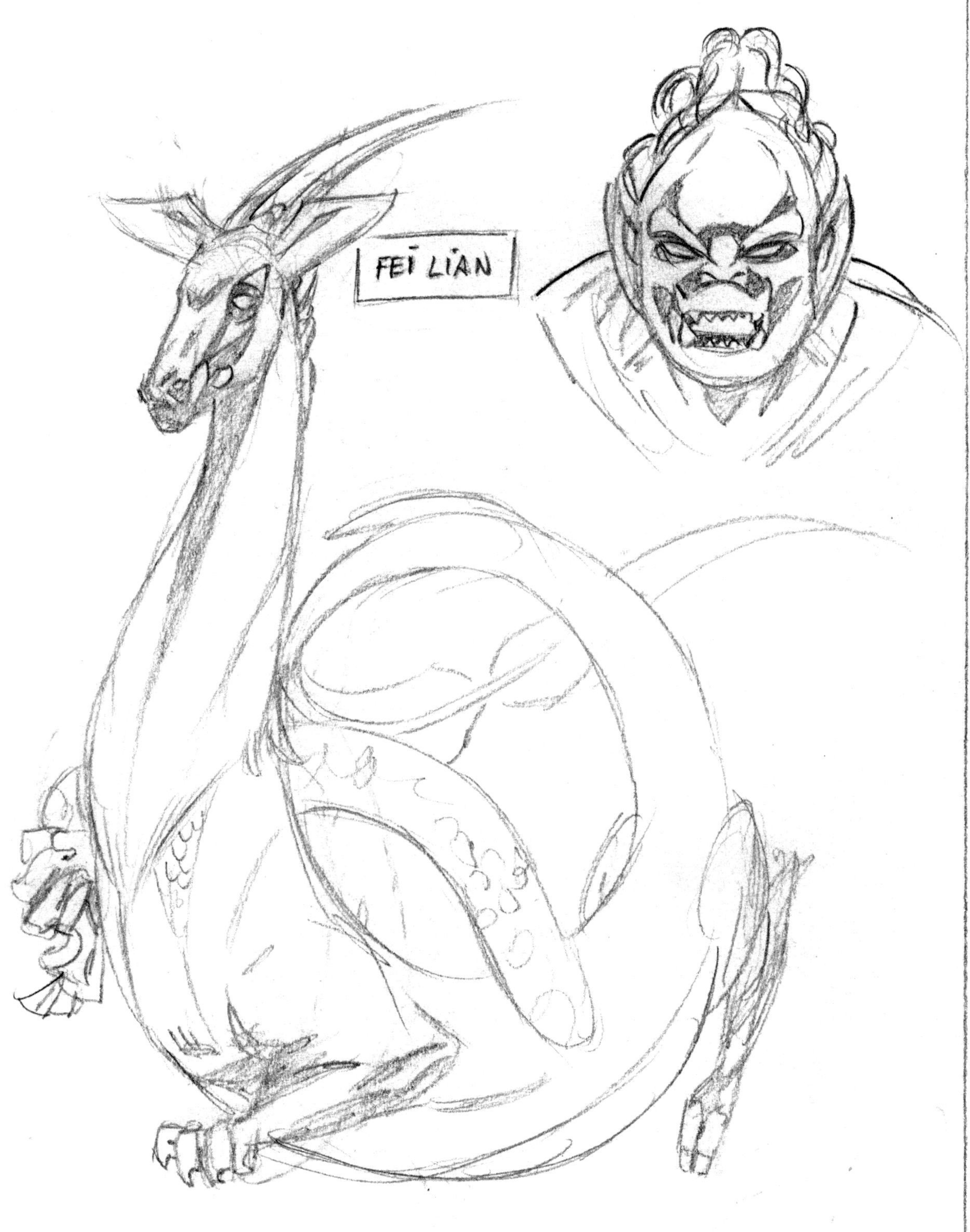
FEI LIAN

OYA
YAPONCHA

A

3
X
A
B
H
1

DC COMICS VERTIGO PENCILLER MARK BUCKINGHAM INKER PAGE# 2

TITLE FABLES ISSUE # 126 MONTH

INTERIORS

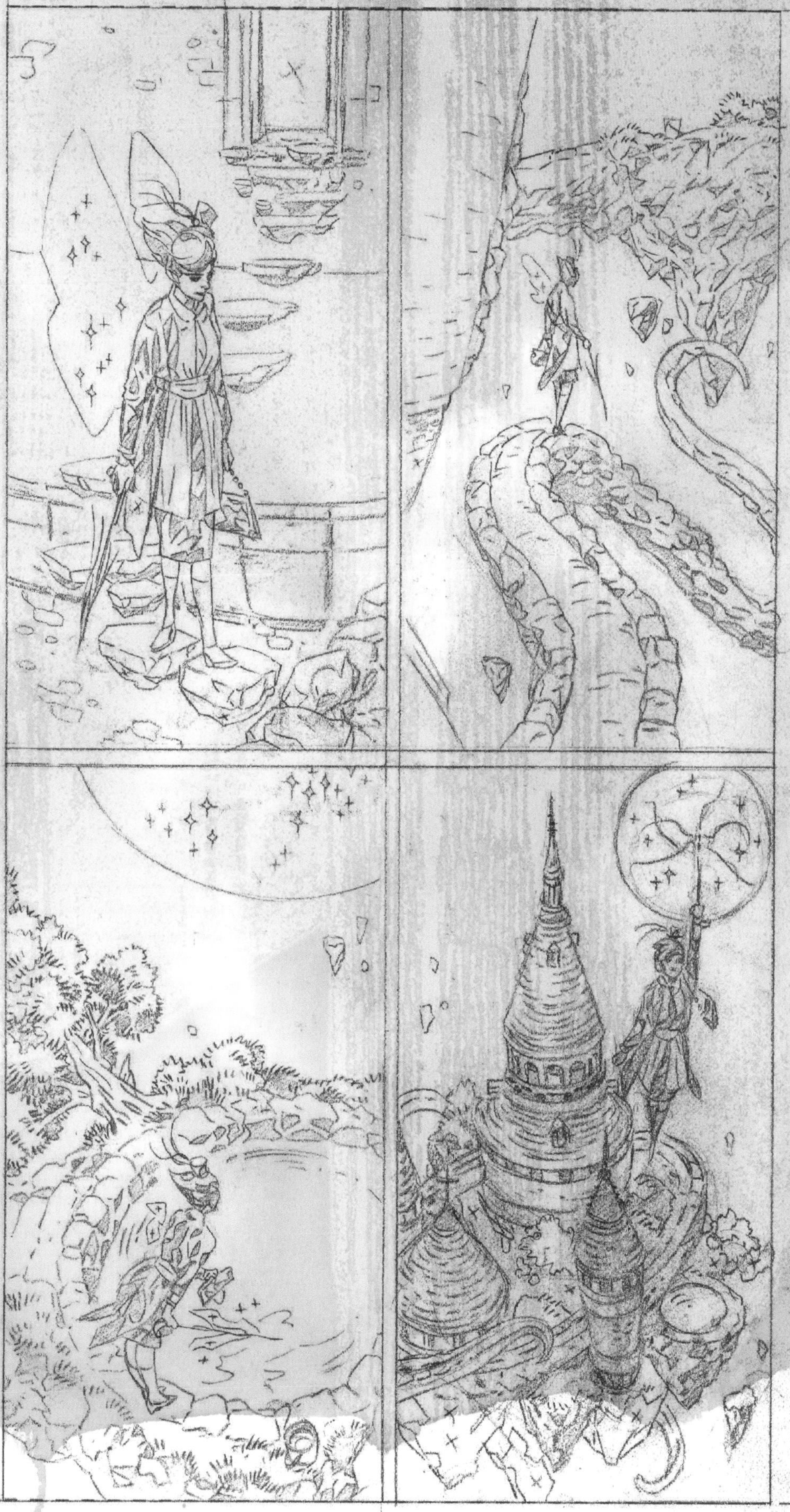

LIVE AREA

TEXT
FABLES
4
HOMELANDS
ADVERSARY'S
ARMY
FLEEING
FABLES
TRANSFORM
INTO
REGULAR
MODERN
CLOTHES
AS
THEY
ENTER MUNDY
WORLD
BULLFINCH
St

5

BACK COVER
TEXT

FABLES

1

FABLE
TOWN
LAW

VERTIGO

2
FABLES
FABLE TOWN
6
FABLES

Bill Willingham has been writing and sometimes drawing comics for more than 20 years. During that time he's had work published by nearly every publisher in the business, and he's created many critically acclaimed comic book series, including *The Elementals*, *Coventry*, PROPOSITION PLAYER and FABLES. His other credits are vast and impressive but far too many to mention here. Currently he lives in his own personal corner of the American Midwest and can be visited at clockworkstorybook.net.

Born in 1966 in the English seaside town of Clevedon, **Mark Buckingham** has worked in comics professionally since 1988. In addition to illustrating all of Neil Gaiman's run on the post–Alan Moore *Miracleman* in the early 1990s, Buckingham contributed inks to THE SANDMAN and its related miniseries DEATH: THE HIGH COST OF LIVING and DEATH: THE TIME OF YOUR LIFE, as well as working on various other titles for Vertigo, DC and Marvel through the end of the decade. Since 2002 he has been the regular penciller for Bill Willingham's FABLES, which has gone on to become one of the most popular and critically acclaimed Vertigo titles of the new millennium.

A 30-year veteran of the industry, **Steve Leialoha** has worked for nearly every major comics publisher in the course of his distinguished career. Titles featuring his artwork include DC's BATMAN, SUPERMAN and JUSTICE LEAGUE INTERNATIONAL, Vertigo's THE DREAMING, THE SANDMAN PRESENTS: PETREFAX and THE SANDMAN PRESENTS: THE DEAD BOY DETECTIVES, Marvel's *The Uncanny X-Men*, *Spider-Woman* and *Doctor Strange*, Epic's *Coyote*, Harris' *Vampirella*, and many of Paradox Press' BIG BOOK volumes. Since 2002 he has inked Bill Willingham's hit Vertigo series FABLES, for which he and penciller Mark Buckingham won the 2007 Eisner Award for Best Penciller/Inker Team. Leialoha also provided pen-and-ink illustrations for Willingham's 2009 FABLES novel, *Peter & Max*.

As a young lad, **Shawn McManus** would haunt the newsstand every other month, waiting for the next issue of his favorite title to date: SWAMP THING by Len Wein and Bernie Wrightson. Their work inspired a young McManus to pursue comic art as a career, and he has since worked for numerous publishers and drawn many characters, including Swamp Thing, the Sandman, Batman and Spider-Man, among many others. He lives in California with his wife Stephanie.

Gene Ha loves Bill Willingham's words, whether in script, comic book or 10-hour road trip form. He is the writer and artist of the comic book *Mae*, and he has won three Eisner Awards for his collaboration with Alan Moore on TOP 10 and one for his work with Brad Meltzer on JLA. Ha and his lovely wife Lisa live outside Chicago in Berwyn, Illinois. Find out more at www.geneha.com.

An Eisner Award winner and nominee for the Hugo and Inkwell Awards, **Andrew Pepoy** has worked for U.S., British and French publishers and has inked thousands of pages for dozens of comics titles, including FABLES, *The Simpsons*, *The X-Men*, *Archie* and *Lanfeust*. He is also the creator, writer and artist of his own Harvey Award–nominated series, *The Adventures of Simone & Ajax*, and he has brought his knack for retro glamour with a modern twist to writing and drawing Archie Comics' *Katy Keene* as well as drawing the *Little Orphan Annie* newspaper strip.

Comics artist and painter **Dan Green** began his career in the early 1970s pencilling and inking for a variety of DC titles, including DARK MANSION, TARZAN and WEIRD WORLDS. Through the '70s, '80s and '90s, his focus shifted more exclusively toward inking, and he contributed long runs on such flagship Marvel titles as *X-Men*, *Wolverine*, *Spider-Man* and *The Avengers*, as well as working on JUSTICE LEAGUE OF AMERICA, SUPERGIRL and WONDER WOMAN for DC and HELLBLAZER: PAPA MIDNITE and FABLES for Vertigo. He also co-wrote and provided watercolor art for the 1986 graphic novel *Doctor Strange: Into Shamballa*, and in 2001 Bulfinch Press published a collection of works by Edgar Allan Poe entitled *The Raven and Other Poems and Tales*, featuring 20 of Green's pencil illustrations. He lives and works in upstate New York.